THE CHRISTIAN SCHOLAR

An Introduction to Theological Research

Gregory G. Bolich

UNIVERSITY
PRESS OF
AMERICA

LANHAM • NEW YORK • LONDON

Copyright © 1986 by

University Press of America,® Inc.

4720 Boston Way
Lanham, MD 20706

3 Henrietta Street
London WC2E 8LU England

Printed in the United States of America

Co-published by arrangement with the
Institute for Christian Studies

Library of Congress Cataloging in Publication Data
Bolich, Gregory G.
    The Christian scholar.

    Bibliography: p.
    1. Theology—Research.   I. Title.
BR118.B558   1986   230'.072   85-26416
ISBN 0-8191-5135-1 (alk. paper)
ISBN 0-8191-5136-X (pbk. : alk. paper)

All University Press of America books are produced on acid-free
paper which exceeds the minimum standards set by the National
Historical Publications and Records Commission.

This book is dedicated to those among my students and colleagues who especially deserve recognition and honor of their commitment as students of God's Living Word. To Judi Ryker, Hal Whitman, Bill Johnson, Byron Care, and Carl Sunderman I give this grateful praise, and the charge of the apostle: "Do your best to present yourself to God as one approved, a workman who has no need to be ashamed, rightly handling the word of truth."

ACKNOWLEDGMENTS

While I have tried to acquire some competency in all of the research methods discussed in this text I can hardly consider myself an expert in each. I am grateful for the help of genuine experts in carefully reviewing certain of the methods discussed herein. Special thanks belong to Professors Ronald Kelly and Garry Kenney for not only checking materials in their own areas of special interest, but also for critiquing the ideas about research advanced in this book. Dr. Sandra Wilson gave particular attention to the three chapters on statistics and strengthened my confidence in their contents. To these scholars and all those kind readers who assisted me in the preparation of this text I give my deepest thanks.

A special commendation and my sincerest thanks are due to Margo Dalager, who selflessly labored to make this a better manuscript by her editing and typing. All that is good belongs to her credit; the errors are mine alone.

TABLE OF CONTENTS

PART THREE

Foreword

Ron Kelley, Ph.D.

Gregory G. Bolich has written an insightful and courageous introductory book on theological research. It is insightful in that he has identified critical issues from the perspective of a dedicated and active scholarly theologian. When he suggests research methodologies and data analysis techniques, it is advice founded upon his experience with theological research. His comments on scholarly writing reflect the wisdom of a disciplined and accomplished author.

Courage is involved in that he challenges theologians to expand their investigative tools to include quantitative research models and statistical analysis. Dr. Bolich's guidelines for theologians aspiring to scholarly inquiry are clear, concise, and even provocative, though they reflect a conservative research philosophy. It is conservative because he desires scholarly research approaches that can only be cultivated over a lifetime by motivated individuals dedicated to a more accurate understanding of God's Word. He leaves no room for shoddy service to God.

Theologians should be cognizant that natural theology provided the motivational basis for late medieval and early modern science. During the period 1250-1650, when our present scientific movement was taking form, every major scientist also considered himself a theologian. It is unfortunate that historical events and human frailties have created a contemporary situation where communication is difficult between the various scholarly disciplines. Dr. Bolich is both perceptive and pragmatic when he suggests that theologians should borrow research methods and data analysis techniques from the scientific fields that emerged from the motivational foundations of natural theology.

Dr. Bolich admonishes theologians to rethink research. He urges adherence to rigorous investigative models while honestly admitting the fact that all research is a uniquely human process. This human factor in research is responsible both for our unlimited potential for error, and for our perpetual drive to understand the world. Dr. Bolich superbly discusses the aspects of curiosity, interest, and the desire to answer the unanswered questions as these apply to theological research. He equates these motivations to the puzzle-solving activities of other researchers in the various scientific disciplines. He also provides an interesting perspective on the urge of theologians to respond to the work of others. All of these factors help to give definition to the tasks of scholarly disciplines.

Delightfully readable (unlike so many research texts), this book shows a clear relationship between theologians and **scholarly** research. Dr. Bolich skillfully leads the reader to agree with him that the goal for theologians is similar to that of all other scholarly researchers: to use rigorous investigative procedures that enable one to discern nonsense from reasonable facts. Several procedures are outlined along with the challenge to try them. The issue is squarely faced that all humans undertaking research face the decision to be competent or not; "to be or not to be competent" is **the** question.

Just as all consumers understand the warning "buyers beware," so the consumers of all research should realize that an abundance of data does not exclude human error. Dr. Bolich demonstrates that theological competence is a **sine qua non** for the faithful researcher of God's Word.

I warmly commend this labor to one and all.

INTRODUCTION

The Christian Scholar

Today

Christianity today is so diverse it is impossible to have much confidence in generalizing many things concerning it. I would like to say that today we are witnessing a resurgence of interest in solid Christian **thinking**, a renewal that has entered into even unexpected quarters of the Church. Unfortunately, I cannot say that as yet. If pressed to say something about the intellectual vitality of today's Church, I can report only that in **some** places **some** persons care deeply about Christian thinking and unceasingly work to produce both Christian scholarship and Christian scholars.

I wish that someday the **some** might become **all.**

Today there is still a widespread anti-intellectual temper within the Church. It is difficult occasionally to resist the judgment that religious conviction for many starts with a disavowal of thinking. In pious circles it is often fashionable to disdain reason as a pagan condition from which God's grace rescues. Fortunately, such circles are narrow and few, their influence usually restrained by the common sense of Christian faith. But as long as the mind which God has created is viewed with suspicion and mistrust, for just that long critical scholarship will be subject to fear and avoidance.

The Christian mind has the freedom to quest unhindered after the riches embodied in the Word of God. Faith cannot fear reason because faith engenders a renewed reason. Reason, if the thought be portrayed poetically, is the child of faith. Looked at in another manner, both are good gifts from God. There exists no natural rivalry between them to prompt concern in us that one must strive to gain an unholy ascendancy over against the other. If faith must take first place, it is not to reason's shame. Where reason climbs to new heights, faith is alongside to welcome the view. Where, as so often happens, reason leads downward into depths of doubt and uncertainty, there faith is once more, encouraging without blunting any of the difficulties. In this partnership of Christian liberty, faith and reason are meant to stand and to walk together.

Today this message must be pronounced without fear or hesitancy.

The Church must be reminded of the need to let faith

1

propagate reason. Christian scholars nowhere should permit themselves to be treated as second-class citizens. Scholarship is neither impractical nor inherently prejudicial to feeling and experience. Study cannot be opposed to prayer. Research cannot be restrained by dogmatic limits, or teachers by doctrinal standards. At its best, Christian scholarship respects fully the claims of both reason and faith.

I think we need a call to arms. Christian scholars, for the sake of the Church, must insist on the freedom to work unhindered by any other restraints than those natural to research, and especially dictated by their subject, the Word of God. But to make a call to arms effective it is essential that scholars discipline themselves anew with the call of their vocation. Theological research is service. To insist on the necessity of scholarship is not enough. Scholars bear the burden of understanding their own call and showing their fruits to the benefit of the entire Church.

This means that a call to arms today envisions a double education. On the one hand, Christian scholars are faced with conscientiously looking at themselves and their profession. A normal passion for knowledge must be examined and passed on. To those who are just now becoming scholars must be given values to set alongside methods, and wisdom to complement information. It is time to own up to that responsibility more honestly and vigorously than ever before.

But if scholars work harder to educate their own ranks, they also must redouble their efforts to expand those ranks so that in some sense, at least, every Christian is encompassed. It is inexcusable that any person, any place should fear research. Further, it is inexcusable that any scholar should permit such fear to occur and grow without trying to address it. How can it be that scholarship in God's Church should ever be shrouded in such mystery that it looks, finally, like magic? Not only the results of research, but also the methods that produce those results must be brought more successfully into the popular awareness of the Church.

Obviously, this is a tall order. That is why there is no better time than today for us to begin arming ourselves for the task.

This book is a contribution to the cause I have just espoused. I am not ignorant of the fact that many others share my concern, and I consider that my effort here aims at joining them in a common cause. The scope of this text is to set out an understanding of reasearch. There are research methods here; indeed, it may be that some unexpected ground can be glimpsed in chapters like those on statistical tools in theological research. But this text does not merely intend to serve up recipes for research. My aim is also to lay a foundation where research is made understandable as such. Then upon that foundation can be laid methods and models. So, the direction of the text is from theory to practice. Of

2

course, the best way to **learn** scholarship is to practice it; and so, too, is the best way to **teach** it. The purpose of this text is to exemplify scholarship, to set forth a reasonable course by which it may be practiced, and to lead the reader actually to attempt study along various general and specific lines.

The fulfilment of this purpose belongs not to tomorrow, but to today.

The Plan

The plan of this book is quite simple. There are three parts, each logically following what precedes it. The goal of the whole is to make research comprehensible, from its most basic features and essential roots through to a rather sophisticated example of study. Along the way a great many tasks are undertaken. The reader is asked to examine the theological vocation, learn the characteristics common to all forms of research, consider the demands set upon theology by the Word of God and the Church, and acquire an ability to read and understand the research of others. Then the reader is invited to undertake research. Aids are provided for conceiving a project and conducting it. Guidelines for reporting research are set forth. A good sampling of different research methods is offered together with models and examples. Finally, an actual example of a research study is given as a last comprehensive test of the skills the reader has acquired.

Part One establishes the fundamentals. It is not only the most basic material, it is also the simplest to read and to understand. This material ought not to be skipped or read hurriedly. It is foundational to what follows. While a few of the points made here are repeated later, most of the message of this part is presumed by the latter two parts. To maximize the usefulness of this text, the material of Part One should be mastered thoroughly before continuing on.

Part Two provides many methods and models of theological research. These vary significantly in difficulty, both to report and to understand. Some methods do not readily lend themselves to a brief treatment, especially when one of the objectives of the treatment is to produce a "how to" guide to doing the method. My success in this regard will be variously judged. The methods covered range from library research to inferential statistics. Broadly, this means that both qualitative and quantitative research strategies are offered. The range also is apparent in another important respect. The methods discussed are not limited to those predominant within biblical research. While such study remains a principal concern throughout the book, indications are given again and again as to how different models can be applied to many kinds of theological problems. This material depends on that of the first part of this text. Material in Part Two is not always easy to read and it demands the exercise of patience. Yet it can be understood. Throughout, I assume that the best way to gain

3

even a partial mastery of methods is by actually attempting them.

Part Three may appear in some respects optional. I encourage the reading of it because it can offer important help in at least two regards. First, it is a mixed research design. In other words, more than one research technique is employed. Much research, of course, is like this. It is helpful to study such a design as a way of reviewing much of what is contained in the first two parts of the book. Second, alongside this review should be an analysis of the research from the perspective of a colleague assigned the task of evaluating the study. What strengths and weaknesses are present? Is the study one that properly can be called scientific? Is it clear and understandable? These and other questions can be put to the study and thus test the research, and the reader.

The Challenge

Opportunity is what is made of it by the individual. Whether an abundance of resources or few resources exist the decisive thing is what is done with what is at hand. Scholars do the best they can with what they have. There are no guarantees, but there can always be integrity. It does not matter that this text is imperfect, for it surely is: what counts is what it can yield in positive benefits to those who sensibly use it.

I have tried to maintain a positive and optimistic tone throughout this book, though I confess that at times I am discouraged by the apathy so often evident among God's people. Still, I believe in God and in his Word. I love research. Many things disturb me concerning the way in which research is miscommunicated. I intend this book as a partial response. I am persuaded that today is the acceptable time to renew our minds in the study of God's Word so that we can serve faithfully within his Church.

Come, let us reason together.

4

PART ONE

An Introduction to Theological Research

INTRODUCTION

I am a theologian by vocation. As such, I care deeply about Christian scholarship. Research is a dominant aspect of my daily life, and a beloved one as well. In this first part I set out fundamental ideas related to scholarship and research.

I have been honest in these chapters. My values and biases are disclosed clearly. But these are not merely a matter of personal opinion, for while I adhere to these thoughts they are not simply my own creation, but part of a shared heritage. The ideas here set out belong in some sense to the community of scholars and to their tradition, though the expression and the ordering of them here is my own responsibility. As a member of this wider community I am able to labor fruitfully with others because of our mutual ideas, values, and concerns. Thus there is in these chapters an inevitable blend of myself and what I have received, the essentials of research.

Throughout this first part, I have kept the tone simple and also personal. I am interested not only in teaching, but also in persuading. I believe in the value of research as an endeavor, and I hope to encourage both an intelligent and a purposeful pursuit of this endeavor by all my readers. In later chapters, in Parts Two and Three, the discussion becomes more noticeably academic. But for now, in these first brief chapters, allow me the opportunity to share not just my knowledge, but also my passion.

On Being a Theologian

Introduction

What is a theologian? The question perplexes many Christians today for theology both is loved and feared. All Christians feel a certain attraction to theology that is tempered by concerns about whether they are capable of rightly engaging in theological work, or can do so without jeopardizing their faith. Theologians are individuals, and individuals vary; some inspire confidence, while others create unwelcome doubts. Yet all these individuals belong to a kind of society where they are known as "the theologians." What is it that makes this society?

Vocation and Individuality

The most basic trait shared by members of this society is a sense of vocation. Theology is the vocation of theologians. So in some sense we are all theologians, since we are all called to theology. This is why we experience its attraction: we all are directed toward God. But some experience this vocation as a call to life-long work involving full-time attention. Their vocation also becomes their job. Naturally, their individual personalities color their efforts, and not all people care for the same colors. Thus there is diversity within theology, and even conflict. Should this warn us away?

God has called the Church to theology as a natural aspect of its life and work. There is no promise that theology always will be simple and without controversy. Reflection, formulation of ideas and strategies, debate, reformulation, practice, and more dialog all are the very essence of a creative process wherein God stands at the center of his people's thinking, speaking, and doing. So in the broadest sense of vocation, theology is something to which all who are in the Church are called. This means that this vocation should be studied and understood.

As a vocation, theology is God's call to the study of himself. This may seem inappropriate to some, since we may think that God is better worshipped and obeyed than made the object of study. But theology should not be opposed to worship or obedience since we study in order better to worship and obey God. Moreover, our study is not an attempt to reduce God to a set of ideas or facts. An inescapably personal dimension exists in scholarship. Theology is a listening discipline that presumes God speaks and can be heard, with knowledge as one outcome, and service as both a goal and a fruit of the process. As God's call the theological vocation is measured by faithfulness, not by how much knowledge we possess or dispense.

God's call comes within the Church. Theology is not a matter for ivory towers or private reflection. It is nitty-gritty work involving real people in real situations. Unfortunately, in some places those who pursue theology with seriousness are seen in a rather more negative than positive light. Often this is due to excesses by young theologians who still lack the discipline and humility of the vocation to which they have given themselves. But sometimes this negativity results from people in the Church who regard these still learning theologians (and that includes all theologians, young or old) as relics from a bygone age, or as dangerous radicals more given to upsetting faith than to building it up. Too many Christians are unaware and unappreciative of theology. Hence, they cannot recognize the call to its full-time pursuit that some receive. So misunderstanding can exist on either side, and both the theologian and the fellow alongside in the pew must learn together what mutual respect and service entails.

The theological vocation rests in the decision of God as received and acted upon by individuals. Rightly understood, the call is one to service, a service aimed at helping "to equip the saints for the work of ministry, for building up the body of Christ, until we all attain to the unity of the faith and of the knowledge of the Son of God" (Eph. 4:12f.). Theologians must strive to communicate their call in their work, and their work in clear and understandable forms so that all may see how theology bears concretely on the life and the ministry of the Church. In this way theologians can invite a wider and more meaningful participation in the theological endeavor than has been evident in the recent past.

Naturally, the theological vocation will be conditioned by many things. Personal identity, training and education, individual talent, personal disposition, and unique situations all help form the special expressions by which a theologian becomes known. These expressions lend both variety and depth to the enterprise. Each theologian has his or her own unique history, personal understanding of what God requires, and intensely personal interest in creating and expressing work which is linked irrevocably to the self. So this vocation which comes from God, and is shared with others, is still one's own as well. The outworking of theology in the Church and the world is—and should be—passionately personal.

The desire remains to explain explicitly to people what that vocation is and how it comes. I wish I could set down a formula to clarify God's call. But none exists. The theological vocation starts as it also ends, in a personal relationship which

10

transcends either formulas or easy answers. All I can offer is some common sense: we must all develop a sensitivity to the movement of God in people's lives, whatever that may mean in any given setting. So instructors of theological material should train their ears to hear with novices whatever call exists. What else can this mean than patience with students, a willingness to listen to them and allow them to experiment as they seek God's direction? As truly difficult as it is to give a student much freedom for self-expression, when discipline is what most obviously is needed, it is essential that one exploring a possible call to some vocation be afforded honest opportunities to confirm or deny that call. At the same time, those around the seeker owe to him or her a debt of honesty. Few, if any calls come in a vacuum. The one who finds a call in silence and in isolation ought to mistrust it. God generally confirms his gifts and call through the agreeable discernment of others.

Another stricture needs to be communicated to those who find themselves attracted to theology. All theology belongs to God and to the Church as well as to the theologians. This joint ownership means a measure of accountability that can never be set aside. The creative expressions of individual theologians are to be subject to the very real needs of the Church. So young theologians need to learn—and older theologians need to be reminded—that they cannot be arbitrary or undisciplined in their work. Their theological expressions, as genuinely unique as they may be, nevertheless stand under the sign and stamp of Jesus Christ, the Lord of theology, and of the Church.

Among other things, this means that some of the most decisive influences on theological expression must come from outside of the theologian. He or she must adapt, to some extent, to these. Such influences begin with God himself, and include Holy Scripture, the contemporary Church situation, tradition, the mission of the Church, and the objective demands of whatever particular area of theology draws the interest of the theologian. Theology, then, is in a pure sense a **discipline**. Theologians are neither merely conservers of a tradition, nor purely inventors. They are stewards charged with receiving what is given to them, and representing it as best they can. This inevitably encompasses refining and extending what they have received. It incorporates the impulse to create, to invent—but never in a vacuum.

If we are to capture all of this in a metaphor, it might be that of a chorus with an orchestra. God conducts the performance, using individuals of differing talents and unequal skills for the various parts. Despite their differences, they are all part of one musical enterprise. In the flow of the music there are points and counterpoints. There are moments of quiet reflection and others of loud exuberance. The choir features young voices and old, poised ones and inexperienced. Yet the themes developed belong to all, and they blend together better than we often credit. Within the chorus and the orchestra there is room for conservative and liberal alike. The instruments of God's orchestra range from the pleasing resonance of the woodwinds to the sharp insistence of the brass. God alone hears the whole and judges each part in accordance with his own counsel in the Gospel of Christ.

Values

Alongside the influences that contribute to theological expression and bring the theological vocation to life are values. Some of these values are personal investments brought by the theologian to the work. These color and enrich the theology of that person, and often mark it out in a distinctive fashion. But some values are more societal in nature. These are values that arise from the nature of theological work itself, and which are therefore shared by all who participate in that work, whether they are professionals or not. It is these values that greatly determine the day-by-day course of a theologian's work.

Values which can be considered personal investments vary widely. For one theologian the value of joy might be so personally important that she or he imbues all her/his work with light and gladness. Another might feel compelled to measure all theology by the value of compassion; work that does not exemplify this value is then judged incomplete or flawed. Probably the preeminent example of this kind of value is the often heralded passion for "Truth." When a theologian brings this passion to his or her labor and invests it into the work, then that theology will bear the marks of it—especially in the dividend of an increased perception of truth. There are many different values that could be mentioned as personal investments.

More relevant to our discussion are **shared** values, for these enable a better understanding of the theological vocation as such. Shared values arise inevitably from the work of theology and impose themselves as necessary conditions for complete success. Because theological work is heavily dependent upon research, these values are largely associated with such research. A theological **scholar** is a careful **researcher**. I believe that these research values are also shared by other disciplines where research plays an integral part. All research is fundamentally more alike than it is different; all research sets certain conditions that must be met for complete success to occur.

At least five basic values should be mentioned because among them they involve most of the chief concerns of theological research, and thereby, of theological work. Each of these five in reality names more than a single value. Each specifies a set of related concerns. These values may be known by different names to different scholars, but the substance of what is expressed by each truly is fundamental to theological work. These values more often are held and practiced unconsciously than drawn conspicuously, but they are no less real because of this situation.

The first value is a commitment to **truth**. This is not "Truth" as the poet's vision; that is a personal investment. This commitment is to truth in the acquisition of facts. It is the integrity of an open and honest approach to whatever is being studied, and a dedication to truthful reporting of the means and results of study. Unlike the powerful urge to **know**, this is the simpler necessity of dealing faithfully with things so that something **can** be known. Without this key value theological work plainly is impossible. The Bible warns, "For the time is coming when people will not endure sound teaching, but having itching ears they will accumulate for themselves teachers to suit their own liking, and will turn away from listening to the truth and wander into myths" (2 Tim. 4:3, 4). Such a thought might be applied to this value: failure to discipline one's self to keep to the facts is no different than acquiring a teacher to tell only what is desired to be heard. In either instance the truth no longer is being listened to, and wandering into endless speculation becomes a sure matter.

The second value similarly evolves from practical necessity. It is the pursuit of **control**. The term itself may be striking and quite unfamiliar in theological circles; control as a value more often is associated with the social or natural sciences. Control means, among other things, a commitment to understanding, to practicality, and to significance. Theologians want to control the information at their disposal by understanding it, not by manipulating it for selfish gain. Likewise, theologians generally are much more interested in showing the practicality of their research than they are credited with by the few who persist in believing that all theology is an exercise in wishful thinking. However, for a scholar, practicality, or utility, is primarily measured in terms of prediction: if others following the same course of research perceive like things, then the study is useful, both in its methodology and in its consequences (products). This is not to suggest that theologians are not also vitally interested in the practical effects of their work for daily life. They want to effect positive change in the Church and in society, too. But utility begins with the idea that the work can be repeated with similar results. All theologians also want to know if their work is significant. But this, too, is measured by a definite criteria. Significant work is **powerful** in its meaning to the degree of its ability to explain matters adequately and consistently. Thus, significant theology is not simply creative but sound.

The third value is **order**. Order always seeks to produce work bearing a true likeness to the reality being studied. Theologians assume that their work to some degree can mirror, or reflect, the things they study. Moreover, they act on the basis that reality is itself ordered; even chaos is subject to a greater order. This order can be investigated systematically. That investigation may yield a variety of plausible explanations for various matters, but scholars, because of a preference for

13

finding order, will tend to accept the simpler explanations over more complex ones. Similarly, they will adopt the clearest and the simplest tools available to conduct their studies.

Tolerance is the fourth value. Of course, tolerance can be a personal value investment, as in a tolerance of other theologians' "obvious aberrations." But tolerance also suggests other important ideas. For a theologian, tolerance means an ability to cope maturely with error, failure, and incompleteness without despairing or giving up the struggle. Tolerance for human limitations when daily dealing with divinity also entails learning to be content with plausible explanations when exact ones are lacking. No theology can be exhaustive. Rather, it must settle for being sufficient for the needs of a particular people at a specific time in a given place. If the work is plausible it need not be perfect. But it must make good sense in light of the other values. Tolerance means, too, the willingness to seek a true likeness in one's own theology to the theology of the Church. This is not always easy because all theologians would like to believe that their work "corrects" or "refines" or "extends" the Church's theology to some degree. A healthy dose of tolerance is needed for an openness to self-criticism, and an even more important openness to the Church's efforts to "extend," "correct," or "refine" one's labors. But if we would speak, we must also learn to listen.

Finally, undergirding all of these values, and bearing the most remarkable resemblance to the nature of theological work as I know it, is the value of **discipline**. Among the various facets this value encompasses are self-control, diligence, and submission. Theology requires a discipleship of self-control in handling an occupation that bears on the whole life of man. There is no room here for careless pranksters or sloppy laborers. Coupled with this caution, though, is the need for diligence in urgently pursuing the manifold important concerns that distinguish theology. Theology ought to be a vocation marked preeminently by disciplined passion, because theology holds God's urgent summons to all mankind. Under this sign theologians also stand, and to the author of the summons they must give answer. The only acceptable response is a disciplined faithfulness.

The Theologian as a Student

The influences and values that surround the theologian and so shape his or her vocational expressions could be characterized legitimately by any one of several headings. It seems to me, though, that one term stands out clearly as superior. The theologian is a **student**. The word "theology" carries this basic meaning: **theos** is the Greek word for "God," and **logos** is the Greek term for "word." When the term **logos** is joined to another word in English (as "-logy"), it conveys the idea of study. Thus, biology is the study of life, geology is the study of the earth, and theology is the study of God. Even

14

though theology is a term which has come to embrace a number of shades of meaning for different people, at heart it means **the study of God.**

Let us examine four critical characteristics of a student. Being a good student is requisite to being a competent scholar, for these traits sustain scholarly endeavor. All that will be said later about research begins with the values we already have examined and with these student characteristics.

First, a good student is **earnest.** For anyone in any work to accomplish the best possible job, that person must be convinced that the work is important. An earnest student approaches every task with the conviction that somehow, in some way, what is being done really matters. Yet earnestness is incomplete in itself. It supplies a motivating drive which yields a second important trait: **zeal.** This is the quality of applied hard work. Energy must be applied to the matter at hand. A zealous student will not let the subject loose until it has been handled as completely as possible.

But not even zeal can produce solid or dependable scholarship without a strong measure of a third trait: **discipline.** A student's labors must be systematic and progressive. Study is to a certain extent a reflection of life; students successful in life understand the need for careful self-control. Sincerity alone cannot accomplish very much. Unchanneled or unfocused energy also is largely wasted energy. Not only must the student concentrate on what is at hand, to the exclusion of competing demands, but there must be a plan in operation. Discipline entails both a personal dimension (self-control) and an objective dimension (a systematic, purposeful plan of action).

Finally, the student must be **submissive.** For a student this is a **sine qua non**; without submission a student cannot qualify as a student. This is true because study requires the student to be put under the rule of the subject. The subject must control the scope, direction, and even the processes of study. For a theologian this means allowing God, as the object of study, to dictate the terms and conditions by which knowledge may come. If God has chosen faith as the avenue of true and dependable access to knowledge of and about himself, then the theologian also must choose faith. Thus it is faith that establishes reason, not the other way around. Relevant and accurate theological facts cannot be divorced from faith, though the exact relation between facts and faith can be explained in many various ways.

Alongside these student characteristics should be set complementary study ideals. Simply listing ideal study traits may make us wonder if there are many (or any) scholarly studies being done in today's classrooms. But, of course, these traits must be developed; they do not suddenly appear in a perfected state. Excellence in study is an acquired matter, and the only way to reach the goals exemplified by these traits is through intelligent and diligent practice.

First, then, study combines **creative reflection** with **investigation**. Creative reflection can take the form of contemplative speculation, imaginative projection, or simple daydreaming. It is a process of permitting what is being studied to work its own way unhindered through the mind. Free from many complex rational structures, creative reflection seeks insight. But this facet is only a minor aspect of study. Investigation, with all its commitment to structured ways of analyzing the object of study, is the principal part. While solid, methodical investigation can profit from creative flights of the "sanctified imagination," study remains peculiarly a **discipline** of the thought processes.

Next, study demands a **sustained application of sound thinking**. It is not truly study to rely on creative, spontaneous insight. While the helpfulness of serendipitous moments of inspiration gains media publicity, it is hard work that accounts for most results. Scholars rely on a sustained application of those qualities that make for sound thinking, things like caution, an insistence on evidence to support all assertions, and an openness to data that does not support their own ideas. These qualities only work as they should when they are used in a sustained fashion. There is no such person as the once a week scholar. Study takes time, hard work, and intelligent use of well-constructed principles of investigation.

Thus, third, an excellence in study depends upon an adherence to **rigorous investigative models**. The principles of investigation are found in models which are theories, that is, collections of hypotheses rationally systematized and empirically supported. Theories, naturally, are not sacred, and can be challenged, and occasionally even overthrown. But they are aids to profitable study and they should be employed with the understanding that as imperfect as they are, they are still the best conceptual tools presently available. Theories are both a means to explain facts that are discovered, and a means to discover facts. In other words, theories predict that certain facts consistent with other, already known facts, should be subject to discovery if methods appropriate to the theory are used. Thus, by utilizing particular methods, the theory is tested by the search for new supporting evidence. While there are a variety of models in theology, all of them share the above characteristics and have in common the fact that they are self-consistent ways of approaching, observing, and explaining the objects under study.

Finally, an excellence in study means ultimately a personal investment into the work of all that a person has and is. Theological work is done by theologians, by persons called by God to put **themselves** into the theological task. It takes persons to conceive of theories, persons to extend and refine them, and persons to test them. Excellence in study requires a **personal integration** and also a **personal expression** of the learning that has been participated in and so acquired. Study excellence is

16

never confined to a recapitulation of material obtained from others. Instead, it is the result of a mutual participation with others. It is a dialog and an interaction expressed in uniquely personal forms and terms.

Study is for Service

The task of theology is circumscribed by the **purpose** of study, namely, **service**. This service has a two-fold expression: first, in serving God, and second, in serving man. Both of these are actually reflections of the same thing; each is determined by the Word of God. Service is the theologizing that completes the theological vocation.

Study and service are both linked to the Word of God. Yet, as often as I have invoked this phrase, I have yet to explain what it means. Today, the Word of God is used commonly and popularly to refer principally, or even **only** to the Bible. But this restricted use of the term is recent and quite inadequate. The Bible itself names three forms as proper aspects of the one Word. These are Jesus Christ (Jn. 1:1-3, 14), the Holy Scriptures (Mk. 7:9-13; 2 Pe. 3:15, 16), and the preaching of the Gospel (1 Th. 2:13; 1 Pe. 1:25). These forms are in union without fusion, and distinct without separation.

The service of God occurs under the dominion of this Word. The precise activities of this service are many and varied, but all can be characterized broadly as **witness**. Because the theological vocation is one of students of the Word of God, the theologian's chief service of witness lies in studying the Word for the benefit of the Church's own multi-faceted ministry of witness. Of course, theologians are expected also to participate in other functions as members of the Church. But first they serve as students, equipping God's people as ministers to the world.

Theological witness is conditioned and directed toward the Word of God. Theologians cannot legitimately say something fundamentally at odds with what God's Word claims. In fact, their words derive all their legitimacy from this source. Theologians aim at interpreting the meaning of what is found within the Word and applying it to the concrete situation of today. What theologians say intends to help others to hear and comprehend what God communicates in the Word. This theological effort is not a narrow one. Creativity, including the use of materials and ideas outside the Bible, is often helpful in accomplishing the task. Still, the Word stands first. It is because of this primacy that sometimes the Bible, as the most accessible and easiest to handle form of the Word, is granted a standing and usage not truly fitting to its intended purpose and place. The result is bibliolatry.

The Bible **is** important to the theologian as an objective form. Standing midway between Christ and Church proclamation, the Bible represents Christ's own Word in and through the ministry of the Holy Spirit's witness. Scripture acts as the

17

canon ("rule") of the Church in bearing witness. But the Bible cannot stand alone, and a naive biblicism is harmful.

God's Word also delineates the service of man. This service is characterized by proclamation in word and deed. The theologian's concern is not simply to formulate ivory castles upon which others may build homiletical towers of grandeur, beauty, and poetic insight. Theology goes beyond that artifice to the muddy, earthy, dirty work of confronting a humanity in all the morass of its sin, depravity, and need.

Here, too, confession is preeminent as the Church proclaims the Gospel. Theologians assist in that work by striving to render for the Church a confession both faithful to the Word and relevant to a modern age. Theologians explore God's Word in order to help the Church help others. This is why theologians make free use of other resources, and why they make certain things outside the Word the subject of limited inquiries. Faithfulness to serving a needy world makes it necessary to embrace a wide and sensitive scholarship.

A Final Note

Study is basic to the mastery of a vocation, **any** vocation. What distinguishes theology is what the student studies. In theology the scholar stands in a peculiar relation to the Word of God. This relation binds the student to the Word, and sets the student free.

The proper use of this freedom in Christian scholarship rests with values, character traits carefully cultivated, and conscientious development of an excellence in study. These things, with God's call, bring a student to research and make that research profitable. And that, after all, is what we think of first when we talk about Christian scholarship.

2

Theological Research

The Theological Vocation and Research

Anyone called to be a theologian must master the practice of research. To accomplish this, it is first necessary to understand what research is, and why it is important to the theological vocation. I am going to begin with this latter consideration. Research is essential to theological work because without it theologizing cannot take place. The conceiving and doing of research is the heart of theological work.

Now I realize that such an assertion is unfamiliar, and probably somewhat suspicious at first glance. After all, isn't there something profoundly theological in feeding the hungry, or visiting the sick? I have no wish to deny that many theological services operate in a manner that makes their connection to research quite invisible. Of course, whether this is a desirable condition is another matter. But what theological service does not begin with research of some kind?

A recollection of the basic features of the theological vocation may make my contention easier to accept. All of us are called to the task of theologizing, of being students of the Word. Most of us, most of the time, rely on others to provide the scholarly rationale for what they, or ourselves, are doing. Research remains in the background. But whenever we study we experience to some degree things integral to research. Theology incorporates the values of research, and the practice of it as well. All this takes place at many different levels, some very simple and others not so simple. But research is never very far from theological labor.

The Word of God demands research. This demand arises from logical necessity, historical distance, and the divine will. Theology works with materials that only yield maximum benefit when they are subjected to careful, i.e., **scholarly** inquiry. The Scriptures, for example, embody an ancient collection of documents. Time separates us from them in such a way as to make research necessary. Our own desire for order and sense leads us to research so we may clarify, organize, and comprehend theological materials and ideas. God, too, seems desirous of our giving his Word careful and constant attention (cf. Jas. 1:22-25).

Let us return for a moment to the example of the Bible.

9

The composition of its ancient materials spanned hundreds of years, with the most recent writings being removed from us by nearly two millenia. The languages used in the Bible, the cultures described there, and the ways of life and patterns of thinking are all different from what is familiar to us today. To make these things intelligible to modern men and women the Church, in **every** generation, has fostered study and encouraged research. The work of Bible translation, of exegesis, of the application of Christian truth to life (to name but a few), all these rest on the foundation and continuing exercise of research.

Research: A Human Process

If research is this important, it is essential to understand what it exactly entails. Especially crucial is a comprehension of how research can take the form of **theological** research. I think a proper view of research in general enables a clearer, more accurate perception of theological research in particular. To be sure, there are a few differences. But the similarities are more basic. Comprehending these basics will aid in the mastery, later, of particular models and methods.

All research is a human process. Theological research is not at all different in this respect. Theologians stamp the indelible imprint of their own personalities onto their scholarly expressions. Yet, as we have seen, too, theologians cannot be arbitrary in this because theology also belongs to the Church. Thus, theological research as a human process incorporates the involvement of individuals and the community as a whole. The research shares the strengths and the weaknesses of these participants. This last point scarcely can be overstated.

All research is affected by its participants. In fact, the essential humanity of all research rests precisely in that. All persons share a commonality of human experience, personal knowledge, purposeful activity, and reliance on conceptual models. Despite the immense variety and complexity in human existence these are common facets of life. Each individual is connected to every other. This networking connection makes research possible and productive because it eliminates the need for endless and pointless repetition, at the same time that it encourages efforts to extend advances.

A commonality of **human experience** means an ability for persons to relate meaningfully to the struggles, thoughts, and feelings of others no matter where they are in time and space. In other words, because men and women are united by their capability to experience the world in similar fashion, irrespective of changing historical and cultural conditions, the study of history and the attempt to relate to one another cross-culturally both can have meaning. This is not to suggest that differences in time and culture make **no** difference, but it is to say that those differences are not so great as to make historical study or cross-cultural ties impossible. For theologians, this commonality means that the Word of God is addressed to all peoples. Theology can take advantage of this commonality to communicate the Gospel in appropriate ways to various individuals and cultures, without sacrificing faithfulness to the message or intent of the Word (cf. 1 Co. 9:19-23).

A commonality of **personal knowledge** means that everyone has something meaningful to contribute to humanity. This something stems from a unique relation to God and his creation. The philosopher Michael Polanyi has said that we all know more than we can express. Yet this knowledge influences what we do express. Theology is enriched by all who take part in it, just as it can enrich each of its participants. People discover that they can contribute important insights, share a mutual sense that great and wonderful things are left inadequately expressed by everyone, and delight in realizing how their own ideas are often similar to those of others. Personal knowledge provides a base for the exchange of ideas and information. It comprises an important element of research as a comprehensively human inquiry after knowledge.

A commonality of **purposeful activity** means that all individuals seek to engage themselves in those activities that provide meaning to their lives. Research, because it embraces as its tools feeling, common sense, and physical labor, parallels this striving by providing structured forms for persons to use in their purpose-seeking activities. Thus research encourages people to use what they already have at their disposal, namely emotions, intellect, and physical energy, to accomplish effectively meaningful work. Theological research provides people the means to channel their personal resources into a creative obedience to God's Word, which is meaningful not merely for the individual, but also for the Church and the world.

Finally, the commonality of a **reliance on conceptual models** means that people are aware that they are not alone in the world, and that they do not have all the answers themselves. Everyone needs a perspective on life. Something has to be created or adopted that not only makes sense of reality, but also can serve as a basis for communicating ably with others. Research builds on the commonalities of human experience, personal knowledge, and the need for purposeful activity. It builds a framework of various methods and models that can, at least partially, satisfy the necessity of making sense of things and being able to talk about it to others. Theological research does this in accordance with God's Word, thus providing an "outside" perspective (cf. 2 Co. 5:16). This perspective is one that carries with it the authority of God's experience, personal knowledge, activity, and structure.

Necessarily, then, theological research always returns to God and his Word. This fact makes theological research distinct from all other research, although the manner in which this returning takes place always bears the character of **human** repentance and faith. Theological research is formulated within the Church and by theologians as a human response and activity. This kind of research complements all other research endeavors; it does not replace them. Theological knowledge is not the only valid knowledge. Still, it does enjoy a singular position of eminence in the total life of God's Church.

The humanity of all research, including theological research, demands several critical conclusions that reflect the nature and the limitations of human inquiry. First, research is the work of people. It is a human process and product. The knowledge gained can be easily, if not completely accurately, attributed to man himself. Thus people are tempted to one of two equally wrong ideas. On the one hand, they may despair that there is anything more to know, or that can be known. They may feel trapped by human limitations. On the other hand, they may conclude that they know all they need to know to "save" themselves in this life, and any that might follow. The first idea fails to see how God works within human limitations and provides what we need. The second idea erroneously concludes that knowledge is a kind of salvation. But not even theological research can promise any ultimacy of human knowledge.

Second, research encompasses and utilizes both thought and feeling, reason and experience. But these are imperfect and limited despite their genuinely awesome capacities. Research, likewise, is imperfect and limited. The fallibility of research menas the ongoing need for correction and, by logical implication, for dialog and continuing participation in the process. The limitations of research require a development that simultaneously recognizes that research cannot become perfect, but still strives to come as close to perfection as possible. Theological research, because of its imperfections and limitations, must continue to rely on the infallible Word of God, and do so in humility and openness to reform.

Third, research depends on certain exterior, "objectifying" elements to avoid arbitrariness. "Objectifying" means creating research that is not overly dependent on the researcher but rests primarily on the existence and qualities of whatever is being studied. Therefore, any elements that can be introduced to limit the individuality of the researcher and increase a true perception of what is being studied are quite valuable. But such objectifying elements also place limitations on the research in terms of its scope, methods employed, and results. Obviously, the more objectifying elements that are present, the more dependable is the research.

Research and Faith

In theological research the Word of God provides these needed objectifying elements. While this has several dimensions, at root it means that God, as the object of the theologian's research, himself determines the appropriate accesses to knowledge about himself. He sets the limitations to human knowledge

22

which best serve his own purposes. The stress in theology on the **revealed** God is hardly accidental. God's own free self-disclosure to us in his Word means everything to theology, since without it there is nothing concrete, objective, dependable, and therefore, authoritative.

Because God sets **faith** as the only way to attain theological knowledge (cf. Heb. 11:3, 6), it is necessary to understand faith and its place in theological research. Faith is **not** empirical or rational knowledge. Faith can lead to such knowledge because it is an intuitive, indwelling trust that permits God's Word to speak for itself and be heard in obedient submission. I say that it is an intuitive, indwelling trust because the Bible speaks of faith as in God, or in Christ (Gal. 3:26; Eph. 1:15). From this **inner** vantage point God's Spirit, "searching the mind of God" (1 Co. 2:6-16), communicates factual knowledge of God by means of the objective forms of the Word (i.e., the historical Christ, the Bible, and preaching).

Theological research accordingly takes on the character of what Anselm termed **fides quaerens intellectum**, "faith in search of understanding." The objective knowledge to which a theologian gains access by faith still requires the application of rigorous thought. Although faith is the precondition to attaining knowledge and making right use of it, it is accompanied by a following-after intellect. Faith in the quest for understanding makes capable use of reason and empirical knowledge. The knowledge, however, rests on a foundation not of **cogito, ergo sum,** "I think, therefore I am" (Descartes' rationalism), but of **credo, ut intelligam,** "I believe, in order to understand."

The question is likely to rise as to how it is possible for a disbelieving researcher to attain to theological knowledge, since many obviously do. Have they succeeded apart from faith? Personally, I understand their work as being made possible by the faith of the Church. It provides all men with objective knowledge attained by faith, regardless of the personal investment of any particular individual. Of course, their knowledge is of limited utility, but it can still be used by the Church. I am unwilling to contest this point too strongly, as there are other viable ways of accounting for what is a remarkable situation.

The faith instrumental in theological research is not **credulity.** By this I mean a readiness to believe on weak, or insufficient bases. Credulity is an abuse of faith, and occasionally its counterfeit. It is not the search for understanding, but an easy giving-in to whatever looks believable. Faith, on the other hand, accepts the inevitability of a growing rational understanding, with its consequences, as surely as it also expects obedience. Faith resists credulity by an intense desire to **know** as well as to **believe.**

Faith does distinguish theological research from other research, but not in the manner that it might be expected to do this. All research involves some kind of "faith" investment, some form of an intuitive, indwelling trust. It may be in a particular theory, teacher, or insight ("hunch"). But faith for the theologian must be in the Word of God, that is, in God himself. It is not, therefore, the mere presence of faith that distinguishes theological research, but once again its object: God. Faith is important in providing access to the objectifying elements that research craves.

Scientific Theology

Inasmuch as theological research is not separated from other kinds of research by the practice of faith, and since it does share much in common with all research as a human inquiry, can it legitimately be called "scientific?" To answer this correctly depends on two points. First, it must be assumed that on the basis of its fundamental likeness to all research, theological research can at least be **possibly** scientific. Second, what is "scientific" must be determined.

Most people think that they know what science is. It is both a way of doing research, and a set of research disciplines. Thus, for many people, science means the "empirical method" used by natural scientists. Some extend this idea to include social scientists and, perhaps, one or two other groups. If this is science, then much of theology may not qualify. But, interestingly enough, scientists themselves rarely hold such a view. They recognize that science is much broader than such a conception.

As a term, "science" means something close to both "research" and "study." Science is the rigorous and the systematic pursuit of knowledge. It utilizes both study and research. Science is related to research in much the same way that research is related to study. Science is a more comprehensive concept, at least in the sense that it further qualifies the basic notion of human inquiry embodied in the terms "research" and "study." Science represents the most sophisticated and methodical approach to research. It is an approach that is strongly oriented not only to the research values described above, but also to empirical tools.

Science possesses at least three basic characteristics. It limits its work to tested or testable tools, it adheres to the development of a definite and self-consistent set of values to undergird all of its methodologies, and it views progress and success in terms of predictability and replicability. In short, science is very conservative. It wishes to proceed with human inquiry cautiously, with repeated checkpoints, and according to an established, carefully prepared plan. As it proceeds, it seeks evidence that can be tested as to its dependability. Evidence that cannot be replicated (i.e., repeated and duplicated) by the work of others is not considered too trustworthy. At the same time, really helpful evidence "fits," it helps to put together a framework for making sense of other things and also predicting as yet unknown things.

In all of these senses, theology can be considered a "science," and theological research "scientific." It, too, is very conservative, heavily depending on evidence (not "proof"). It also depends upon replicability (that criteria is the foundation for hermeneutics), and predictability (which permits cautious inferences and systematizing). Theological research upholds the values of science, and practices its work in a scientific manner, with a scientist's reserve. The Word of God helps discipline this scientific inquiry by placing stringent demands on those who approach it seeking an ever deeper, more comprehensive understanding. Through faith, with all of the natural tools of reason and experience, scientific theology can be practiced.

3

The Elements of Research

Introduction

Theological research is both like and unlike other kinds of research. Once it was called the "Queen of the Sciences," and I like that designation. Theology rises above other scientific endeavors becuase it concerns itself with the highest object of knowledge (God), and the most certain ground for understanding (God's Word). Theological research follows after the inquiring Spirit as he searches the "thoughts of God" (cf. 1 Co. 2:6-16). Unlike other kinds of research, theology openly acknowledges the fundamental importance of faith. It is its glory, not its shame. Reason and experience are made the companions of faith.

The likeness of theological research to other kinds of research rests largely in the manner in which reason and experience are employed. Theology is not, ultimately, the articulation of a mystic vision. It is the proclamation of the Gospel as God's self-disclosed knowledge of himself. This proclamation uses the mind and human experience to form creative vehicles of expression. These expressions are aimed at renewing the Church's understanding in each new generation. Theological reform, then, is the work of nudging the Church to faithful and contemporary expressions of God's Word.

Reason and experience do not create a knowledge of God, but explore it. They create relevant likenesses of what faith receives in order to aid the understanding of successive generations. In short, faith sparks reason and experience so that scientific research can and does occur. With this ground firmly established, we can examine six basic phases utilized in all manner of research efforts.

Interest

The first of these phases is the **motivation** that moves a person from being a non-student to a diligent researcher. Obviously, **interest** is essential. An individual whose curiosity is pricked by something will very likely look into it enough to either satisfy the initial interest or increase it. In this manner, people's general interest in living things may lead them into more specific lines of interest such as microbiology or botany. As they pursue their interest, they may either satisfy it enough to leave the subject for another interest, or decide to follow it into special and related interests.

How does interest relate to a theologian's vocation? Does God call persons to theology independent of individual interest? Perhaps we should ask which comes first, the call, or curiosity? Personally, I am not persuaded that answering such a query is very important; what matters is that both the call and the interest are prsent in a theologian's life. Naturally, theologians possess an interest in their work. As in any vocation, liking what the work requires is an important concern. Theologians use research to help satisfy their own curiosity about things. In fact, their research begins with their interest, which motivates them to act. When the call to vocation is added to natural interest, a glad union occurs, one in which theology is a joy, no matter how difficult the work might become.

Exploration

Through faith the Holy Spirit communicates the knowledge of God. But reason and experience are not left without their proper tasks. The theologian's interest in what the Spirit discloses stimulates reason to a diligent application. Likewise, the experience of God and his Word, as well as the experience of the world, prompt exercises of trying to make communicable sense of everything. Faith unites with reason and experience in ordinary practice so that our attempts to distinguish where one begins and another leaves off are largely unprofitable.

Nowhere is this unity more evident than in the exploration of God's Word. Theological research, like all research, depends heavily on sustained and accurate exploration. Faith contributes a confident trust and willing submission to the Word. Reason gives studied contemplation. Experience adds observation and manipulation. But all work together, often simultaneously, to complete a thorough examination. This interaction makes theological research one exploratory process no matter which aspect is emphasized at a given time.

The examination of the Word entails two primary facets. The more basic of the two is the **source** actually being explored. For the theologian this source is ultimately God himself. But as we have seen, God has disclosed himself in the three-fold form of his one Word, so that Word is the scholar's source. Yet, because this Word does possess three distinct forms, any one of these may serve as a source. So, in a sense, there is both one source and yet many sources.

The Word, in its three-fold form, provides diverse sources, all corresponding to its own nature. Thus, the second form of the one Word, the Bible, takes the shape of sixty-six documents, some of which are themselves the results of multiple sources. These documents bear the different characteristics of various literary types. Any one of these can serve as material for detailed exploration. Yet obviously, some are more concrete and susceptible to a full examination. This idea holds true for all sources of the Word in any of its forms. More tools, for instance, can be brought to bear upon the Bible than can be brought into play when studying the first form of the Word, Jesus. However, it is crucial to understand that all the forms are constituent parts of a unified, greater whole, the Word. Thus, while an examination of the first form of the Word is in itself restricted and indirect in many ways, it can still be explored by the thorough, direct examination of the second form of the Word, since both forms belong to **one** Word. Accordingly, we can and do study the Bible to learn of Jesus although we also recognize that there is much about him we cannot know from the Bible.

Coupled with sources are various **methods.** The examination of God's Word requires both direct and indirect methods. Let us once more use the figure of Jesus as an example. Our study of him will employ indirect methods, that is, tools which recognize that any immediate and direct access to his person is not included in the study. Since at present Jesus is not experienced by our senses like other living people are, the study of Jesus must be like the study of any historical figure. Documents, artifacts, and the recorded testimony of those who knew him when he walked upon the earth provide for us indirect ways of acquiring dependable knowledge about him. Of course, this evidence gained indirectly must be critically assessed but this need not dismay us. Criticism seeks to affirm truth, not to deny it. At the same time, scholarly study does not deny that the person of Jesus can be known directly. It does suggest, however, that theological tools to directly explore the Jesus immediately revealed by God's Spirit are either lacking or deficient for research purposes where replicability is at a premium. Scholarship, then, is cognizant of its own limitations in such a matter as direct examination of the Risen Lord. Expressed in another way, theologians recognize that an exploration of the first form of the Word requires an examination of the second form in order to be valid, reliable, and replicable for the community of the Church at large. Everyone can learn something of Jesus by indirectly approaching him through the Bible. **That** examination can be verified and repeated.

Indirect methods of examination are probably more common to the researcher because many things cannot be directly explored. Even when they can be, indirect methods may still be quite useful. The Bible can be directly examined; a cultic practice which it may describe cannot be. Of course, the Bible can also be indirectly explored by interrogating students of the Bible, asking them questions designed to contribute to the researcher's own understanding. This is one reason why theological researchers value archaeological artifacts and nonbiblical, ancient documents. They add to a fuller understanding of the Bible.

Description

As exploration takes place, and after a particular investigation is completed, the researcher typically experiences the desire to describe what has been observed, as well as his or her explanation of it, or thoughts about it. But where explanation aims at making some sense out of what has been examined, **description** merely points out what has, in fact, been examined. Thus, description is more basic than explanation, and undergirds it.

When a theological researcher describes the Word of God, or any of the contributory sources of knowledge, he has at his disposal both numbers and words. Words, of course, are the predominant tool used. They may describe what has been explored by presenting quotes, allusions, records, translations, or factual reports. They are appropriately used if their presence actually does describe, at least in part, what has been looked at. For instance, describing Paul's use of the Law may entail alluding to some of the key passages in his epistles, quoting an important text from Romans, and presenting a detailed summary of what Paul actually said.

Although too often overlooked, numbers can also be profitably employed in description. To describe Paul's use of the Law might also mean compiling descriptive statistics that clearly show what is really there. Thus the researcher might note the frequency, or the number of times, that Paul uses the term "Law," or compute the ratio of texts devoted to this subject compared to others interested in "faith." These statistics do not "prove" anything about what Paul meant; they only describe what Paul wrote. But this function has value too (cf. chapters 15 and 16).

Explanation

Description almost inevitably gives way to explanation. It is easy to see why. A researcher cannot avoid interacting with what is being explored and described. Scholarly interest is rarely satisfied by just these activities. Instead, the researcher seeks meaning, the significance of what has been studied. This is a turning to the critical labor of finding an explanation for what has been observed.

Theologians try to explain the Word of God. Often this task is seriously misunderstood. Some people look at theological activity with profound distrust, and even disgust. They believe that what theologians are really doing is creating their own thoughts to take the place of God's thoughts. If this perception is accurate, then theology is indeed dangerous when it supposes itself to be representing accurately God's Word.

But what actually takes place in theological explanation? This activity should be understood as a natural and desirable outcome of the Church's recurrent response to the Word. Even within the first decades of the life of the Christian community the need for theological explanation was perceived. Paul viewed his communication as "interpreting spiritual truth to those who possess the Spirit" (cf. 1 Co. 2:13). Yet even Paul had to be interpreted because in his writings are "some things . . . hard to understand" (2 Pe. 3:16). The need has never diminished.

Theological explanation is the declaration of the sense of what has been examined and described by making clear its meaning, significance, or reason. Practically, it carries both a positive aim and a negative function. Positively, it works to clarify, highlight, and account for the meaning of things. Negatively, it functions as a corrective to misunderstandings of the meaning of things. Either way, its importance and necessity are beyond reasonable doubt or dispute.

The real problem lies in the fact that explanations cannot be dispassionately objective. They involve human beings who **declare** the sense of things in their own individual ways. But is this truly arbitrary? Of course not, because the actual **sense** lies behind the declaration, and exercises its control over it. If, for example, I explain Paul's use of the Law by inventing my own conception of justice, it only takes someone else a minimum amount of consideration to conclude how foolish I am. But if I explain his use of the Law by clarifying his arguments in various biblical texts, then others are aided in their comprehension. They are also made more secure in their awareness that the actual sense of Paul controls my explanation of his work. If I cannot explain it as Paul might, I nevertheless can explain it in a manner helpful to my hearers, and faithful to Paul's meaning.

Actually, the coloring of theological explanations by those who make them, including theologians and the Church, is right and good. The Word of God uses these activities to maintain its relevance for each generation. There is sound reasoning behind the decision not to use 1st century, 16th century, or even 19th century theological expressions as our own. To adopt their expressions as ours is to isolate the Church from the world. If different groups within the Church adopt various communication vehicles belonging to disparate periods of the past, then the Church also becomes relatively isolated from herself. The vehicles of communicating truth, of explaining God's Word, become substitutes for the real meaning, because they are **different**. The differentness draws attention to itself, and more and more people lose sight of the meaning as they focus on the time-conditioned vehicle bearing it. Let God himself be our instructor in this: he used common (Koine) Greek to a 1st century world, not classical Greek, Hebrew, or some "heavenly language." Likewise, let the Church's example be our own: the 16th century Reformers recaptured the sense of God's Word without succumbing to a fruitless revival of the 1st century world view, or the peculiar expressions of the 1st century Church. Indebtedness to the past does not mean bondage to it.

At the same time, contemporary explanations of theological

matters are quite free to draw upon the rich resources of Church tradition. The past provides excellent and poor models to instruct present labors. Current explanations can correct, renew, or extend helpful insights from the past. There is nothing wrong with retaining confessions, or repeating them. We can enjoy our continuity with that "great cloud of witnesses" which surrounds us (Heb. 12:1). But though we align ourselves with past confessions, they are not our own so that we may escape formulating contemporary words that have been forged by our own reflection and experience in a modern age. God's Word comes to us as well as it did to them.

Theological explanations embody one or more of four principal activities. At heart, all explanations are an **analysis** of something in order to see the constituent parts and arrange them in a manageable form. Naturally, this carries with it the temptation to believe that an analysis of some part of the Word carries with it a mastery of that part as well. But the Word of God is not fettered because we can analyze it! Analysis exists to help relate researchers to the material in a more meaningful manner. By analysis a theologian can discover what makes something tick, and then put it back together in such a way that others can also see why it ticks.

A second activity is the formulation of **hypotheses**, or **theories**, or **synthetic statements**. These are not all the same thing. An hypothesis is a proposition that is yet unproven. If it is asserted that Paul's use of the Law contradicts the rabbinic understanding of his day, that is an hypothesis. It explains something, and does so in a testable manner. A theory is a body of such hypotheses. A theory might, for example, propose that the New Testament uses the Law in a radically different manner than 1st century rabbinic thought. Now the hypothesis about Paul's use of the Law is a subset under a more comprehensive heading. Of course, this example also shows that an hypothesis and a theory may be the same idea but in different contexts. An hypothesis, in other words, might be used as a theory, but a distinction between hypotheses and theories is generally useful. Theories like the example above are also testable. A synthetic statement simply rearranges things so as to highlight some feature, or make the whole clearer. If, for instance, scholars have always analyzed Paul's use of the Law along certain lines to draw one portrait, then a reorganization of the evidence to create a second valid picture creates a synthetic statement. Like the standard portrayal, it also is subject to being tested by the evidence.

Hypothesis testing, then, is the third activity of explanation. It bears this name because theories are tested by their member parts undergoing testing, and synthetic statements are very similar to hypotheses. Hypothesis testing seeks to validate the explanation upon the basis of evidence. If Paul's use of the Law really is in opposition to the rabbinic thought of his time, there must be evidence to show it. In hypothesis test-

32

ing, one piece of contrary evidence may disprove the explanation where a thousand pieces of corroborating evidence can only establish its (high) probability of truth.

Model building results from successful hypothesis testing. The evidence which substantiates the explanatory hypothesis and theories mounts. Theories are combined into more comprehensive models of conceptual perspective. Thus, Paul's use of the Law is fitted into a Catholic, or Lutheran, or Reformed, or Wesleyan model. Model building tries to incorporate various explanatory statements, most particularly theories, into a unified, systematic, global body with characteristic features of expression and emphasis. Thus a Roman Catholic theologian and a Wesleyan theologian, in explaining Paul's use of the Law, may be in substantial agreement, but utilize quite different expressions and emphases consistent with their different theological models and traditions. Some remarkably successful models actually create new traditions. Both models and traditions greatly influence theological research.

One other important activity of explanation available in many instances to theological researchers, but rarely used, is **inferential statistics.** The primary reason they are not used more often is that most theologians are not trained in them, so they do not think about their use. However, inferential statistics could prove very valuable in many instances because they provide a numerical statement of relative probability designed to yield a degree of certainty where uncertainty might otherwise go unchecked. Statistical analysis techniques like the parametric t-tests, analysis of variance (ANOVA), and multiple correlation, or nonparametric alternatives like the Chi-square and Spearman rho, can be adapted to the task of theological explanation (cf. chapter 17).

Reporting Results

Explanations, like descriptions, beg for reporting. Again, the tools are numbers and words. Numbers incorporated into graphs, charts, or tables are one way to pictorially represent an explanation. If, for example, an inferential statistical test disclosed that Paul's use of the Law bears strong resemblance to an early Christian understanding, but a poor likeness to the Judaic use of the time, then an appropriate table might report in brief and plain fashion the exact statistical similarities or dissimilarities, the specific variables examined, and the level of significance (i.e., a statement of probability of the test results being due to chance). Such a compact, reliable, testable, and clear manner of reporting is manifestly desirable in the face of today's often long, obscure, and unverifiable writing.

Nevertheless, words will remain with us. But to benefit the Church most, these words need to be organized effectively, without needless dross, and in coherent form. Brilliant explanations of perplexing problems fall on deaf ears if the speaker cannot find an appropriate, and that means "understandable," way to express him- or herself. The whole purpose of reporting is to **communicate**, not to make a spectacle of one's self. In theology the aim of reporting should always be a faithful and clear communicating of truth, not an arm-waving effort to acquire attention to one's own supposed genius in thought or speech.

Peer Review

The principal practical aid to achieving and maintaining humility in the theological vocation may very well be peer review. The colleagues of a theologian scrutinize his or her work, separating the gold from the lead. Their critiques challenge, refine, correct, and (yes) hurt. But attended to with care they can greatly assist in a growing process. Peers also applaud remarkable efforts and express indebtedness. Always, peer review reminds individuals that they belong to a **community**. For theologians, peer review is a sign and a work of the Church.

There are many ways by which peer review takes place. In an academic setting, where theologians most often practice their work, there are reappointment committees, promotion and tenure committees, and various other formal and informal opportunities for peer review. In the scholarly community at large there are society meetings, or, if they have published material, there are journal review boards and critical reviewers. In a myriad of ways, theologians can check themselves and one another. This process encourages the development and refinement of theological activity, when it functions correctly, and it is itself an essential element in the total task of theological research.

Conclusion

Theological research, much as any kind of research, is a continuous and involved process. I have, for the sake of description and explanation, divided research into the six basic phases given above. But I would be remiss in my duty if I did not conclude with a mild warning. Research is a human endeavor, and a complicated one at that. Research "in the real world" of practitioners, is not as orderly as my arrangement may make it appear. But despite the mix that occurs in practice, all six of these elements play their part in good research. And always, in theological research, above the toil and tribulation of human reason and experience stands the beckoning Word of God.

4

Understanding Others' Research

Learning How to do Research

There are two roads to learning how to do research. Those individuals who become successful theologians learn how to travel both roads. The first is the **practice of doing one's own research.** Nothing can take the place of learning by doing. But theologians are not condemned to an apprenticeship of random trials and errors, until, at last, they stumble onto a right course. Rather, they can choose also to walk the path of **studying the research of other scholars.** It is this path which, initially at least, is clearest. While studying the scholarship of others cannot replace practice, it certainly can make practice a more fruitful venture.

Many people take occasional glances at theological research. In truth, though, most profit little from their time and effort, and some quickly dismiss it as "an ungodly waste of time." Such an unfortunate judgment may be understandable, and perhaps even forgiveable, if the research is trivial, or reported obscurely, or is misleading. But often this judgment is unfair. Gaining an appreciable amount from theological work requires taking time to study it, then reflect upon it, and finally relate it to other labors in the same area. Likewise, theology cannot have its right effect if a person insists on reading personal ideas, biases, and conclusions into the research so that what the researcher is trying to say simply falls on deaf ears. Instead, when dealing with the research of others, **exegesis** (which is the reading of the researcher's meaning out of the words) should be the goal.

Research Sources

A surprising abundance of theological resources exist for those who would take advantage of them. Usually, it is a matter of having our eyes trained to recognize these resources, then having our minds made up to seize upon them whenever possible. These resources can be divided into two major categories: **written documents** and **oral presentations.** We tend naturally to think first of written materials because we are accustomed to dealing with textbooks, journal articles, and the like. Even within this group, however, a variety of less known sources, like archival collections, are too often overlooked. More frequently bypassed are the wealth of helps available in oral resources.

Each Sunday morning the sermon offers an opportunity for the attentive student to review theological research. Of course, a first responsibility must always be to hear the Word of God. But then a reflection can follow on how that Word has been researched and presented. Other oral sources abound. Classes on Sunday morning or evening, and others through the week, are almost always available as resources. Classroom lectures and discussion provide models of research and forums for a lively exchange of ideas, complete with opportunities for testing one's own theological efforts. Often, public speeches by guest scholars and various research society meetings are overlooked chances to be exposed to first-rate work. Even television and radio offer a few reputable resources. Finally, discussions with one's peers are almost always very instructive and stimulating.

Written sources, because they are relatively more structured, and afford an opportunity for repeated examination, are generally preferred for the study of other scholars' research efforts. Sources that are most visible include books, articles in general periodicals as well as specialized journals, and scholarly monographs (often issued in book form). Yet other written sources can prove quite valuable. Theses and dissertations, booklets and pamphlets, unpublished papers, and correspondence are all rich resources that too often remain untapped. Because of the vast amounts of literature embodied by these different sources, it is helpful to recognize a few basic facts in order to select the best and most appropriate models of research.

The first fact to keep in mind is that authors, publishers, and magazines have **reputations**. Some enjoy an esteem earned by long years of producing quality theological literature. Others are in the midst of changing their image; some for the better, and others for the worse. Finding what the reputation is can be helpful, as long as it is not permitted to establish an unyielding prejudice (i.e., "nothing good ever comes out of ___"). Good publishing houses make mistakes, while poor publishing houses occasionally find a gem. All knowing the reputations does is help find the better places to begin looking for quality work.

The second fact worth noting is that authors, publishers, and magazines often have **specialties**. A general knowledge of these can save time and effort in getting at the most abundant sources for any particular project. It does not require that much effort to discover and record somewhere who is doing what and how much.

Finally, authors, book publishers, and magazines are often the **representatives** of definite religious **traditions** (what I termed "models" in the last chapter). Looking for sympathetic materials on liberal theology in a very conservative magazine is generally fruitless. Knowing what traditions, if any, are represented is another valuable time-saver.

36

When the sources of theological research have been located, the task of understanding them as models has just begun. In this part, and in the following one, I want to set forth two ways of approaching the research of others. The first approach attempts to regard research products in light of the research process. Therefore, the six basic phases discussed in the last chapter provide the elements for analyzing and evaluating the research. Interest, exploration, description, explanation, report of the results, and peer review afford criteria for assessing research.

The first question that should come to mind when studying anyone's research is, Why was it done? This is the question of interest, or **motivation**. Most research proposes to satisfy a persistent question, or respond to an urgent need. Identifying this factor is an important first step in understanding both the research and its significance. Comprehending how this interest on the part of the researcher led into the work can help show ways to bridge the gap between motivation and effective labor.

The next area to consider is what the researcher explored. Here three simple questions should be asked: What was examined? How was it examined? Were direct, or indirect, methods of exploration used? The first question will pinpoint the subject under consideration. The second will uncover the process of examination utilized. The third will assess the limitations of the research exploration.

The next phase of research is **description**. Two fundamental queries pose themselves: What did the researcher actually see? How is it described? Because it is very easy to pass straight through description to explanation, it is critical to discipline one's self to a patient, thorough inspection of the researcher's description. The researcher should be able to make his or her readers see what he or she saw. The description should be accurate, and as full as needed to undergird adequately the explanatory remarks. If the description is indistinguishable from the interpretive remarks, how can anyone be sure of what was actually there to see? Description is crucial because it displays the basic materials of evidence.

The manner in which that evidence is diagnosed and built upon constitutes the researcher's **explanation**. Since this is the part of the research which generally sets it apart (in practical terms it is what often gets it published), this explanation must have several questions put to it. What was found? What does it mean? Why is it important? (Or is it important?) What kind of analysis was done? Are hypotheses advanced? Are theories defended? Are creative synthetic statements offered? Are these hypotheses, theories, or statements tested? Does the research bear the marks of some model (tradition)?

The first three of these questions reflect upon the

significance of the research. Asking what was found serves as the transition from description, with its presentation of evidence, to explanation, with its ordering of the evidence so as to highlight the more important pieces and set them into an argument of some kind. The other two questions mirror the concern, "So what?" Does the research matter? Would it have made any difference if it had not been conducted, or published? The burden of establishing significance must rest with the researcher. Ask, does the researcher assume that the work is important, or show how and why it is important?

The questions following these first three are roughly methodological. These kinds of questions about how the research was conducted are often all that a student focuses on. In our day of learning by the reader's digest method, it is all too easy to look only for a cookbook approach to research. Obviously, understanding how the analysis took place is important. But it must not assume an importance out of line with the whole research process.

Being able to follow another person's arguments, watching the building of inexorable logic upon a foundation of indisputable facts, can be an exhilarating experience. It can also be an instructive one if the student applies him/herself to understanding how it was done. In such learning are the seeds of a successful venture; for understanding how another has done a thing makes it easier to do it one's self. An added benefit also accrues to this understanding. If the work is flawed, so that the explanation is not sufficiently sound in light of the evidence advanced, then the student should be able to see that, and learn from it. Thus this understanding can guard against being swept away by persuasive, but empty, rhetoric.

Closely linked with both description and explanation in anyone's research is the **report of the results**. Four questions can be asked in this regard. Is the research clearly understandable? Are definite conclusions reached? Do they make sense? Do they appear to be reasonably consistent with the explanation? The first question is broader than just the results. The whole research should be free of obscurity. However, this does not mean that it must necessarily be uncomplicated, and so easy that fourth-grade readers can comprehend all of it. Some research grapples with very complex and conceptually difficult questions. Some research needs to use technical language to communicate more exactly. Yet, all research should aim at being comprehensible.

The latter three questions specifically are concerned with the legitimacy of the author's conclusions. They should be relatively easy to identify, consistent with the rest of the research, and validated by the appropriate use of the evidence. It is not unusual, particularly in early attempts at research, to find that the conclusions appear strangely out of touch with the rest of the work. They look tacked on. Closely examining the way good scholars have their conclusions flow smoothly and inevitably from their research can help overcome this awkwardness. Good conclusions are conservative, sticking discernibly to the facts, and open-ended, awaiting more evidence or sensitive response.

Finally, there remains a responsibility to seek out the reactions of a responsible **peer review**. Three questions should be asked in this phase. Has the research been reviewed or responded to by any other research? How has it been evaluated by the researcher's own colleagues? Why was the scholarly reaction what it was? Naturally, not all research is reviewed in print. But some books receive many reviews, in publications with varying perspectives. Then, too, in most periodicals there is either a letters column or some other format for readers to respond to recently published work. If even these resources seem to be lacking, a little creativity may be quite in order. Pastors, teachers, and informed friends often are very capable of providing a learned and perceptive review of whatever study the student is examining.

When peer reviews have been found they ought to be assessed carefully. First, of course, their evaluation of the research must be considered. Are the reviewers fair in their criticism? If some reaction appears to stem from a misreading of the research (which is more common than many suppose), then the review is severely limited in its utility. Yet, perhaps the misreading has been prompted by misstatements on the researcher's part. These should be pointed out. But if a reaction is built on solid evidence, or a sound analysis of the research, then the review becomes invaluable, either as a source confirming the research, or warning against its flaws. Paying attention to accurate reviews can sensitize a researcher to the needs of readers. This will pay dividends later in better research more clearly reported.

Structural Model

The process model of studying others' research has the great advantage of focusing attention on the basic components of well done research. But for a variety of reasons much research simply does not report all these phases in its published form. Yet it would be a mistake to simply pass a negative judgment on the work. This next model, then, attempts to start with the premise that theological research in its published form can be evaluated profitably by focusing upon three aspects of structure. These aspects are style, formal structural components, and substantive structural parts.

Style in this model refers mainly to the characteristic qualities of the researcher's writing (or speaking), and not to those highly formalized peculiarities which are supposed to characterize academic and scholarly work. Since individual expressions can, and do vary greatly, it would be pointless to try to be more particular than to single out those three special measures by which all good writing and speaking are marked. These qualities are clarity, coherence, and cohesiveness.

Clarity is the quality of transparency. Is the scholar's meaning unfolded by his or her expressions, or is it obscured? Generally, clarity is produced by short, simple, direct prose statements of distinctive, unambiguous conceptual thoughts. Not all research always lends itself to a simplicity of conception or expression. But every researcher should strive to be as lucid in his or her remarks as is possible.

Coherence is the quality of comprehensibility. Does the work make sense? Can the scholar be understood? A matter can hardly be more fundamental than this! The people receiving the research must be able to understand it if the scholar's task is to be fulfilled. A sermon falls on fallow ground if it fails to lay bare the Scriptural text and sense. Lectures pass over students like threatening rain clouds unless they are within the conceptual grasp of the hearers. The research must be understandable, and that means it must be clear.

Cohesiveness is the quality of consistency within the work. Is there a logic in the movement from one part to the next? Does the research hold together as a whole? Cohesiveness completes clarity and coherence by joining them smoothly throughout the research. Cohesiveness aims at a consistency of thought and expression so that the person examining the research is not distracted by lapses but is instead drawn inexorably into the whole work.

Clarity, coherence, and cohesiveness should characterize all of the **formal structural components** of the published research. These components include:

1) an appropriate title, and table of contents;
2) an identification of the subject area or object of study;
3) a specification of the research methodology and its limitations;
4) a presentation of the content of the research including:
   (1) a description of what was seen;
   (2) a distinction between the more important and less important pieces of information;
   (3) an interpretation of the meaning or the significance of the evidence (i.e., What is it evidence of? What does it mean? What difference does it make?);
   (4) a testing of any hypotheses, theories, or synthetic statements advanced;
   (5) a statement of conclusions reached on the basis of the research;
5) reference notes to supplement the content;
6) citations of pertinent research sources;
7) appendices for additional information; and,
8) indices for ease of reference to the parts of the

research.

Again, not all research that is published either in writing or by oral presentation will embody all of these structural parts. But the presence or absence of these parts helps the one wanting to use the research; they make the research more accessible and accountable. An awareness of these parts can train the beginning researcher in discriminating between more and less complete reports of research. They will also aid in distinguishing the basic phases of research and how they relate to a publishable format. It is no random accident that the structure of good research reporting parallels the process of good research work.

The interior structure of the reported research is embedded in the **substantive structural parts.** This aspect is, in many respects, the most critical element of the structural model. These parts all answer to the demands of coherence. Among these parts are the purpose of the research, the audience addressed, the line of argument employed, the logic of it, the evidence advanced, the conclusions proposed, and the stated significance of the research in its parts or as a whole. Each of these concerns is explicit or implicit in all good research. Even where one or another formal structural part is absent, these substantive issues should be present.

The **purpose of research** is most often disclosed right at the beginning, sometimes even in the title. Identifying it may be easier if it is remembered that the purpose is almost always linked to the interest or motivation of the researcher. The purpose is also closely associated with an address to a particular **audience,** which the researcher believes will share his or her interest. Thus, a scholar reporting on archaeological finds at a dig in Israel is unlikely to submit his or her findings to **Good Housekeeping.** The audience may not be directly named, but it is generally obvious by the periodical in which it appears, or by the publisher which issues it, or simply by the nature of its contents.

The **line of argument** used should be scrutinized carefully. Is the researcher trying to accomplish a **tour de force** (i.e., do with ingenuity what cannot be done with evidence)? Or, is the argument **ad hominem** (i.e., in the hope that discrediting someone's person will discredit their arguments)? There are multitudes of erroneous, fallacious lines of logic. The research argument and its **logic** should be assessed for its adherence to the evidence cited and its reasonableness. (But please note: not all reasonable arguments are also strictly logical; logic is **not** a criteria for truthfulness.)

The **evidence** should always be conspicuous and not merely assumed. Of course, well-known and established evidence might be briefly referred to without a full recitation of it. But good research is conservative in its handling of evidence: it wants to put it out where it can be seen by all, but only that evidence that is pertinent to the study. Unfortunately, some researchers

41

think that the only pertinent evidence is what supports their arguments, so they ignore discrepancies or anomalies. However, good research is ready to acknowledge significant evidence that cannot be presently accounted for by the researcher's arguments. Good research takes stock of any important rival hypotheses (i.e., alternate explanations for the evidence).

The **proposed conclusions** are quite important. They are the researcher's last word on the subject, and generally they are meant to put a best foot forward to the reader. Hence, they may represent the strongest evidence and most compelling line of argument. If the conclusion is not manifestly **significant**, then the rest of the research is not likely to be significant either. But if the research is meaningful, the conclusions will draw attention to that fact, and try to make it as explicit as possible.

The structural model may be more feasible to employ in some instances. In others, the process model will prove more useful. Each should be mastered. Both can aid in understanding research.

Conclusion

The study of others' research need not be tedious. It certainly will be work, and occasionally difficult work at that. But tedium can be set aside by adopting the positive, and correct, stance of a partner in dialog with whomever is the author of the research being studied. Learning need not be unidirectional. If the research is a beneficial model, then it can be utilized when the time for practicing research arrives. If the research is flawed, or unclear, then the author can be answered by better research, clearer expressions, or actual contact (i.e., by writing the author). Theologians, like any intelligent people, crave constructive, edifying conversation. We are all parts of a wide and diverse community that hearkens after a clear and comprehensive understanding of the Word of God. Under that Word we are all students, all peers, and all accountable to God and to one another.

5

Doing Theological Research

The Road Less Traveled By: Practice

The well-traveled road of learning how to do research through studying the research of others should lead regularly to that less-traveled road: the pathway of practice. Despite its advantages and necessity, this second road is often shunned. It is easy to imagine some of the reasons. Many unreasonable fears disguise its appearance, and occasional glimpses may reveal only its many twists and turns. The whole road may look unsuitable to travel. Who would hazard such a path? If the knowledge of God's Word can be gained by following the research of others, then why not let them simply be our guides? Why test an unknown, hazardous road?

Why bother indeed? An old saying assures us that "experience teaches," and so it is with research. No better path presents itself for acquiring a personal and meaningful understanding than that of using our own earnest sweat in study. Certainly we ought to make full use of what others have won for the Church by their faithful, and sometimes costly service. Still, each of us has also our place in which we are to stand and serve. No one can do our work for us. By participating in the practice of research we can immeasurably enrich our labors, and fulfill our responsibility to study and show ourselves approved, workmen who can stand unashamed (cf. 2 Ti. 2:15). It does not matter that many individuals are called to vocations other than theology. Even the briefest participation in theological study will return rich dividends.

For those who are called to the theological vocation a regular, intelligent practice of research is indispensable. This is true not only for the teachers and academicians who write massive tomes, but also for the ministers of youth and Christian education in the local church. It holds true for the pastor who faces weekly sermon preparation, and the lay leader who finds that special calling to the study and service of God's Word. Unfortunately, some people try to escape this responsibility. But the theological vocation is one reserved for practitioners only. Those who aspire to this calling **must be doers** of the Word and not hearers only (cf. Jas. 1:22-25); for theologians, study and practice are equally "doing."

Theological research is colored by the individuals who

practice it. This practice can and does take many shapes—some of which are better suited to the service of the Word than others. Even a quick glance at the many published products of theological study reveals how varied the practice of this vocation is. Such a situation makes any step-by-step approach to research rather artificial. Obviously, though any outright prescriptions for each detail of research may be beyond reach, there is the possibility that broad, guiding suggestions can be set forward. That must be our goal even while recognizing that in many respects each student of the Word must learn a uniquely personal way of answering God's call. (This same basic observation must be remembered later when examining various models and methods. Practitioners of these methods adjust the methods to their own needs and styles. No one right way exists to conduct research, though certain parameters establish what is appropriate or inappropriate in the use of a method.)

There is a profound difference between artifice and arbitrariness. The basic guidelines that follow are expedient and possess a demonstrable utility. They are not arbitrary, but the results of logic and practice. The basic elements of research discussed in our earlier chapters not only makes the research process more understandable, but they also provide a suitable structure to guide the doing of research. They thus serve as "steps" for mastering a first attempt at practicing research.

Interest

How does anyone begin an involvement with research practice? In all likelihood, the first formal practice comes in school when an instructor assigns some topic to be investigated, or problem to be solved, or question to be answered. Yet, in a more rudimentary sense, people first practice research as children when they begin to methodically and purposively interact with their environment. Theological research begins for the children of God when they hear his Word and respond with a desire to study and to understand it. In other words, involvement in research begins with an interest, a motivation of one or another kind.

The variations of interest are too numerous to list. But among them are five fundamental motivations that persistently emerge: curiosity, the desire to answer the unanswered question, the urge to respond to the work of others, need, and puzzlement. These different motivations frequently intermix. Yet each is capable of providing the interest needed to sustain long and involved research.

Curiosity is both famous and ill-understood. Essentially, it is nonspecific interest directed at something that may be quite specific. For example, an encounter with the Bible might produce a curiosity about its general message, or an interest in the particular theme of forgiveness. In either instance, an

44

interest is nonspecific because it simply desires an acquisition of more knowledge about the subject, whether the subject itself is very general or specific. Curiosity does not aim at some particular kind of knowledge, but at an increase of knowledge in general.

The desire to **answer the unanswered question** is a special motivation. An encounter with the Bible might produce the question, How can a good God permit evil to exist? In the absence of any satisfactory answers, the questioner might be driven by an intense desire to answer this question for himself or herself, and for others too. This motivation is similar to that of **puzzlement**, which is the desire to solve a piece of a model which remains unresolved. Much of research is of this puzzle-solving variety. It might arise by the finding of a short text in the Bible which does not appear to fit the model to which the student adheres. Finding no satisfactory explanations by others in the tradition, the student turns to solving the puzzle. If it cannot be solved, the puzzle may lead the student into a diffferent tradition.

The urge to **respond to the work of others** also is specific. A student interested in the Bible may enocunter a text or an article that sparks a very direct response to the author of the piece. This in turn prompts a desire to do research in order to respond to the author's contentions. For example, the book, **The Battle for the Bible** aroused much intense interest in the subject of biblical inerrancy. It prompted many people to study the issue in order to respond to the author's arguments. The response might be favorable, a way to take up the defense of someone and buttress his or her arguments with additional or corroborating evidence. On the other hand, the response might be polemical, or critical, aimed at showing how the author needs to rethink his or her arguments or reexamine the evidence.

Often motivation stems from a perceived **need**. Perhaps the Church situation is such that God's sovereignty has fallen into disrepute, or the divinity of Christ has been denied, or the value and importance of social ministry has gone unobserved. A student of the Word may turn to research to provide information and tools to help the Church be directed back to a more faithful service.

Exploration

Whatever the interest, or source of the motivation, some means of exploration must be determined upon for research to take place. This means four concrete steps. First, the researcher must **select appropriate sources**. Interest leads to the identification of a problem that is to be examined. That examination relies on sources of information that seem to promise a yield of dependable knowledge. Thus, if the biblical concept of justification by faith is to be explored, appropriate sources must be selected, like Paul's discussion in Romans, and the text of James 2. To these sources there might be added others that are relevant, like important books from theologians on the subject. If these sources are literary in nature, this step is commonly called a **review of the literature**. But in some instances, sources may include information gathered directly from people through surveys or interviews. Whatever the sources are, they should be carefully selected and clearly specified.

When the sources have been collected a methodology must be employed to draw out the required information. **Determining the methods** to be used is a second critical step. To choose the correct methods for the particular research depends on several factors. It should be obvious, for example, that using a survey of lay people in a local church to discover what Jesus meant when he said, "Think not that I have come to abolish the law and the prophets; I have come not to abolish them but to fulfill them" (Mt. 5:17), may indeed produce interesting information, but it will not help us understand Jesus' meaning in the same way that an exegesis of the biblical text can. The **instruments** or **tools** selected must be appropriate ones. Likewise, the **presuppositions** behind the research should be acknowledged openly. If, for instance, it is presupposed that people cannot be raised from the dead, then research into the resurrection is going to reflect the restrictions of this assumption. The researcher must also take into account such factors as personal ability (i.e., do not use methods far beyond present competency), audience (i.e., do not use methods incomprehensible to the audience unless an aim is to teach the method), and inherent limitations (i.e., because of the topic or the availability of evidence).

Clarifying the study's limitations is too seldom done, but it is a very important step. It is a public confession of what the study is able to do alongside what it simply cannot do. The limitations might stem from the **sources** that are available. For example, a study on religious art in the eighth century B.C. may be quite limited by the number or quality of available artifacts. The limitations might also arise from the **distance** in time or space which is involved. Thus, a study of events in Abraham's time is a more restricted work than, say, reviewing twentieth century affairs. In this sense, distance is also a matter of the sources available. But distance can refer, too, to whether direct observation is possible (i.e., immediate proximity) or only indirect (i.e., mediated closeness). Limitations might exist in the nature of the **evidence** that can be culled from sources, regardless of how abundant they are. All of the evidence might be of a similar, restricted nature, or of poor quality. Finally, limitations might be imposed by the **purpose** of the research (e.g., to present only Paul's view of faith), or the constraints of its **published form** (e.g., only a brief summary of methods may be permitted, etc.).

Once sources have been selected, a methodology determined, and limitations recognized, the fourth step must occur: **the actual thorough and methodical examination of the object of**

study. This labor is the heartbeat of research, the essence of its excitement and life. Of course, this is only romantic rhetoric **until** it has first been experienced. Then it is the joy of discovery, that sublime experience that constantly entices researchers. The discipline of a thorough and methodical examination is not to constrict what might be found, but to create a kind of freedom for the object so that it can make itself known to the researcher.

Description

Three ideas establish the essence of research description. The features of whatever is being studied must be made known, the most important of these should be highlighted, and the facts should be permitted to represent themselves. Recall that the aim of description is to see what is really there, and then accurately communicate it. At this point maximum effort to limit interpretive comments is necessary. While these may not be totally eliminated, they should be kept as much as possible to their proper place. The aim is for others to first see what the researcher has seen, then understand what he or she has understood.

Accordingly, the first rule of description is always to **clarify the features of whatever is being studied.** A theologian studying St. Anselm's arguments for the existence of God must first clearly enumerate these arguments so that others can see them also. If he or she first jumps to a critique of Anselm's thought, an audience that is not fully familiar with the arguments is at the mercy of the critique. They can only decide whether to trust the scholar, not the evidence. There may be contexts where the features are already known to the audience. Then, a brief recap can suffice.

Why should an issue be made of what seems such a minor matter? The Church does not need Christian gurus with their esoteric wisdom; Christians are to hear God's Word (cf. Mt. 17:5). What this means practically is an examination of all teaching on the basis of its evidence, not merely the credentials of the teacher or author. The clarification of an object's features is the introduction of evidence.

Not all evidence is equally important. The second part of good description is to **highlight the most important evidence.** Naturally, this calls for an interpretive element. Still, most research objects provide pretty clear indications of their most prominent features. A study of Pauline theology, for example, should note his treatment of the topic "apostolic authority," but also observe that his christology is relatively more important. The key here is caution. Highlight the obviously more important features, and avoid too much of hairsplitting judgment.

Caution is the watchword of the day in description. The third principal feature of good description is to **let the facts represent themselves.** It is self-defeating in research to engage in too much speculation. An elaboration on the facts endangers

47

a study more than any hoped-for insight can add to its value. Facts have much more power residing in them than one would care to acknowledge. With a smart use of highlighting the most important facts, together with an avoidance of elaboration on them, the evidence may emerge so compelling that only a few brief and restrained explanatory notes will be necessary to carry the day.

One important aid to letting the facts represent themselves is the use of **descriptive statistics**. Many more people are familiar with certain kinds of these statistics than is true of inferential statistics. A limited use of an appropriate statistical technique often can be just the right finishing touch. **Frequencies** are an easily understood statistic which can be employed without sophisticated tools in most instances. If a researcher states that the terms "light," "Spirit," and "door" are important in John's Gospel, and backs that assertion with a report of exactly how frequently these terms occur, then the statement takes on greater credibility. If the researcher goes still further by computing a ratio of these occurrences compared with other terms in the Gospel, then the description may become clearer yet. **Measures of central tendency** (i.e., mode, median, and mean) can be helpful too. If, for instance, a scholar wanted to examine the incidence of the term **agape** ("love") in the New Testament, he might compute the frequency of occurrence in each book as a ratio, put these ratios in a list from highest to lowest, and determine the most frequently occurring ratio (the mode), the ratio that evenly divides the ratio list in half (the median), and the figure that represents an "average" ratio score (the mean). These simple statistics sharpen the description. Other kinds of accessible descriptive statistics include **measures of variance** (range, variance, and standard deviation), and **correlations** (which aim at describing relationships between things; they can also aid in inferences). Any clear basic statistics text can be consulted with profit, but for some applications to specifically theological problems see chapters 15 and 16 of this text.

Explanation

Despite its difficulties, explanation is a favored activity of all researchers. It is here that the joy of discovery can be expressed best, in creative explanation. A dozen scholars can examine the same text of Jn. 3:16 and explain its significance in different, if complementary manners. Of course, it is important that creativity be disciplined by a real faithfulness to the evidence. Biblical interpretation put away allegorical explanation centuries ago. What matters, naturally, is the object itself. But creative explanations can help others to attain to a better understanding of that object.

Many different parts comprise explanation. If these were to be put into some kind of reasonable order, perhaps these six would emerge:

1) Analyze the evidence.
2) Determine its significance, if any, and elucidate why it is important.
3) Decide if any hypotheses, theories, or synthetic statements are appropriate.
4) Test the explanation by the evidence. Is the explanation reasonable? Does it fit the evidence? Reflect on any rival hypotheses.
5) Clarify the difference between the vehicle of explanation (i.e., one's own manner of theologizing) and the substance of the meaning.
6) Consider whether the explanation fits into a model. Is it a model in which the researcher is already at home? Has the model determined the explanation, or does the explanation independently confirm the model? (This step requires searching self-honesty.)

These six components need further consideration.

Analysis itself encompasses more than one thing. In fact, in a few respects analysis can be envisioned as belonging to either description or explanation. At least four activities are central to analysis. The first is descriptive in nature, being the **identification of features,** but particularly their identification as **units of the whole object.** Since analysis means the breakdown of the object into its constituent parts, this first activity of unitizing the object's features is basic and inevitable. The next step is the **naming of various parts of each larger feature.** To illustrate this step in conjunction with the first step, consider the student whose research object is the composition of 1 Jn. In an analysis of the formal structure of the English version of the book the researcher may note first that it has five chapters. But each of these "features" (i.e., the chapters) has parts which make it up, namely paragraphs and sentences, or, viewed somewhat differently, verses. The third step is to **try to visualize the function of each part.** The researcher of 1 Jn. could note that verses function as easy reference aids to the material of the text. Finally, the last step is the **attempt to discover what makes each part function as it does.** Why are there verses? The student might conclude not only that they exist as aids, but that they really do help because they are arranged in numerical sequence and are short, thus making reference to material much easier.

Analysis should never suffice for explanation. A clear statement of the **significance** is what matters most in explanation. If the study reveals little or no significance then that should be faced. In the example above, the division of the biblical text into verses was very briefly analyzed. But is verse division significant? If so, to

49

what degree? Where there is meaning and significance it should have attention drawn to it consciously, clearly, and thoroughly. Thus, a study of the life of Jesus cannot be complete without something being said about his significance. If the research is strictly historical, then the significance should be stated in those terms. The idea of significance, in a narrow sense, can be determined by statistical means (for which the chapters on statistics should be consulted). But determining significance as theologians generally do is far less susceptible to hard and fast rules. One rule of thumb is this: if it is significant it has a perceivable or measurable influence or effect. Since this can apply to many, if not most things, an ability to talk about the **relative importance** of the meaning or significance is very helpful. Thus, the Synoptic Gospels place relatively more importance on Jesus' death than upon his birth, and more upon his birth than upon his childhood.

Almost invariably explanation makes use of hypotheses, or a theory, or synthetic statements. Sometimes all three kinds of explanatory formulations are used. What is essential is that the kind of formulation selected be consistent with the research. An hypothesis with regard to already established facts would be ludicrous. A comprehensive theory where a simple hypothesis would suffice would also be absurd. If the evidence can be best organized and explained by an original hypothesis, then make one. If it is best served by an existing theory, then use it without hesitation. If a synthetic statement is sufficient, then avoid needless complications by using a theory.

However the explanation is framed, it must be supported by the evidence. Contrary to the practice of some individuals, this is not guaranteed merely by saying so. The explanation must be tested by the evidence. If James, the brother of Jesus, is asserted to be the author of the book which bears his name, that assertion does not at all prove the matter, no matter how eminent an authority it is who makes the claim. The assertion must be tested by the evidence of the text and any pertinent outside evidence. Few things make an argument stronger than relating evidence to an assertion. Theological research is not rhetoric, but calculated explanation built upon the strategic use of understood evidence. A valuable aspect of this testing process is an honest appraisal of important rival hypotheses. Thus an important alternative explaining the authorship of the book of James is that it was written pseudonymously (i.e., by someone using the name of the Lord's brother). This rival explanation must be fairly considered, and the evidence should be tested against it as well.

Unfortunately, many people cannot easily separate the vehicles of an explanation from the explanation itself. The result is that they are easily put off by the manner of expression and never get to the meaning. Therefore, if a student is going to address the folks back home all about the form criticism of Matthew's Gospel, he or she had better find a suitable vehicle for so doing or the folks will react in righteous (and I do mean **righteous**) anger. Restraint in one's creative vigor is always advisable. After all, the purpose of explanation is to **explain**, not to show off. Help people to see the difference between the substance and the form in which it comes.

As a late step in explanation, consider whether the explanation fits into a model (a theological tradition). Is it consistent with the conceptual structure of the researcher's tradition? For example, a student whose membership is in the Reformed tradition but whose research leads to such conclusions as the necessity of the Sabbath (i.e., Saturday) worship, and soul sleep, might consider Seventh Day Adventism a more comfortable home. Of course, a theologian can be a staunch supporter of a tradition without adhering to its every part. But he or she has the responsibility of continually weighing his or her work against the model in order to sense movement toward or away from it. Such a process, practiced conscientiously, is a first step in offering reform or renewal for that tradition in the Church.

At the same time, researchers must always beware the temptation to let their tradition provide them answers independent of their work and in its place. Thus a student who proposes to research the idea of tongues as a valid current-day spiritual gift, but who only advances a defense of dispensational thought on the subject, is not engaging in scholarship, but pseudoscholarship. It has the form of scholarly work but not the substance. Once a theologian has done his or her own work, then it is appropriate, valuable, and desirable to review it by the tradition. But this sequence cannot be reversed without denying the legitimate process of research.

Finally, as a possible additional tool to traditional theological methods, some consideration should be given to the use of **inferential statistics**. In the vast majority of individual research studies, this kind of strategy is never even briefly contemplated. This is understandable, however, in light of a theological education which, traditionally, never mentions the utilization of numbers as research tools. But in the modern world statistics play an important role, both in communicating information and attempting to get at more certain knowledge. Inferential statistics enable a researcher to get beyond simple description to more generalized statements. By them inferences may be made that are based on numerical information.

Inferential statistics rely on the notion that valid methods exist for generalizing from the characteristics of a small group to those of a larger, unmeasured group. In other words, the characteristics of the larger group are inferred from the smaller group. The ability to do this with a high level of confidence in the results has many advantages: it saves time and expense, renders dependable results, expresses these results in a simple form, and permits legitimate access to the study of large group

51

characteristics which might otherwise have to go unstudied. The application of this concept, and of the many methods built upon it, is long past due in theological research circles (cf. chapter 17; please note, however, that I am not unaware that more is done with statistics today by theologians than ever before. It is still not nearly enough.)

Report of Results

A traditional problem in research is deciding exactly what to report. In the next chapter this issue is dealt with at length. But here I wish to address the more specific concern of reporting the **conclusions** of the research. Three ideas should predominate in reporting results. First, conclusions should be formulated that are a **natural and inevitable outcome of the arguments based on the evidence.** If a theologian argues that the evidence all points to the resurrection narratives being literary myth, but concludes that the body of Jesus actually was raised, it may be questionable how that conclusion depends on either the arguments or the evidence. On the other hand, if a student argues that a world-wide flood really occurred, presents evidence for that contention, and concludes that it is therefore reasonable to treat the Genesis account as one firmly rooted in history, then the results can be said to be truly consistent with the research. This does not guarantee that the research is right in its conclusions. What it does mean is that if the researcher is to be debated, the whole research process must be addressed because the conclusions are firmly tied to it. The former researcher can be challenged more easily because the conclusions are not obviously connected with the arguments or evidence.

Second, the **conclusions should be tested.** Research is inherently conservative, being very cautious about all its methods and statements. Because the conclusions are the most important of all the statements they require the most attention. They should be congruent with the research process, consistent with the arguments, based upon the evidence, and aimed at making the most significant results of the study stand out. This last point may seem obvious, but, occasionally, research appears where the most important results receive little attention while the researcher beats the drums for a minor motif. When this happens, it signals a surrender to motives other than to produce sound research, or reveals the researcher's incompetence. In the pressure to use research to advance a career it is all too easy to pounce on the unusual and make it important in the hope that by calling attention to it, it will bring attention to its champion. Unworthy motives like this must be resisted.

Finally, third, **the best way to represent the conclusions** should be given careful consideration. Nothing spoils a research report quite like an incomplete, obscure, or long-winded conclusion. Once the results have been formulated and tested, they should be stated briefly (but not **too briefly**), clearly, and forcefully. Good conclusions draw attention to themselves as bearing what is most memorable in the research. They are good, not because they are clever, or pretentious, but because their significance clearly stands out.

Peer Review

When the research report is ready, three simple steps should be taken. The researcher should **solicit the criticism of others** before going any further. The better the critics are, the more trust can be placed in their remarks. The best critics are good readers who pay close attention to what they read, observing both the way that the research report has been put together and the substance of its message. If these critics also have an extensive knowledge in the field in which the research was conducted, their criticism becomes even more valuable. However, I practice the regular inclusion of at least one reader who does **not** have any expertise in the area of my research in order to better ascertain whether my report is accessible to a wider audience. After all, the more people who can profit from the research, the more potential benefit it has.

Once the criticism has been received, **listen to it and learn**. I am afraid many researchers solicit only a pat on the back. They want their egos scratched because it feels good. We all like praise, but learning is the object of research. The learning does not stop with the writing of the research report. Good criticism teaches. It can greatly enhance the report. It may even cause some constructive changes in the manner in which research in the future will be pursued. Unless a researcher intends to listen and to learn from his or her readers time is being wasted soliciting their comments.

Third, **revise the report where needed and resubmit it.** Once corrections are made, take the report back to the original readers. There is always the possibility the revision will be worse than the original. Let the readers see the changes and evaluate them. This process makes for better readers as well as for better researchers. If one revision does not suffice, repeat the process until a readable product at last emerges.

At this point, one caution may be needed. The researcher must always serve as her or his own final editor. Readers are hardly infallible. Sometimes their suggestions are wrong. The researcher is ultimately responsible for the content. If a change seems incorrect, do not make it. Readers offer advice, not commands. But every researcher needs to be sure that a rejected suggestion is being rejected on its merits, not because the researcher's feelings have been hurt.

After a researcher has submitted a final, polished copy of the work to a teacher, journal, publisher, society, or someone else, the work is still not finished. Further peer review may be forthcoming in a variety of formats, such as grades, letters to the editor (or the author on occasion), editorial revisions, or public response. These reviews of the work should be utilized as an invaluable education. They ought to be taken as resources to help the researcher in his or her continuing labors of study.

A Scientific Checklist

In the interest of producing scientific research in theological work, I have established a checklist of twelve sets of questions. It is valuable to ask these questions of the research as a whole, then to apply them to any specific part of the research where they may be especially appropriate. The checklist:

1) Is the research **honest**? Does the researcher have a hidden agenda, or is everything aboveboard? Can the researcher point to the evidence without having to play games?

2) Is it **replicable**? Does it exist as a unique feat of insight, or can it be repeated by others?

3) Is it **verifiable**? Does it leave itself open to being checked by others? Can it bear the weight of the evidence?

4) Is it **reliable**? Can it be trusted? Would someone else doing the research the same way find the same or very similar things?

5) Is it **valid**? Does it really do what it purports to do? Can the process or the tools handle the task?

6) Is it **consistent**? Does it rest alongside other research? Or, is it remarkably unique? If it does not fit into a model, why doesn't it? Should it give birth to a new model?

7) Is it **simple**? Does the research search for the simplest way to do the task adequately? Can the research be explained equally well by a simpler interpretation of the facts?

8) Is it **predictive**? Does it point the way for other research? Can it help others see different things that might be hidden otherwise? Does it suggest the existence of previously unguessed matters?

9) Is it **restrained**? Does it try to do too much? Can its limitations and weaknesses be accounted for? Is it cautious in its use of evidence, and in its stated conclusions?

10) Is it **reasonable**? Can the results be accounted for by chance? Is the level of error tolerable?

11) Is it **significant**? Can it mean a difference in anything, or to anyone? Does it effect some kind of change?

12) Is it **faithful to God's Word**? Does it give to faith its proper place? Can it represent the Word it has studied?

54

Most of the items on this checklist are understandable and easy to accept as "scientific." Some, however, may balk at my final item. Yet I am persuaded that the essence of **all** research is faithfulness to the object being studied. In theology the object is the self-disclosed God in his Word. Therefore, faithfulness to that Word is indispensable to scientific theology.

May I add another note? I realize that much of what has been presented so far is simple and almost embarrassingly obvious. What may seem worse, I repeatedly reemphasize the same basic points. A kind of inertia can set in unless this procedure finally succeeds in communicating the fact that certain fundamentals **must** be realized and mastered if research is to become all that it can and should be.

Mission: Service

Both roads to learning research, the study of others' efforts and practice, point to the same destination: knowledge. Theological knowledge, though, is **never** knowledge in itself, for itself. Rather it is always instruction given by God through his Word for the glad obedience of a free and faithful service. Learning to do theological research is a discipling unto Christian service. Those enrolled by God in the theological vocation must put aside the criticism of those who will not understand this, and press on in the service to which God has called and equipped them.

6

Reporting Research

Proclaimed Research

Theological research studies God's Word in order to serve. But that service is expressed principally in the theological vocation by the publication of theological studies. God's Word is a proclaimed Word; it is God himself speaking. Theology studies the Word, and publishes the results. No matter from which angle the matter is examined the conclusion is the same: theological research is proclaimed research.

To proclaim the studied Word does not mean to mount a favorite soap box and propagate popular opinion. Nor does it require any particular style of expression. Certainly it does not necessitate "experts" rendering "proofs" for a gullible public eager to cling to innovative fads. The proclamation which theology appropriates for itself is the humble repetition, interpretation, and application of truths it has not derived by its own initiative. Theological proclamation is witness. Theologians are called to testify to what their research has disclosed, not to invent stories. The fabrication of theological research is sin.

The whole Church, of course, participates in the proclamation of God's Word. But theology serves the Church's proclamation by sharpening it upon the basis of sound study. The particular discipline within theology in which this task is most acutely focused is called **dogmatics**. The dogmatic theologian works to renew and to reform the proclamation of the Church in each generation so that the Word is effectively translated into the language of the people of God at that time. However, the dogmatician does not labor alone. Theological research is constantly contributing to the dogmatic effort.

These contributions come together under the Word for the same purpose, service. Yet, they can only mesh together because the researcher is willing to expose his or her work. Without exposure how can the research contribute to service? Its fruit would remain untasted. So it is of genuine significance to the whole theological enterprise that research not only be conducted, but also reported to as wide a section of the community as possible. Research must be advertised in action, whether by publication in print, speech, or by affirmative deed.

The responsibilities placed upon theologians by their research reach an ultimate moment of accountability when a report is issued. That is why many students of the Word are afraid to expose their work. They fear the accountability. But this fear can be overcome so that the study benefits others. Individuals can learn to trust the community to which they offer their service. Naturally, theologians place themselves on the line by presenting their work. But more importantly, they put the Gospel on the line, the Gospel of which they need not be ashamed (Rom. 1:16, 17), not even in its tiniest details. To those committed to faithfulness, fear must be set aside in the interest of service. Moreover, by an attention to the processes of research and by an attentiveness to proper ways to express research, needless fear can be alleviated.

Avenues of Publication

Not everyone should write for publication. I think it is one of the greatest misfortunes of academic life that so many who excell at teaching are penalized for their struggles to communicate through the written word. The expectations that a good thinker must also be a fine writer, or that a capable writer is necessarily a sound thinker, are both roots for some senseless practices and unneeded misunderstandings. Institutions built for the communication of instruction need to recall the primary value of oral skills. Writing is important; so is speaking. Rare is the individual who excells both in writing and speaking. On what basis ought one to be elevated above the other? Yet many institutions routinely provide higher rewards for those whose greater competency is in writing. Research can be conducted by anyone, and reported orally or in writing. Yet the rewards are for those who do capable research and then write. I have no wish to see writing become unimportant. But I cannot see that students are well served by rewards based primarily on their talent for writing.

Theological research can be published through many avenues, of which writing is only one. Research does not become better when it is written down. Published writing does, though, make the study accessible to more people than is generally true of other publication avenues. However, what is of fundamental value is the research finding expression in some public fashion. That manner should be determined by the researcher's setting, audience, and personal strengths and weaknesses. When these factors dictate a speech instead of an article, then that is the avenue that should be taken. A bit more common sense in these matters, with a lot less senseless pressure, can only help the maturing of the theological vocation and religious education.

Although many may not readily recognize **programs** or **projects** as legitimate expressions of theological reporting, they can be very creative outlets for publishing theological research. If, for example, someone has researched the environment of a local church and found that the evidence for widespread dissatisfaction among the people is the lack of Christ-centered preaching, perhaps this research can be published by a project designed to reproduce the findings in the midst of the congregation, thus inducing a constructive response. Such projects or programs typically aim not only at publishing completed research in a usable format, but also reproducing it and then extending it. Generally, either oral reporting or a written report accompany the affirmative deed.

I have no desire to quarrel with anyone about whether that kind of reporting is true reporting or only a consequence of the research report. Either way, programs and projects are sure to incorporate words spoken or written. Competency in both is desirable, though excellence in either is always as much gift as skill.

Although there are genuine differences between an oral and a written report, the likenesses are more important. Both formats share the same basic responsibilities of sound reporting. Both can profit from the same general guidelines.

Guidelines

Researchers who struggle with how to report their studies often wrestle with several interrelated concerns. They want to know what form is the most appropriate, how much they can or should include, and what ways exist by which to increase or enhance the quality of their work. **Appropriateness**, as already mentioned, is a matter of setting, audience, and personal factors. Of course, research often assumes more than one avenue of reporting. A speech, for example, might be requested to appear as a journal article. Or, a book might provide the material for a lecture series. Once an appropriate form has been decided, then other concerns move to the forefront.

There are at least three general guidelines to observe in coming to a sensible determination about the **quantity** to be included. Each guideline answers a natural and specific question researchers must ask themselves. Most basic of these questions is this one: How much of the research should be reported? The answer invariably is: **Report only as much of the research as is needed to permit the audience to know what it needs to know.** In other words, the audience is the decisive factor. If the audience is neither interested in, nor needs to know the precise methodological steps employed, then spare them what would only appear to be needless, confusing, and obscure details. Determine what the audience needs (not **wants**), and give that to them. For instance, a graduate student who has researched the problems of ascertaining the authorship of the book of Jude may be invited to speak both to a graduate forum class in critical problems of the New Testament, and a local adult Sunday morning class. Obviously, his presentation must vary. But so, too, must his quantity. He need not, and should not give to the Sunday morning class

what he gives to the forum class. Their respective needs, not
his ego, should determine his service.

How does this advice square with what I said earlier
about all the elements of research, and the evaluating of others'
research? Have I taken away with one hand what I sought to
give with the other? I think not. The point here is this: the
report of research is designed to serve a particular audience.
The elements of research which are reported are those the audience needs. I personally am of the opinion that most often
that requires some indication, however general or brief, of all
the elements. But that does not require an in-depth explanation of every element. To return to the example, what fasci-
nates and educates a forum class may bewilder and frighten a
Sunday morning class. Honesty and creativity should go hand
in hand.

Other factors besides audience often influence quantity.
Perhaps the nature of the research itself sharply limits the
report. If there is only enough material to write an article, do
not try to write a full book. Perhaps the time allowed for a
report is limited. Then do the best with the time available by
selecting only the most important bits to report. It is better
to do a few things well than many poorly. The amount reported is always a matter of judgment, and practice sharpens
that judgment. When in doubt, a little less is most often
preferable to a little more.

A second natural question is: What elements of the research should be given proportionately more attention? A good
guideline here is: **Give the most space to the most important
parts of the particular research.** It would be nice to be able
to say that explanation should always receive the most attention. But the most important element might vary from study to
study. Research, for instance, into the book of Jonah might
be of such a nature that description is the most important feature. A report emphasizing the significance of Jonah's message, then, would not be consistent with the research that was
done, even if that report was completely true. The report
should mirror the research that was done, not the study that
might have been done. If explanation was most prominent, then
it should be so displayed in the report.

The third question is: What can be left out? Here the
guideline is: **Leave out any material that is unnecessary, too
unsupported, obscure, confusing, or distracting.** A good
report aims at making the research accessible to a specific
audience. To accomplish this it should adopt a strategy of
using its assets and limiting its liabilities. Material that is
peripheral, cannot be substantiated adequately (or at all), or
that detracts from the thrust of the research should be
avoided. By deleting it, that which remains can speak with
more clarity and force.

Like quantity, quality is also a constant concern. The
two are closely connected. A strict handle on quantity will

facilitate the development of quality. Still, three further guidelines might be helpful in making decisions about the quality of a report, or of its material. First, **put the most important research material at both the beginning and at the end of the report.** There is little sense in saving the best for last if the audience is not around at the end. Lead with the most important material and the perceived quality of the report is likely to rise dramatically. This is not to suggest that everything that can be said about what is most important need be said at once. The idea is to capture and then sustain interest. Write a good first page and there will be readers for the second one. When repeating material, care should be exercised to restate it so that the repetition is not merely redundant.

Next, **aim at sufficiency, not exhaustiveness.** This, of course, is the concrete relation between quantity and quality. Many initial attempts at research and reporting founder on the treacherous shore of exhaustiveness. Lacking the discipline of many efforts, beginners almost invariably try to do too much when they try to do anything at all. But even proficient scholars can stumble at this point. It is easy to reach just a little too far. A standard mark of quality is the sense of completeness that flows from work that is exactly sufficient. Thus, if reporting on Paul's view of the Church, do not feel compelled to discuss his soteriology as well.

Finally, **strive for the best descriptions, evidence, explanations, and conclusions, not the most.** This suggestion differs only a little from the one offered above. It is intended as a safeguard against the notion that quantity equals quality, or "bigger is better." One well-done explanation for an event is more valuable than an interminable list of possibilities. This is not to decry the value of variety in looking at reasonable alternatives. But it is to place the emphasis on doing a few things well rather than many poorly.

After a researcher determines what goes into his or her report and begins the task of forming it, a new group of difficulties step forward. What style should be used? Should he or she aim at profound expression or a simplicity of prose? What kind of vocabulary would be suitable? These questions should be answered in a manner agreeing with prior considerations. So the student invited to speak to the Sunday morning class may decide to use an uncomplicated vocabulary instead of one filled with technical terms (which may or may not be appropriate even to the forum audience).

Again, the basic criteria of clarity, coherence, and cohesiveness should take center stage. Clarity can be aided by simple prose, in short sentences and paragraphs, with an economy of difficult concepts and expressions. Coherence can be helped by breaking the complicated ideas into their basic parts and utilizing simple, direct illustrations. Cohesiveness can be facilitated by paying attention to transitions between the parts, by remaining consistent in thought and expression, and by using repetition without redundancy. Not surprisingly, practice is the key to increased success.

Reporting Each Basic Element

Not every research report directly states all the basic elements of the research process. A good report very likely provides an indication of how each element participated in the process. But it is not always necessary or desirable to explicitly indicate each phase of the research. In fact, since they blend in actual practice, it is often misleading to do so. Good reports are good not because they do lip service to the elements of research, but because they relate only what needs to be told, and tell it well.

The **interest** or the **motivation** that prompted the research needs only to be reported when it is of special interest to the audience, or when it addresses some specific concern apart from which the study is harder to understand. Accordingly, a speech to the local biblical archaeology society on artifacts from ancient Jerusalem hardly needs to begin with the observation that the speaker is interested in archaeology. The audience can safely assume that fact. On the other hand, a paper urging the Church to repentance is helped if the author clarifies how her or his research is in answer to a need. The clarification of the needs helps clarify the research.

The **exploration** or the **examination** at the heart of the research cannot be passed over. The audience must know something of what object drew the researcher's attention, how it was approached, and what sources were utilized. However, this phase of the research might very well be reported in a discussion of the description and explanation of the object. Wherever it occurs, this aspect of the report should leave the audience with a precise understanding of the path to information and knowledge which the researcher took. Without this the research cannot be comprehended as **research**, and the conclusions will emerge as only opinions.

The **description** of the object, no matter how brief, is also indispensable. Research without evidence is quite impossible. A report must enumerate at least the most essential evidence. Sometimes, this element is mixed with explanation in the interest of an economy of time and effort. There is nothing wrong with this procedure unless it conveys a false impression that the researcher's explanation is its own evidence. In other words, avoid the appearance that the explanation is true because "I" say it is. The audience deserves more than "me", it deserves the evidence.

The **explanation**, despite its apparent importance, can actually, in some instances, be deleted. Some research is interested only in description. The history of King David's realm according to the information of 2 Sam. might be the subject of research aiming simply to summarize the narrative. The only explanatory comments might be imbedded in the description itself. Their intent, then, is just to elucidate the description, not to analyze it or state its significance. Still, it is comparatively rare that a statement of explanation or indication of meaning is not desirable. Such statements should stick to the evidence, with speculation never being more than a modest projection of inference from hard fact.

The **conclusions** should always be stated clearly, although sometimes a literary conclusion is used which follows the logical conclusions of the research. Thus, the research results might be stated, then followed by an exhortation to further study or to some kind of action. The former results are logical, the latter conclusion is literary. Since the researcher's conclusions are almost surely to be a focus of interest for the audience, they ought to be as strong and as plain as possible.

The **peer review** is hardly ever expressed explicitly in the research report. This is likely to be because it has not yet happened. It may not be pertinent to understanding the research. But there are occasions when a research report includes an interaction with a peer review. Suppose the research is a follow-up to earlier work which has already been reviewed. To make the new research make the most sense a peer review might be mentioned. Another situation is far more common. The **discussion** section or the **literature review** frequently found in research is a kind of peer review. Better, it is an interaction, or dialog, with others. No research is conducted in a vacuum and it is often helpful to reflect that fact.

A Reminder

There is, finally, no substitute for practice. Reporting work is something that requires repetition for skill to be developed. Yet good scholars learn from others and the continuous study of what others have done in conducting and reporting research helps. It is useful not merely in gaining information, but also in acquiring good models against which to judge one's own work. Insight into how a report has been put together makes it easier to do so one's self.

Too much helpful research is lost by the failure of the scholar to work hard at publishing a good report of it. Theology need not be printed in a major journal or by a major publisher for it to serve the Church. Once research has been done it should be given to others.

PART TWO

Methods and Models

INTRODUCTION

In the chapters to follow there are discussed many methods and models available to the theological scholar. These range from the relatively simple to the more complex, and from qualitative to quantitative. To understand any of them fully demands a recognition of those essential features of research discussed in Part One. Among such features, the most fundamental are these:

1) Research is a human endeavor. All of the potential and the limitations inherent to human experience and thinking are also inherent to research. No research is ever able to attain to the status of "revealed truth."

2) Research methods are always only tools, and never ends in themselves. When the method receives disproportionate emphasis the other benefits of research are limited unfairly.

3) Researchers are more important than their methods, and their goals and needs are more decisive to the research endeavor. The appropriate methods and models employed in any given research project depend less on the methods and models themselves than on the scholar's decisions and subject.

Such ideas as these will continue to surface occasionally. No one should be allowed easily to achieve false ideas such as, "Research is too difficult for most people to do," or, "That kind of research is too simple to warrant real effort, or yield real significance." The truth lies between such extremes. Some methods are harder than others, but none are beyond the reach of the diligent. Some yield more than others, but any can prove best for a given project. The doing of research is not a matter of magical incantations producing guaranteed results. Instead, it is sweat bringing forth fruit from the earth.

Trying to specify a logical progression to the methods and the models in the following chapters is unnecessary. The only exceptions are the quite intentional ones of placing Bible study after the critical approaches (for reasons specified in that chapter), and the leaving of less familiar quantitative strategies for the later chapters. As much as is possible, each method has been discussed briefly and practically. An emphasis has been placed on uniting theory and fact. So assumptions precede principles, but both are set forth as being indispensable to a method.

A prime aim of each chapter is to render enough information to make possible an attempt of the method. The degree of completeness varies. Some methods are more amenable to brief analysis than are others. Some of the chapters may appear very elementary and others quite demanding. Hopefully, whether easy or hard to absorb, all of the information is presented clearly and intelligibly. Since confusion and misunderstanding are major enemies of scholarship, I have tried conscientiously to shun them. Still, I will not claim infallibility in what appears here. To gain the best use of this material will take a discerning mind and a willingness to consult other books.

Perhaps it is too obvious to merit much attention, but there are many methods and tools not represented in the following chapters. The selection basis for the material included followed two considerations. The first, and more important, was including basic and historically important approaches to theological research (chapters 7-13). The second consideration was advancing quantitative strategies useful to theological research (chapters 14-17). Some might well question the absence of methods like redaction criticism, structuralism, and narrative analysis. Manageability of size demanded the line be drawn somewhere, and so some important methods were excluded. Those that remain, however, are sufficient to get new researchers on the road of practice.

Please be mindful that research is for all people. **Try** these methods and models. **Share** the experience with others. The gain will prove to be not only personal, but of benefit to the Church.

7

Library Research

Definition and Value

Library research is so common to the more comprehensive research designs discussed in this book that it merits first place for attention. In fact, as any student can attest, it is library research that usually is thought of when the term "research" is used in the classroom. But while library research shares characteristics true of any research process it is also unique. In library research the preeminent goal is the utilization of collected resources so as to acquire particular sources useful for study. Library research can be defined by this goal. **It is the searching out of particular relevant sources for study from a collection of many diverse sources.**

The value of libraries is their ability to provide vast amounts of materials, many of them highly specialized, to the public for general use. No scholar has the funds ready at hand simply to buy everything likely ever to be useful in a career, then house them in a building designed to maximize their protection and usefulness. Libraries, then, are indispensable hunting preserves for scholars. In most cities and towns there is ready access to more than one library. Because every library collection varies it is to the decided advantage of students to discover the particular makeup of those in their local area.

The value of library research is its ability to teach the most profitable use of libraries. It creates a full awareness of library resources, which over time renders inestimable assistance in the pursuit of many different kinds of research. Library research can make possible a better application of other research methods, becuase it supplies them with intelligently gathered aids. So, for example, when charged with the assignment of doing a historical study of the early Church, a library's collection is the natural place to begin. Library research soon produces materials relevant to the historical study. These may include articles from reference books, specialized studies of the subject from periodicals, standard texts by respected scholars, and translations of early Church documents. But the library research does not replace the historical research method; it complements it. The student must still employ an appropriate methodology in order to fulfill the assignment.

It is this profoundly complementary nature of library research that makes it such an integral aspect of many research methods. It is a basic and preliminary process that make other methods both possible and complete. It is little wonder, then, that so much time is given by teachers to encourage their students to frequent libraries, and to learn how best to use their resources. Unfortunately, too often a misconception is passed on to students. The concentration on library research can lead to the incorrect idea that it is a complete process in itself. A far better conception is one that views this effort as preliminary to further research. Library research is rarely, if ever, complete in itself.

To properly conduct library research requires a knowledge of library resources as well as a plan of how best to use them. Schools often provide regular instruction in these matters, for undergraduates and graduates alike. Just as regularly, though, some students neglect this instruction. Later they are forced to learn in a more tedious and painful manner—on their own. While libraries provide personnel trained to assist students in certain matters, it is unfair to expect them to do the student's research. A student who hopes to prevail on the mercies of a librarian will still find, after all the assistance rendered, that it would have been far better to learn the system of library research when it was first offered.

Library Resources

The resources available in a library are determined by many factors. Libraries differ according to size, their special interests, and the funds available to them. Some libraries are able to maintain an impressive number of subscriptions to periodicals, while others are limited in this capacity. Some libraries specialize, as those at seminaries, while others, like public libraries, seek to maintain very general collections. This means there is no substitute for spending time to discover exactly what resources are available in a given library. Of course, this does not mean that only these resources are available. What a library does not have may be available through a book store. Certainly, all scholars wish to possess some books. But the limitations of time and money make libraries irreplaceable. Thus it is wise to become well acquainted with what is available.

While any given library may have some, or all, or even more than the following, these twelve resources serve as a starting point in discussing library resources:
1) Assistance from trained personnel,
2) A system of cataloging to help searching,
3) A special section of reference materials,
4) Indexes,
5) Stacks,
6) Periodicals,

7) Archives,
8) Audio-visual materials,
9) Microfilms or microfiche,
10) Copying capabilities,
11) Typewriters, and
12) Inter-library loan.

The proper utilization of these resources is not a matter that can be fully explained in this chapter. There is too much variation among libraries on particular points of policy. A more useful effort would be to take the equivalent time and simply chat with the local librarians. However, in the appendices at the end of this text are two classification systems for religious books. It is likely that one or the other of these is in operation at the libraries nearby. As for these twelve resources, while they cannot be discussed at any length, they do merit a summary paragraph describing their basic character and place in the whole.

Assistance from trained library personnel makes it possible for anyone to gain some use from any library. Larger libraries are able to maintain a staff in which different functions are expertly handled by various individuals. This means that time can be saved both for the library staff and the researcher if it is determined beforehand who is the appropriate person to approach with a given question. Generally, there will be a desk or area marked out for assistance in research matters. As indicated earlier, many libraries offer regular classes on using their resources. These may be as short as a half-hour, or based on a long-term, regular exposure to the library and its resources. The classes are led by experts, who ought to be noted, listened to, then consulted as the need arises.

A **system of cataloging** exists in every library. The two best-known systems are outlined in the appendices. It is absolutely necessary to master the classification system, and the sooner the better. This does not require memorizing every detail, but having a feel for the general location of broad subject areas. A little looking around will probably turn up simplified visual aids outlining the system used by a particular library. A centrally located and easily found area will contain the card catalogs, where the books kept by the library are listed according to author, subject, and title. One section will have listings by author in alphabetical order. Another section will list the books by subject and title, also in alphabetical order. Some systems of classification are accompanied by volumes which list many alternative subject headings. Thus, if a researcher cannot find material where it is expected, these volumes can guide the search to another area where the materials are listed.

A **special section of reference materials** is regularly maintained by libraries. This section is set in its own place but still conforms to the classification system employed for all books in the library. It contains materials that cannot be removed from the library. The kinds of material most likely to be found here are encyclopedias, dictionaries, atlases, and special sets of specialized information, such as **Who's Who in America.** Reference materials are frequently a good starting place to acquire basic information on a topic.

Indexes provide a key to locating material without having to search through vast amounts of documents. The kinds of indexes are many, and the degree of sophistication in them varies from the very simple to the outright baffling. Indexes may serve as guides to periodical literature, to books, or to other kinds of documents and materials. Which index should be used depends on the nature of the study being conceived by the researcher. In some instances a very general index, such as the **Reader's Guide to Periodical Literature,** is appropriate. By consulting it on a given topic the researcher may be pointed in several different directions. Or, if the researcher desires to be confined to a particular field, an index to the literature in that field will be most helpful. The study of biblical literature, for example, might lead to any number of indexes, such as **New Testament Abstracts, American Theological Library Association Index to Religious Periodical Literature,** or **Christian Periodical Index.** Obviously, these, too, vary in specialization of their contents. The first named of them is a guide that provides not only the location of material but also an abbreviated summary of its contents. Periodicals themselves also issue indexes, normally at the conclusion of each volume and occasionally at five- and ten-year intervals. Though every index used may require a new and unique understanding to follow its presentation, the consultation of indexes can save considerable time.

The **stacks** are those structures of bookshelves utilized to compactly organize and store a library's documents. In common usage, the term designates where the library's books can be found. Quite naturally this is the part of the library that requires the most space and usually commands the most attention. The organization of the books is in accordance with the classification system, at least it is in theory. Unfortunately, there always seems to be at least one indifferent user who by indolence creates chaos out of order. The stacks may not be the researcher's best friend, but they must certainly be numbered among the intimates.

Periodicals, materials issued on a recurrent basis, are another major part of a library and take up space accordingly. These vary as much as books do. Some are simple, some technical; some are general, others are specialized. They are organized alphabetically, with current issues kept on display and back issues, usually bound together in volumes, maintained on shelves. Periodicals are quite valuable to researchers since they not only offer many specialized studies of interest, but also indicate the concerns of current scholars in a field. It takes a substantial amount of time to get a book into print and periodicals may offer the latest available research on a subject.

Since every field today seems to enjoy journals without number, it has become increasingly important to master indexes and abstracts keyed to the periodical literature. Otherwise, what might seem a simple topic to study can become lost in a sea of materials, or a vast empty desert where no relevant article can be found.

Archives are a very valuable, if too little used, resource. Several factors contribute to this situation. Most archives are restricted to access by qualified researchers who have definite business. Archives contain material which, by their very nature, require special care for their preservation and handling, and are irreplaceable. An awareness of this, reinforced by the presence of an anxious archivist, can make even approaching a library's archives an uneasy experience. But somewhere along the line a young scholar is likely to find that the materials of an archive are absolutely indispensable to a study. Why? The answer lies in the nature of the materials. Archives preserve original and unpublished materials. Studying the ideas of a certain theologian by examining unpublished notes and letters can produce a level of understanding that might not be possible any other way. So, if a study can make use of archival material, a researcher should follow whatever accepted policies exist to gain access to it. Then, exercising great care and respect, obeying all the relevant procedures and instructions, this invaluable resource can be employed.

Audio-visual materials are often incorporated into a library. Today these might include video cassettes and recorders as well as the familiar phonographs and records. Sound recordings and films can often be added to the written materials a researcher might examine in order to gain information and understanding. This equipment can probably be found in some less frequented part of the library, in an area where the sound will not disturb others. Again, there will be policies to consult, and steps to follow to gain the use of these things. Whether or not any of these materials or the equipment can be removed from the library will be included in the library's policies about them. The creative use of such resources may add a vital element to a study.

Microfilm and/or microfiche has become a popular feature in today's libraries. Through them libraries have been able to increase their ability to store materials. Special machines are needed to read the microfilm or microfiche materials but these are easy to master, and the instructions are right on or next to the machines. Some of these machines offer the added bonus of copying the material on the screen onto a large, easy to read print-out. Materials commonly put into this kind of format include newspapers, magazines, booklets, pamphlets, brochures, and government publications. The exact extent and nature of this kind of collection should be noted so that it is remembered as a possible resource for a given study.

Copying materials is a frequent desire of researchers.

Almost all libraries have machines available to do this at a reasonable cost. Many libraries, conscious of copyright restrictions, insist on knowing what materials are to be copied, and do the actual copying, too. Virtually every copier found in libraries has both a set of operating instructions and information regarding copyright laws and restrictions near it. A scholar does have the privilege of copying some materials under what is known as the "fair use" provision of copyright law. Essentially, this means the privilege of making copies for private use, and only in such a manner that it does not impinge on the copyright owner's rights. Any researcher who has doubts about whether or how much may be copied should consult the librarian for guidance.

Typewriters are often made available to users of the library. This makes it possible to take some materials and retreat to a room where notes or a paper can be composed. Recently, libraries have also begun using electronic typewriters, computers, and even word processors. Seldom are these available to the general public. But it seems safe to say that in keeping with the character of libraries, it is only a matter of time before tools like these will be commonplace to users.

The last resource listed above is the **inter-library loan**. The network of libraries that any particular library is a part of may be small or large. But by being involved in a cooperative network a library is able to greatly extend its holdings. If materials are not available in one place, perhaps in another location in the network they can be found. Special procedures and policies govern the use of inter-library loan. It is necessary to have the assistance of a librarian to make use of this resource. The inter-library loan is a last resort, when the researcher has determined that the materials he or she needs cannot be found close at hand.

One point bears repeating. There is no substitute for becoming personally aware of local resources. A little time and attention used early in the game will save time and effort later. Researchers who are creative in seeking information are more likely to produce work that enjoys breadth and depth. Library research, to be as useful as it can be, depends on an awareness of what is available and a creative application of those resources.

Library Search

Armed with a knowledge of what is available, and charged with the task of completing some assignment, how can the library best be used? There is no one right system that answers this question. Different assignments may require different strategies. The gathering, for example, of bibliographic data necessitates a much more restricted use of resources than a sweeping study of Reformation politics. Still, while recognizing that flexibility is a desirable trait in a researcher, there are seven basic steps that can help many library searches.

74

They are:

1) Start with a clear idea of what the topic being researched is. In other words, know what the research goal is.

2) Form a general idea of what is available that is relevant to the topic or purpose. This means consulting the card catalog, indexes, and bibliographic guides.

3) Before looking at any books or magazines on the subject, have a bibliography in hand. A bibliography should be a natural by-product of step two.

4) From the bibliography select the most promising titles.

5) Collect these materials and see if they are as relevant as they promised. Use them to suggest other places to look.

6) After gathering the materials needed, shape the study in light of them. This may mean considering special needs and moving on to the use of some of the special resources of the library.

7) Make the collection of materials as precisely relevant to the study as possible, and make the study as reflective of the information as possible. The study determines the selection of materials, but the materials determine the shape of the study.

At any step, if help is needed, seek it! The secret of success in library research is learning how to coordinate a study with the available materials. Remember, library research is concerned with locating materials. The analysis of them requires some other method. An intelligent application of library research steps will produce relevant material. Then that material should be allowed to suggest its own most appropriate usage in accordance with the needs of the study and the demands of whatever methodology is being used. To put this into larger perspective, think of the research process as entailing two broad phases. In the first, a topic or goal is determined and materials collected. Here is where library research is introduced. In the second phase, the materials are examined by some method such as historical research. The two phases need to be coordinated, and the coordinating phase uses steps six and seven above. Library research is guided by the specific methodology to be used, but the materials collected then modify the study design in light of what the methodology has available to work on.

A review of each step can be instructive. The first step entails making decisions before reaching the library. It is not impossible to discover a good topic by visiting the library, but it is most certainly easier to use a library if some goal is fixed in mind before walking in the door. Clarity of purpose goes a long way toward making sense out of where library research should start and how far it needs to extend.

The second step involves two processes that occur at once. On one hand, the idea with which the researcher started is somewhat modified as it is seen what is available in the library. The card catalog and indexes (and whatever other guides are used) may disclose that the study as first conceived is infeasible. Or, they might suggest some alteration in the study's scope, design, or nature. At the same time, an investigation of these guides will begin pinpointing the most relevant parts of the library for the researcher's work. These areas should be fixed carefully in mind. It may later happen that in one of these areas just the right document will be found that somehow was missed in the search of the various guides.

Still prior to actually going to collect documents is the forming of a bibliography. This should be a natural result of step two because as various guides yield likely titles the researcher is noting them in writing. Once several titles have been noted they should be organized. This may follow any of several methods. If all that is desired is a bibliography, an alphabetical listing is what is needed. But for a library search this procedure would mean a lot of unnecessary footwork. A more sensible procedure is to list book titles under their classification within the library system. This means that all books listed in one part of the bibliography will be found close together on the shelves. Article titles can be listed under the periodicals in which they are found, and the periodicals can be listed alphabetically. Then when looking for the material the researcher will be able to proceed in a methodical fashion.

The fourth step is selecting the most promising titles from the bibliography. This step might be included in step three. At times it is possible to be highly selective as titles are viewed in the various guides. But more often, a substantial number of titles rapidly accumulates. There are likely to be more titles than a researcher can manage in terms of actually collecting the documents they represent. So as a very practical consideration, once the bibliographical list has been put together a first selection of things to look at will need to be made. This is a best-guess operation, and it may well be that adjustments will be required later.

Once the selection of titles is complete, the fifth step ensues. This entails collecting the materials. A sound knowledge of the floor plan of the library can save steps now. Organize the titles further by grouping them according to their proximity to one another. That means that rather than proceeding from one section on the first floor to another on the second floor, then down to the basement, plan so as to save time and energy. Start with the materials closest at hand and proceed in a methodical fashion to the next closest section, and so on. The whole purpose of organizing the bibliography was to cut haphazard wandering. In collecting the material make full and

76

practical use of the bibliography. As each section is visited and the titles are found, they should be given at least a cursory examination to verify whether they are, in fact, relevant to the study. It also cannot hurt, if time permits, to glance at surrounding titles. One of them might prove to be exactly what is being looked for. If the material itself suggests other places to look, do not immediately run to those places, but do immediately note them to be checked later.

The sixth step is critical. Once the materials have been gathered, the study should be reevaluated. This means spending time with the collected materials while reflecting on what the study aims to accomplish. If the materials are relevant to the study, but the study now appears to be too broad, too narrow, too loose, or too inflexible in light of the materials, then it is time to make a hard decision. Either the study should look for other materials, judging the present ones to be insufficient (though relevant), or the research should adjust itself to the reality of the materials and undergo some revisions. The unacceptable choices are to press on with the original plan whether it is really appropriate or not, or to play around with the material so that it is misused. A responsible study uses its sources responsibly, which means maintaining an honesty about them and about what they say with regard to the study's aim. It may be that in this reflective process the idea occurs to try some of the special resources of the library, like the archives. Whatever the case, it cannot be emphasized too strongly that this is a critical step if success in the later employment of a research methodology is to occur.

Finally, seventh, with a determination of the materials completed they should be organized so as to maximize their relevance to the study. As initiated in step six, from now on these materials will be interacting with the study design so that each shapes the other in a creative manner. The study has determined what was selected; it now begins deciding what parts from each document should be used, and where and how. The materials, meanwhile, shape the study by their very nature. If they are to be used correctly the study must recognize their character and limitations. The research, then, becomes a dialog between the researcher and the collected materials.

This last step should be viewed as an extension of step six. It differs principally in that step six is the last clearly independent step of library research; yet it, too, contributes to the transition to the employment of a research methodology. Step six can be seen as the first collision between the materials available and the study as first conceived. A basic decision about what this collision signifies is then made. The seventh step assumes that the library search has accomplished its purpose, at least for now. It brings the weight of the materials fully to bear on the study design.

Doubtless there are many legitimate conceptions as to how

best to pursue library research. As a matter of fact, there are entire books on the subject; these may be profitably consulted. The seven steps offered here are simply one convenient and effective way to get at the resources of a library, particularly the most fundamental ones: books and articles. Every researcher discovers over time a personal approach to using libraries, one that works best for her or him. In this endeavor, as in so many others, experience teaches.

Conclusion

Library research, like any research, is a process which places certain demands upon people. Competency in library research can only be acquired by practice. But it is certainly made easier by taking full advantage of the help offered by librarians in mastering the use of the wide range of available resources. Because this kind of research is so fundamental to success in school and scholarship it cannot be exaggerated in importance. To succeed as a scholar or as a student is (or ought to be) impossible without sound library research skills.

The following exercises may help in acquiring greater facility in library research.

Exercise 1. Make a list of all the libraries in your geographical area. Categorize each library by the nature of its collection, i.e., whether it offers materials of a very general nature, whether it is a specialized library (as museum and seminary libraries are likely to be), or whether it attempts to maintain a general collection alongside certain special interests. Note whether it is a public library, school library, private collection, etc. Note, too, its size (number of volumes, periodicals, etc.), and the extent of its available resources.

Exercise 2. Visit the library where you have most frequent access. Obtain a floor plan of it (many libraries provide these). Note where the card catalogs, reference materials, stacks, information desk, etc., are located. Check the cataloging system to see whether it is Dewey Decimal, Library of Congress, or some other system. Take the time to visit different sections of the library, acquainting yourself with what is available.

Exercise 3. Select a specific topic from those listed below and conduct a library search:
1) The political situation in Europe at the start of the Protestant Reformation.
2) The meaning of "Son of man" in the Gospel of Mark.
3) The idea of "justification" in the theology of Karl Barth.
4) The origin of the idea of the separation of Church and State.
5) The development of the practice of tithing.
6) The current situation in American Christianity with regard to the ordination of women.

Remember, library research paves the way for other specific research methods. Use the library search to make the best possible collection of materials for a study.

8

Translation

Translation as Research

Translation is a process of transfer or conversion. What has been communicated in one fashion may need to be communicated in another manner. Accomplishing the transition from one to the other is the act of translation. As an idea, translation is common to many scholarly efforts. For example, a scholar must translate his or her work, which may be highly complex, into intelligible terms for one or another audience of nonspecialists. More often, though, the term is used to refer to **that process of rendering one language communication into another.**

In theological research the translation of the Scriptures from the original languages has always occupied a prominent position. What other effort is as fundamental to the study of the written Word? In point of fact, translation precedes many research projects and rarely is distant from many others. Yet researchers are not the only ones who depend on translation. The millions of people who are able to read the Bible in their own language are also greatly indebted to the scholars who have given themselves to translation work.

However, it may seem odd to think of translation as research. Certainly, it appears to be a different kind of labor than, for instance, a textual analysis or a statistical analysis. Yet translation shares with other research methods a common passion for understanding. The translator pursues a knowledge of language so complete and reliable that what is comprehensible in one domain can be rendered intelligible in another. To accomplish this end the translator engages in all of those familiar traits of research: interest, exploration, description, explanation, and report. Motivated to help others understand something, the translator explores the avenues of expression which are available for conveying meaning. Expressions in one language must be described or explained in another so that the meaning of the original is preserved. The end product, the translation, is itself a research report.

The Necessity and Priority of Translation

Without translation, communication as we know it would not exist. Knowledge gained by one person, or by a few persons, would be largely limited to them. The very process of inquiry, relying as it does on convenient but specialized forms of communication, would be obstructed because without the ability to translate the human mind is locked. Translation is the key to insight which makes possible rendering a simple observation into a profound generalization that many others can profit from and build upon.

Apart from the translation of communications from one language to another a global awareness would be impossible. Translation, obviously, is both a necessity for human existence and a critical priority for human affairs. Nowhere is this any truer than in the Church. It scarcely is imaginable how different things would be within the Church if every Christian had to have a thorough understanding of the biblical languages in order to read and study the Bible.

From the earliest period of the Church's history the Bible has been translated. No other document has been so important to the gradual development and refinement of ideas about translation than the Bible. The manner in which the Scriptures have been translated has always been an item of great interest, not only to scholars, but to all believers. Even today it is not uncommon to hear lively (occasionally heated) debates about the relative merits of one Bible translation or another. It is commonly recognized how important translation is to gaining a reliable understanding of the Bible.

Difficulties in Translation

The importance of translation is underscored by the response people give to different translations. But what also is highlighted in the responses is the inherent difficulty in satisfactorily rendering one language into another. What is one in the original can become many in the translation. In other words, a single communication in Greek, when rendered into English, may take several forms. To verify this it is necessary only to look as far as the nearest parallel Bible. Each version represented there is dealing with the same original. Depending on many factors, those who read those different translations will prefer one and take issue with another.

Such a situation inevitably puts pressure on any translator or team of translators. On the one hand, the translator feels keenly the responsibility to **faithfully** render the original. On the other hand, an equally important aim is rendering something **meaningful** in the language of the readers. Ideally, of course, a good translation succeeds in accomplishing both intents. But no matter how excellent the translation, it is certain that somebody, somewhere will question either the translator's success in being faithful to the original or maintaining a meaningful contemporary version. To make matters worse, the general run of criticism is to the effect that a translation in honoring one aim spoils the other. In such cases the translator is tempted to opt for either faithfulness or meaningfulness when, of course, he or she must provide both.

Translation is the first step in biblical interpretation. That entails an awesome responsibility for the translator, particularly where the original is susceptible to more than one possible understanding. To render the text one way will be to direct the path of interpretation along a route that will be different from what would occur if the text were translated differently. Later in this chapter this kind of difficulty will be illustrated from the New Testament. But at this point it only is necessary to note that a constant danger in translation is to extend the interpretive element further than the text itself warrants. A tendency to read more into a text than what is there can seriously diminish the value of a translation. Such a move represents a certain scarificing of faithfulness to ensure meaningfulness. The problem, though, is that the meaning that is ensured may be the wrong one!

Another difficulty, and a rather strange and unfortunate one, is caused by the success of a translation. The most famous example of this is the success of the **Authorized Version** (the **King James Version**). Though written some centuries ago, though based on a critical text inferior to that possessed today, and though misleading in places because of archaic vocabulary and style, this translation in some quarters still brooks no rivals. It is pathetic and tragic that godly scholars who contribute to modern translations should be subjected to ridicule and scorn by other Christians. Unfortunately, the word has too seldom been passed that no one translation has been dropped from heaven, fresh from the lap of God.

Why does such a situation exist? Why does it persist? Of course, there are many factors at work to produce and maintain this kind of situation. One that needs to be marked here is the severe misunderstanding of the essential nature of the translation process itself. If it is missed that translation exists to communicate to the people of the translator's time and place in an effective manner, then it almost will be inevitable that a successful translation in one time and place will be enshrined as the best translation for all times and places. But translation is needed in every generation and place if the Bible's message is to be faithfully and meaningfully communicated.

Another difficulty faced by the translator entails the large amount of background information useful or needed to accurately render a passage. A good translator hardly can avoid being, or relying upon, scholars schooled in both the history and the culture of the people who produced the material now being translated. A knowledge of the situation of the author and the audience of the original document unlocks the possibilities of translation. But rarely is this as straightforward a matter as it may appear. Scholars disagree on many matters pertinent to understanding a text; this can affect confidence in translating the text. If the work is to be translated at all, the translator must adopt a stance. Accordingly, the translator's viewpoint inescapably becomes involved. That viewpoint at least ought to be as informed as possible.

So far the kinds of difficulties enumerated all have been rather general in nature. But the actual work of translation is one in which a myriad of particular problems surface. These may have to do with idioms in the language, morphological problems, stylistic difficulties, and even punctuation. An example often cited to me when I was in college concerned Eph. 4:28. The text is rendered (correctly): "Let the thief no longer steal, but rather let him labor . . ." (RSV). The Greek original had no punctuation, and by misreading the text as to word order and intent the text could be rendered: "Let him who stole, steal. No longer let him labor . . ."! Of course, this is an obvious and poor example of the very substantial problems that can beset a translator.

To illustrate this more adequately, let us examine briefly some of the difficulties surrounding terminology important to understanding the kingdom of God. It is well known that the preaching of the kingdom was central to the message of Jesus. Its prominent place demands efforts to understand it as carefully and fully as possible. The translator is a part of this effort by rendering the discussion of the kingdom in a manner faithful to what Jesus intended, and also meaningful to today's readers. Right from the beginning this is a difficult task since to retain a term like "kingdom" may be as misleading as it can be descriptive to a modern reader. But other problems also abound.

In the age of modern theology a reawakened interest in the eschatology of the New Testament gave rise to a view that the coming of the kingdom of God is a totally future event. Later reaction to this viewpoint argued that the kingdom was, at least partly, realized in history. Both sides of the debate appealed to texts for support, but several of the most critical passages in the debate are obscured by very difficult terminological obstacles. This situation, of course, has created many implications for theology, depending on the viewpoint adopted. Biblical scholars have had to wrestle with the alternatives and determine what seems to them the most likely meaning of words and passages. In the midst of this, translators have had the unenviable task of rendering these hard portions in such a way that they reflect what they think was meant, but without overstating their case. For better or for worse, once the decision has been made, and the translation offered, many readers without a strong realization of the issues involved will be influenced in one direction while remaining ignorant of the plausibility of a different translation. For some of these readers a subsequent encounter with the alternative rendering can produce confusion and even hostility as they react against what seems to them an obvious perversion of the Bible.

Let us begin with Lu. 17:21. The text can be translated: "Being asked by the Pharisees when the kingdom of God was coming, he answered them, 'The kingdom of God is not coming with signs to be observed; nor will they say, Lo, here it is! or There! for behold, the kingdom of God is **in the midst of** (ἐντός) you.'"

The term in parentheses (pronounced "entos"), rendered by the words in bold print, can also be translated by the English words "within" or "among." Modern translations offer different choices; "within" is used in the King James, American Standard, and the paraphrased Living Bible, among others. The New English Bible prefers "among"; Philips adopts the term "inside." Generally, one term is selected and an alternative noted in the margin in a footnote.

Now it is fairly obvious that there is a significant disparity in meaning between "among" (or "in the midst of") and "within." The Greek term is a rare one, appearing in only one other place in the New Testament, where it clearly means "inside" (". . . first cleanse the inside of the cup," Mt. 23:26). This means that there is little help from other usage to determine its proper rendering. But there are some very basic things about the word that are instructive. It is an adverb of place, not a preposition; but used with the genitive case, as in this passage, it functions very like a preposition. It is an antonym to the term ἐκτός ("ektos"), meaning "without," in the sense of "outside." Generally, then, the natural or expected meaning of the term is "within," or "inside."

Two passages in the Greek writer, Xenephon, have suggested the legitimacy of the translation "among," or "in the midst of." However, the relevancy of these other texts has been disputed. Usually the rendering is supported by an appeal to the context. How could Jesus have meant entos to say "within" when he is addressing the Pharisees? To mean that the Pharisees have the kingdom within (as in "inside") themselves has nothing to commend it from the context. Rather, so the argument runs, Jesus is reflecting that while they profess to be eager for a sign so as to know when the kingdom is near, it is in fact already right under their noses, "in the midst of" them. Of course, to read the context in this manner is to presuppose the kingdom is "realized," that is, as already present in some manner.

It can be argued that whether the rendering "among" or "within" is adopted, either way the saying reflects a present kingdom. If this is the case, then certainly the context indicates "among" as the preferable translation choice. But the matter should not be so quickly resolved. The English "within" is versatile enough to be maintained here without necessitating an understanding that Jesus meant the kingdom of God was inside the Pharisees. "Within" can also mean "within the reach of," or "within your perception." Both these senses fit well into the context. Moreover, to retain "within" used in these ways allows the text to have either a future or present understanding of the kingdom. The added advantage of maintaining the normal, expected rendering of entos should make this alternative a very desirable one.

But to communicate either of these senses with "within" requires adding words that cannot be directly matched to corresponding Greek terms. In other words, the Greek entos must be interpretively stretched. Since this seems to already be the case in translating it "among," this consideration perhaps should not be overstressed. Now, the text might be paraphrased: "Behold! The kingdom of God is still within reach, and it will certainly be obvious to you when it has suddenly come!" Such a rendering carries a strong future sense of the kingdom.

Both the above paraphrase and the use of the term "among" can be avoided. A more "neutral" reading is possible. So the text can be translated: "Behold! The kingdom is within your reach." Such a translation permits the kingdom to be understood as either already present or still coming. It stresses continuity with the thematic element in Jesus' preaching of repentance. The translation: "Behold! The kingdom is within your perception" is likewise temporally ambiguous and stresses continuity with the Pharisees' statement. Yet both of these renderings make presumptions that can be challenged. The translator has no clear and easy choice in such situations. Having made a choice she or he can only partly and mildly indicate the many issues behind it by placing off to the side, or in a note, the recognition that another translation possibility exists.

Let us consider three other lexicographical difficulties, although not in as much detail. The Greek term βιάζεται ("biazetai") and βιασταί ("biastai") are, in their contexts, very difficult to understand. The relevant texts are Mt. 11:12 and Lu. 16:16. These read, respectively:

"From the days of John the Baptist until now the kingdom of heaven **biazetai**, and **biastai** take it by force."

"The law and the prophets were until John; since then the good news of the kingdom of God is preached, and every one enters it **biazetai**."

The translation possibilities are numerous: almost as many as the guesses as to who the biastai are. At root, the term means "violent, impetuous men." Biazetai is a verb form which can be rendered in either the middle or passive voice, and understood as either transitive or intransitive. Thus, alternatives for the phrase in Matthew range from "the kingdom of heaven uses force" to "the kingdom of heaven suffers violence." In Luke the reading can be "every one enters it violently," or, "every one who enters it passes through violence." Indirectly, at least, the alternative chosen will influence not only an understanding of the nature of the kingdom in its coming, but also, in the context, the time of its coming. About all that is clear is that any rendering advanced can at best be a tentative one. This is one of the more difficult statements to be found in the Bible.

Another problem surrounds the term ἤγγικεν ("engiken"). It is the perfect of the verb ἐγγίζω ("engizo"), meaning "to bring near," "to come near to," "to approach." The term can mean either that the kingdom has drawn near enough actually to have arrived, or it is very near but not yet here. The word appears in many critical places (Mk. 1:15; Mt. 3:2, 4:17, 10:7; Lk. 10:9, 11). Closely linked to Jesus' proclamation of the kingdom, this verb is, arguably, the most important for determining the time of the kingdom of God. A primary example of this importance is found in the summary text of Mk. 1:14, 15. With the Greek term transliterated and supplied, the text reads: "Now after John was arrested, Jesus came into Galilee, preaching the gospel of God, and saying, 'The time is fulfilled, and the kingdom of God **engiken**; repent, and believe in the gospel'" (RSV). Depending on how the word is rendered, the passage can read:

"The time is fulfilled, and the kingdom of God has come";
or,

"The time is fulfilled, and the kingdom of God is near."
One reflects a present ("realized") kingdom, and the other a still future kingdom. The common alternative, "the kingdom of God **is at hand**" theoretically may retain a temporal ambiguity, but most readers doubtless understand the meaning as "is present." Where this word is concerned a translator faces an unavoidable, yet critical, interpretive decision.

This is true also of a term similar to engiken. The word ἔφθασεν ("ephthasen"), found in Mt. 12:28 (parallel in Lk. 11:20), is the first aorist form of the verb φθάνω ("phthano"), which is found just seven times in the New Testament. This verb, like engiken, can carry more than one time sense. It may mean "to arrive before," or "precede." It also may mean "arrive," "come," or "reach." Unlike engiken, however, there is more agreement that this verb can be expected to carry the sense of the most acute temporal imminence, that is, it is more likely to signify arrival than just closeness. The Matthew passage reads: "But if it is by the Spirit of God that I cast out demons, then the kingdom of God **ephthasen** upon you" (RSV). Again, the options are clear. The text can be read as, "then the kingdom of God has come," or, "then the kingdom of God is very near." It is possible to render the passage to retain an element of doubt about the time: "then the kingdom of God is certainly before you." But this reading suffers from a weakening of the temporal element ("before" does not need to be understood as making any notice of time other than an incidental one), and if "before" is understood as referring primarily to place, then the time is present by default. Once more the translator is exceedingly hard pressed to find a way to retain any of the ambiguity in the term being translated. No matter how it is said in English, it reflects an interpretive decision.

These four examples, restricted to just one matter, indicate how involved a translator's task can become, and how critical a task it is. If it does nothing else, the awareness of this situation should confirm that there is no final substitute for learning the original languages and working diligently to grow in an understanding of the multitude of factors that are at play in understanding the biblical message. The wonder of it is that biblical translators do as reliable and readable a job as they do. In an age where the need for translators is greater than ever before, and the number of translators not adequate for the magnitude of the need, the Church ought to be exhorting, supporting, and directing interested individuals into this exciting and rewarding field.

Principles

In light of all that has been said to this point, it might be apparent that enumerating so-called "steps to an effective translation" is a near hopeless task. Translation is an endeavor not bound by rigid methodological laws. In fact, as will be seen later, there are two quite distinct philosophies about translation, and adherence to one or the other of these can produce two quite different products. The student who seeks a recipe for translating is engaged in a futile search.

Still, there are some principles that are general enough and yet fundamental enough to warrant special attention. The first among these already has been indicated: a translator must be both **faithful to the original** and **meaningful to his or her contemporaries**. Any translation failing at either of these goals is inadequate. A translator is creative, but in servitude to the creation of another. That means the goal is not to impress the audience with the translator's wisdom and style, but to get across the original author's wisdom and style. Accomplishing that goal is being faithful. Being meaningful means remembering that contemporary readers want to read the original author and understand him. The translator stands as a mediator, helping to fulfill the reader's desire. In fact, the image of a mediator is a very helpful one, since the translator truly is standing between two parties who cannot make significant contact with each other without help.

A second principle is: translation must reckon with both **form** and **substance**. Regardless of the relative weight assigned to each of these, they are inseparable, and both must be addressed. Form has to do with the way in which something is said; substance is what is said. Obviously, a translator has to handle both at two ends. The original's style and words is at one end, the translation's style and words at the other end.

The original's message is at one end, the translation's at the other. The very best translations are those where a way has been found to transmit meaningfully the original's message in the original's style while simutaneously providing the contemporary reader with a pleasurable reading experience.

A third principle, particularly critical in biblical translating, is maintaining an **aural** sense alongside the **visual** sense. In other words, a translation should sound as well as it reads. The Bible is more than a book for the parlor table; it is a proclamation, the **Word** of God **spoken** to the world. The simple fact that the Bible plays such a central role in the services of the Church, where it is read aloud, necessitates for the translator a close attention to the way a passage sounds. The better translations attain a pleasantness of sound equal to their written beauty.

A fourth principle is: use **background information** as intelligently as possible to sharpen the translation. We already have seen how translation can demand such information in order to make wise selections among translation alternatives. A New Testament translator not only needs a comprehension of Koine Greek, and English, but a fundamental grasp of many other things, such as the background of the author and the audience, the tenor of the times, and so forth.

A fifth principle, and one close to the nature of research, is to make **conservative decisions** when faced with difficult choices. It is better to brave ambiguity than to clearly make a choice that, in retrospect, proves wrong. I am not advocating cowardice but caution. The work is hard enough without adding the hazards that come with too free a hand in interpretive decisions.

A sixth principle, and a rather obvious one, is to pay close attention to **syntax** and **grammar**. Remembering that a translation can be viewed as a kind of research report, the guidelines for such reports should be kept in force. Clarity, cohesiveness, and coherence are important to the translator even where they appear not to have been for the author. A basic respect for language is central to translation.

These six principles provide a broad enclosure within which to work. But what about steps? While I am pessimistic about reducing the art of translation to anything that smacks of a recipe, perhaps a few rather general steps might be in order. In outline form, and without elaboration, these are:

1) Be sure that the work being translated does not exceed the translator's present skills.
2) Be certain that the original is understood before attempting to translate it.
3) Respect the author's manner of presentation, especially his or her peculiar mannerisms and distinctive expressions.
4) Paraphrase the original to gain the sense of having said the same things one's self.

5) Break the original into manageable portions and be satisfied with one part before moving to the next.
6) Take time to resolve fully each difficulty now that a rudimentary translation is complete.
7) Go back and rework the whole, aiming now at enhancing clarity, ensuring cohesiveness, and checking the coherence.

The above steps are demanding, and hardly representative of all that can go on in translation. Yet they may prove beneficial in trying a little translation work. Certainly practice remains the real key to attaining success.

Two Translation Philosophies

At the present time there are two different approaches to the task of translation. Each promises somewhat of a way between various difficult alternatives, but does so by opting to tend one direction over another. At the outset, though, it must be made clear that either approach can provide a helpful translation, and both already have served the Church's needs. Each approach attempts to honor fully the basic principles enumerated above, and to cope satisfactorily with the various kinds of difficulties indicated above. Unfortunately, the contact between the practitioners of the two philosophies often has been unnecessarily limited, and the strengths of each too often undersold in the training of the alternative approach. But this may change.

The older of these two approaches can be labeled two ways. It can be called the **classical** philosophy of translation, or the **correspondence** method of translating. It thrives in institutions of higher learning, and stresses training in the original languages together with related biblical and theological studies. Its aim is suggested by its latter name. It desires renderings corresponding to the original not only in the original's intent, but also in its form. Characteristically, such translations afford a word-for-word correspondence between the original and the translation. This often has made for a style unnatural to the modern reader, but not unfamiliar. Because of the long success of this approach generations of readers have become accustomed to reading Bible translations that are quite different in style from the other literature they read. Some people even think in terms of a "biblical style of expression," and believe that their religious life is helped by Bible versions featuring such a style. The classical approach also tends to adopt a consistency in rendering terms, giving priority to using the same English word to translate a given Hebrew or Greek term wherever it occurs. This can, on occasion, be cumbersome and misleading since the context may indicate that some other English word would be a better choice. In summary, where this translation philosophy errs, it does so on the side of conservatism, opting to be faithful to the original even at the expense of modern intelligibility.

The second approach embodies a **modern** philosophy of translation. It is commonly called the **dynamic equivalency** method. Used by many professional translators trained through translation agencies as well as having received a seminary education, this approach emphasizes a knowledge and use of contemporary linguistics. The focus of translating is shifted from strict correspondence to the concept of equivalency between languages. While the translator is concerned to stay close to the original in structure and usage, still there is greater freedom than under the classical method to depart from these concerns when some other means of communicating the message proves more efficient or effective for the modern audience. In essence, the translator makes a priority of message over form, always seeking the best means at hand to convey the message. Therefore, in this approach there is a greater willingness to depart from verbal consistency in the interest of relevant contexts. The decisive question the translator asks of the ancient author is, What would he say if he spoke today's language? The focus is on translation occurring between meanings, and not primarily on words. The obvious danger in this approach lies in becoming overly interpretive in the translation. As distinct from the classical approach, where dynamic equivalency errs, it is on the side of liberality, opting to be meaningful to contemporary readers even at the expense of the exact style and/or words of the original.

The fact that both approaches exist and prosper suggests two important things. First, each has proven an ability to render products helpful to their modern audience, and approved by their colleagues. Second, neither has demonstrated such an overwhelming superiority to the other that one has supplanted the other. As we have seen, the research work involved in translation is of such a nature that difficult decisions have to be made almost as a matter of routine. It would seem that neither correspondence nor equivalency can ever entirely provide an answer to what ought to be written. The art of the scholar is as critical a key to success as is the science of language.

Conclusion

Theological research depends heavily upon the skills of translators. Scholars who are not themselves primarily translators require the assistance of those who are. Whether a research study involves modern foreign works, ancient works, or the most advanced scientific terminology and statistics, translating is involved. This should mean a greater attention to developing this skill in students, regardless of whether or not they have any intention of becoming professional translators. The idea of translating, its accompanying principles, and its specific difficulties all bear significantly on scholarship. In an age such as ours the task requires persistent attention.

The knowledge of another language may seem indispensable to translation work—and so it is! But even those people who do not know the biblical languages are keenly interested in being able to evaluate the translations they use. An understanding of translation like that presented in this chapter should aid them in their evaluations by informing them on such basic issues as translation philosophy. The first two exercises below are designed to reinforce this material.

Exercise 1. Select several translations of the New Testament to examine. (The use of a parallel Bible will help.) Read Lk. 15: 11-32, then Rom. 7:21-25. What translation philosophy does each version appear to follow in translating these two texts? Can you tell? Is the difference obvious? What indicators do you see that one or another philosophy is guiding the translation? Now, read any introductory material the Bibles you are examining may offer. Does this material reflect a certain translation stance? Was the translation accomplished by an individual or by a team? Of all the translations you examined, which read the easiest? Which reads aloud the best? Why? Which seems most understandable? In answering all of these simple questions the query "Why?" ought to be prominent.

Exercise 2. Find any one of the following pairs of translations: New American Standard Bible and New English Bible; King James Version and Living Bible; Today's English Version (Good News Bible) and Revised Standard Version; the Amplified New Testament and the New International Version. Spend a few minutes reading in the text. What contrasts in style do you observe? Do you find any important differences in the content or word usage? Which translation philosophy does each embrace? What specific examples can you offer to support your claim? Now read the introductory materials to see if they confirm your findings.

A little knowledge can be trouble if we think more highly of it than we ought. But in anything we start first with a little knowledge and watch it grow. Thus, the following exercises provide you with a little information and ask you to attempt some translation work. Do not be discouraged if you find the work difficult—so do the experts!

Exercise 3. The text is Jn. 1:1. It is rendered here with the Greek text and corresponding English words in interlinear fashion:

Ἐν ἀρχῇ   ἦν ὁ λόγος καὶ ὁ λόγος ἦν πρὸς τὸν θεόν, καὶ θεὸς
In beginning was the word and the word was with the God and God

ἦν ὁ λόγος
was the word.

Render this verse into normal English (i.e., put it into a

sensible word order, etc.). Does it make any difference which translation philosophy you use? Why, or why not?

Exercise 4. The text is Rom. 1:17b. You should find this text a little more challenging:

ὁ   δὲ   δίκαιος   ἐκ πίστεως ζήσεται
The but righteous/just by faith shall live.

This probably seems fairly straightforward. Either of the two renderings that follow are possible:
"The just shall live by faith."
"The righteous shall live by faith."
The former of these renderings can be found in the KJV, while the latter is one of two alternatives offered by the RSV. The other choice given by the RSV, in fact the preferred reading, is:
"He who through faith is righteous shall live."
Evaluate this last rendering. Is it different in meaning than the other two choices? Can such a rendering be supported adequately by the Greek?

To answer this second question requires some additional information. The Greek word δίκαιος (dikaios) means "righteous man." The Greek verb ζήσεται (zasetai) means "shall live." The critical words, however, are ἐκ πίστεως (ek pisteos), meaning "by faith" or "through faith." To what do these two words belong? Should they be paired with "righteous man" or with "shall live"? Either pairing is possible. So the third rendering must be considered seriously.

Since there are two viable alternatives in translating this very important Greek phrase, we must turn to other considerations in finding help to make the best selection. First, note that this phrase is a quote taken from the Old Testament (Hab. 2:4). Find this text in several translations. Does one or another rendering of Rom. 1: 17b correspond more closely to the Old Testament passage? Next, consider Paul's theme and teaching in the epistle. Which rendering, if either, do you think better fits the thrust of the Apostle's message? Finally, take the time to tackle one or more Greek grammars or commentaries on this text. See how the preposition ἐκ (ek) can be used, and determine its function in this passage. Which rendering do you find supports your conclusion?

Exercise 5. Sometimes a little word can have large repercussions. One such instance can be found in 1 Co. 12:13. The text has an important beginning:

καὶ γὰρ ἐν   ἑνὶ πνεύματι ἡμεῖς πάντες   εἰς ἓν σῶμα ἐβαπτίσ-
and for in/by one Spirit   we   all   into one body were bap-
θημεν
tized.

The decisive word, of course, is ἐν (en), which can be translated "by" or "in." Select several translations and examine their rendering of this verse. Have they selected "in" or "by"?
Some questions you might ask yourself are:
1) Does en refer to the *element* of baptism, or to the *ruling influence*, i.e., the baptizer?

2) There are six other New Testament texts which use the phrase, "en . . . Spirit." These are: Mt. 3:11; Mk. 1:8 Lk. 3:16; Jn. 1:33; Ac. 1:5, 11:16. In these six texts, who is the baptizer? What is the element? Do these six texts help you decide the best way to render 1 Co. 12: 13?
3) You probably noticed that in some texts the preposition en is translated by the English word "with." Should this be considered another option for 1 Co. 12:13? What does the word "with" do to the meaning? Does it emphasize the Spirit as the element, or as the agent of baptism?

Once again it will prove useful to you to take the time to consult a Greek grammar or some commentaries on this passage. What seems to be the consensus, if any, of the experts? Are all three of these alternatives ("in," "by," "with") acceptable?

Assume for a moment that the text ought to be rendered, "For indeed *in* one Spirit we all into one body were baptized." Does this rendering affect your understanding of baptism, changing it in any manner? Why, or why not? Who is the baptizer? What is the element of baptism? Does this translation support claims for a charismatic baptism in the Spirit? Why, or why not?

Now take the alternative, "For indeed *by* one Spirit we all into one body were baptized." Ask the same questions as above. Also ask, Does this rendering correspond to, or parallel, the other six occasions in which the phrase "en . . . Spirit" occurs? Why, or why not?

I trust these little exercises generate more light than heat, as well as a deepened appreciation of the effort that translation takes. If you desire further practice, work again through the examples afforded in the chapter. If you have language skills, use them!

9

Textual Criticism

Definition and Value

In the scholarly study of the Bible textual criticism is not a luxury, but a necessity. Occasionally referred to as "lower criticism," textual criticism is **the study of copies of a work with the aim of ascertaining the original text.** Such important work is not inferior in any sense to other kinds of biblical criticism and so the term "lower criticism," meant to distinguish textual criticism from the work encompassed by "higher criticism" (which can be used to designate **all** other forms of biblical criticism), should not be used. Textual criticism is foundational to biblical criticism because it strives to establish the original text of the Bible.

Textual criticism, of course, is not restricted to the study of the Old and New Testament manuscripts. It is applicable to any manuscript whose history is known through copies rather than the original. Thus, prior to the advent of the printing press, when handmade copies were the only recourse for reproducing a work, any work copied extensively was sure to give birth to copies containing errors. This tendency is easy enough to visualize. Imagine having to reproduce by hand a favorite novel, or even a short story. The work is tedious and often interrupted. How easy it is for a tiny error to occur.

But suppose that after having copied the original, the original is misplaced. Someone else desiring a copy of the work now has access only to the copy just made. As this is reproduced the new copy also finds small errors creeping in. Repeat this process many times and eventually a complicated and diverse history of the manuscript results. Just how quickly this can become the case can be seen in the diagram below:

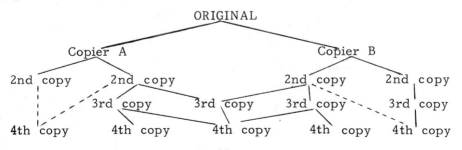

Here are just sixteen copies of the original. But only copiers A and B actually had the original. The others are working from these two prime copies. Each copy probably has errors, and errors from two sources. On the one hand, there are the errors carried over from the copy with which the copyist is working. On the other hand, there are the errors being freshly introduced. Now, imagine the dilemma of the poor fellow who sits down to make a copy and has three copies to work from, all of which vary in small degrees. How is he to decide which copy to follow in any given instance? The answer to that question is the goal of practical textual criticism.

The most immediate value of such work is obvious. The more established the text becomes, the more reliable it is for the person seeking to understand it. This does not mean that the text always becomes easier to understand, for often the results of textual criticism lead to accepting a more difficult reading over an easier reading. But it does mean that a student of the text struggling to understand it can possess a greater degree of confidence that she or he is wrestling with the text as it actually was written, and not as it was miscopied.

But there is a less obvious value to textual criticism, too. By studying the copies and their errors, valuable insights can be attained. In these errors occasional glimpses of the thinking, and sometimes the practices, of the early Church may be obtained. The question as to why a particular change occurs may lead to the sometimes startling conclusion that a copyist has not erred unthinkingly, but intentionally has changed the reading of the text before him. The careful scholar, therefore, can not only contribute to the establishment of the original text, but also offer explanations for the textual variants, which illuminate an understanding of early Christian history.

For the purposes of this chapter, only New Testament textual criticism is considered. Naturally, there are many similarities to the work that goes on in Old Testament textual criticism. After all, the fundamental concepts and processes of textual criticism are the same for any manuscript. But there are differences as well. To facilitate an ease in understanding the basics of textual critical work this chapter is confined to the New Testament.

Manuscripts and Styles

Despite all the different kinds of books seen today, there are some basic similarities. Nearly all books, and shorter works as well, are printed on paper. If they enjoy mass reproduction they are almost certainly set in print of one kind or another. This situation has been normal since the invention of the printing press. But in the period of the early Church quite a different situation existed.

In ancient times many materials received writing, including tree barks and leaves, broken pieces of pottery, and metal. Waxed tablets were used for centuries, as was papyrus (from whose name the term "paper" is derived), and parchment (or vellum). **Papyrus** was a fragile material taken from a reed found in swampy areas of the Nile delta. The stalk of the reed was stripped to its pithy center. This center was cut into thin strips, with one layer of strips running parallel in one direction and a second layer running crosswise, glued on top of the first layer. Such material not only could receive writing, but it also could be rolled, thus becoming a convenient way to produce larger, continuous works in a manageable form. But papyrus was not a durable enough material to persist across the centuries except under rare conditions (such as the barren sands of Egypt). **Parchment,** a kind of writing material made from animal skins, made for strong, durable rolls. Animal skins soaked in limewater, with the hair removed and the skin scraped and dried, were treated with chalk and pumice stone to produce a smooth writing surface. Eventually, parchment came to replace papyrus as the preferred material for writing.

Two different formats were common for ancient books. One, the **scroll,** already has been mentioned. Such scrolls generally did not exceed about thirty to thirty-five feet in length (the approximate length of Luke or Acts), simply because the longer a manuscript was the more unwieldy would be its roll. The second form for books became a popular alternative. Called the **codex,** this form consisted of sheets of written material folded and sewn together. Both rolls and codices characteristically featured uniform columns of writing only two or three inches wide. But as time passed, the columns of the codex gradually became wider and, thus, more convenient to read.

For many centuries the style of writing in these ancient books consisted of capital letters written continuously so that a sentence might look like this:

INTHEBEGINNINGWASTHEWORDANDTHEWORDWASWITHGOD

Actually, with the columns that were typical in the early manuscripts, the effect was more like this:

INTHEBEGINNINGWASTHEWORD   OUTHIMWASNOTANYTHINGMADE
ANDTHEWORDWASWITHGODANDT   THATWASMADEINHIMWASLIFEA
HEWORDWASGODHEWASINTHEBE   NDTHELIFEWASTHELIGHTOFME
GINNINGWITHGODALLTHINGSW   NTHELIGHTSHINESINTHEDARK
EREMADETHROUGHHIMANDWITH   NESSANDTHEDARKNESSHASNOT

Everyday documents were written in a different style. Instead of uncials, a cursive (or "running") hand was used. It is common today to distinguish these hands by what is familiar to our own experience. **Uncials** are roughly similar to our capital letters, while **cursive** is very like our normal, nonformal style of handwriting. But it is helpful to note some further features of these two styles. Uncials were used in ancient works where the writer desired to create a formal and precise manuscript. The letters were carefully inscribed, each

97

separated from the next, and exactly formed. Cursive was used wherever the uncial style was unnecessary; hence cursive was employed for letters, business documents, hastily scribbled notes, and legal deeds. It was a versatile style, one making full use of abbreviations and contractions. In short, it was the style of writing convenience.

About the start of the ninth century, with the deterioration of the uncial style and a reform in the cursive style, it came to pass that books were written with a modified cursive style. These manuscripts, called **miniscules**, featured letters smaller than uncials (hence the name "miniscule," meaning "rather small"), written in a running hand. This style proved very popular for books because the compact writing made book production more rapid and economical, as well as producing works easier to manage in bulk.

Miniscules outnumber uncials for the New Testament by about ten to one. There are a few papyri fragments of portions of the New Testament (less than a hundred), a number of uncial manuscripts, and a large number of miniscules. This abundance of witnesses to the text of the New Testament roughly can be divided chronologically between the uncials (earlier manuscripts, down to the tenth century), and miniscules (ninth century and later). But these documents are not all that are considered by textual critics.

In addition to the uncials and miniscules written in Greek (Koine, or "common" Greek), there are other ancient manuscripts of parts of the New Testament in various other languages. These translations into Latin, Coptic, Syriac, Ethiopic, Gothic, and Armenian are known as **versions**. These versions vary in length and completeness, and some are generally more valuable than others. The Latin versions, for example, are important for the critical role they played in the Roman Catholic Church. The Syriac versions are important because of the closeness of the language to Aramaic, the language of Jesus and his disciples. Versions range from Arabic to Persian to a small fragment in Frankish. The importance of any version resides both in its role in the Church (historical value), and its degree of helpfulness in establishing the original text (textual critical value). This latter function naturally is indirect. But a careful evaluation of a translation can shed light on the Greek text from which the version was made.

Besides versions, other helpful ancient manuscripts include lectionaries and patristic quotations. **Lectionaries**, with their scripture portions arranged in units for Church services, constitute a large group of early Greek manuscripts. These are found in both uncials and miniscules. **Patristic quotations** are so numerous that virtually the entire New Testament could be reconstructed from them! They are found in Greek, Latin, and other languages. The use of the New Testament by the Church Fathers is varied and dynamic. Not only did these writers use different Greek texts, they often quoted from memory, altered a reading, or merely made passing reference by a few words to a passage.

When the number of manuscripts thus available to the textual critic is summed, the result is considerable. Papyri, uncials, miniscules, versions, lectionaries, and quotations provide thousands of texts varying in size and accuracy. To make the fullest use of all of these manuscripts a system of evaluating their worth needed to be developed. Given the likelihood that each manuscript contained some errors, how can these many and varied materials be enlisted in the quest to establish the true (original) text?

The Critical Text

A procedure for evaluating textual readings evolved. In broad canvas, this procedure entails: (1) evaluating the internal evidence for a given reading (which encompasses both its intrinsic probability of occurring and its transcriptional probability of being changed by the copyist); (2) evaluating the external evidence of the individual witnesses, and the family groupings of those witnesses; and, (3) reevaluating the actual reading in light of both the earlier two steps as considered together. While more weight is given to internal considerations than to external, both must be reckoned carefully.

Internal evidence is that material within a reading that reflects the probability of a scribal change. In other words, it deals with the likelihood of errors either intentional or unintentional. This requires a knowledge both of the kinds of errors that might be found, and of the principles used in evaluating the internal evidence.

Most changes, of course, are unintentional. Without spacing between the letters, and without punctuation, the earliest manuscripts lent themselves to copying errors. Some were **errors of sight**, as in the incorrect division of words, the confusion of one letter for another (such as ΑΔΛ in uncials; ξζ in miniscules), the switching of order of letters or words (e.g., ἔλαβον for ἔβαλον in Mk. 16:65; this error is called "metathesis"), the omission of words because the copyist's eye slips from one set of letters, or a word, to the same further down the page (called "homoioteleuton"), or any of a number of less frequent errors of sight.

Some errors were **errors of hearing**, caused by the scribe recording what he heard in his mind for a word rather than what he actually saw. Thus, various Greek vowels and combinations of vowels (called "diphthongs"), which were pronounced alike, might be substituted for one another (like ο, ω, ψ; or like ευ for η). This kind of error, called "itacism," is a very common phenomenon. In English it might happen where "way" is substituted for "weigh."

Other errors were **errors of memory**. So a scribe might substitute a synonym for the actual word. Or, he accidently might change the word order. In some instances, he might even inadvertently change the reading to reflect conformity to a parallel text firmly in his mind. Such errors are not far removed from **errors of judgment**. A wandering mind might overlook an abbreviation, or simply miscopy a letter or word from momentary carelessness. The meaning of the reading might be misunderstood and so be changed in the rendering. Since the margins were often filled with notes and readings of portions that an earlier scribe had omitted, then added to the side, errors of two quite different kinds occasionally occurred. The scribe might include a comment as part of the actual text, or he might omit a reading that belongs because it had been placed in the margin.

Some errors simply were blunders in writing. But what all these errors share in common is this: they were all unintentional. Although much less numerous, intentional changes certainly do exist. These are significant in that they reflect conscientious attempts by scribes to improve the text before them. These scribal "corrections" generally were not inspired by heretical intentions. Instead, they represent concerned efforts by scribes to adjust and improve the text which they had received and found to be (in their opinion) in error.

Among these kinds of changes, those of a **grammatical** and **linguistic** character naturally suggested themselves to those scribes who were particularly conscious of such matters. (Some scribes had a better command of the Koine Greek than did the author of the writing being copied, and the copyist naturally would be tempted to correct the manuscript as he worked on it.) A scribe might replace first aorist verb endings on second aorists, or add a word here or there to smooth the syntax. Especially a document like the Apocalypse of John (Book of Revelation), a difficult book with unusual stylistic features, drew the attention of such scribes. A genitive case might be altered to become dative (as in Rev. 1:15), or a verb in indicative mood changed to a participle to agree with other parts of its context (as in Rev. 1:5-6). Forms a scribe thought less desirable were replaced by those he judged to be more appropriate to the sacred text.

Some changes were for **liturgical** reasons. Some scholars believe that such an explanation accounts for the doxology of the Lord's Prayer (Mt. 6:13). Similarly, some changes were made because of **doctrinal** considerations. The most famous example of this is the passage of 1 Jn. 5:7-8, a reading with only suspect support in the manuscripts. Such changes conform generally to one of two intents. First, some changes were meant to eliminate what a scribe found doctrinally unacceptable (cf. Mk. 13:32). Second, other changes were aimed at adding a supporting element to a favored belief or practice (cf. Lk. 2:33, 41, 43, 48, where changes in some copies were made to safeguard the Virgin Birth).

Some changes were simply meant to **correct a manuscript error**. If a scribe found that the copy from which he was working was in error, he easily could feel obliged to adjust it. These kind of changes occasionally aroused the ire of other scribes. One scribe, who had changed an erroneous reading to the usual (and preferred one) was later corrected by another scribe, who reintroduced the incorrect reading and chastised his predecessor as a "fool and knave."

Other kinds of intentional changes include the **elimination of apparent discrepancies** (cf. Mk. 1:2), the **combining of two or more variants into a single reading** (cf. Mk. 9:49; called "conflation," this was one solution for a scribe uncertain of which of two different readings to adopt), and **harmonization,** where parallel passages were adjusted for accuracy (cf. Mk. 10:18 with Mt. 19:17). Sometimes copyists **amplified or rounded** passages, intending to complete what they judged an incomplete sense (as in adding the phrase "unto repentance" in Lk. 5:32). Somewhat similar to this were changes made to **resolve historical or geographical difficulties,** such as the difference between John's "sixth hour" (19:14) and Mark's "third hour" (15:25) in the Passion Narrative. Likewise, there are changes in **attribution of quotations,** as later scribes, conscious of conflated quotations ascribed to one source, changed the reading to reflect this awareness (cf. Mk. 1:2).

A knowledge of the kinds of errors that might creep into the history of a document must be put to good use. The general principles applied in evaluating the internal evidence for a reading seek to do just that. The principles reflect an awareness of how changes occur. Five such principles can be specified, the first of which belongs to a category all its own. The other four may be conveniently grouped together.

Evaluating the internal evidence is first and foremost a matter of weighing its **intrinsic probability.** This means judging the likelihood that a particular reading is what the author would have written. Various factors enter into making such a judgment. First, is the reading consonant with the style and vocabulary of the author as it is found throughout the work in question? Second, is the reading supported by the sense of the immediate context? Third, is the usage of the reading essentially like that employed elsewhere by the author? Fourth, does the reading reflect the influence of the Christian community and tradition? This influence on the formulation and transmission of a passage can have critical bearing on the rejection or adoption of a reading. Other factors are pertinent to particular parts of the New Testament. For example, in the Synoptics the matter of Mark's priority must be kept in view. It is also wise to remember the Aramaic background, particularly, of course, in the teaching of Jesus. In general, a thorough knowledge of the author is most beneficial to weighing the intrinsic probability of a reading.

The other four principles gauge what might be termed the **transcriptional probabilities.** This task measures readings according to what might have happened to the original text in the process of copying. Here, naturally, is where a knowledge of the kinds of errors that might occur becomes crucial. In brief, the four principles applied here are:

1) The shorter reading is generally preferred.
2) The more difficult reading is generally preferred.
3) The reading least explainable in terms of possible changes is generally preferred.
4) The reading which best explains the others is generally preferred.

The **shorter reading** is generally preferred because longer readings can often be explained as the result of errors. Thus intentional changes are more likely to add material than delete it (through conflation, harmonization, or rounding). Unintentional changes, however, might either add or delete mateiral, depending on the cause of the change; thus, repetition might add material, but homoioteleuton delete material.

The **harder reading** is generally preferred, especially if reflection shows that it does make sense. Again, this is because the other readings are easier to explain in terms of possible changes. Intentional changes would aim at smoothing the sense or style. Even unintentional changes tend in this direction as the scribe unconsciously makes selections to make the reading of the text easier.

The reading **least explainable in terms of possible changes** is almost a catch-all principle, since it easily can be seen that all four principles adhere to this essential idea. But it covers areas not explicitly in mind by the other three principles. Thus, mindful of changes caused by harmonization, this principle would suggest that readings involving verbal dissidence (i.e., disagreement from the parallel) generally are preferable to ones that are concordant (i.e., harmonized). Again, the replacement of a word by a synonym common to the scribe, but not to the author, may not change the length or difficulty of a reading, but does affect a reading's intrinsic probability and can be explained as an unintentional change.

The reading **which best explains the other readings** has a natural counterpoint. It also should be the reading **least explained by the other readings**. This principle embraces the other three. Any kind of error can be reflected here. But the logic is compelling: the original text is unlikely to be as explainable by later changes as the changes (especially intentional ones) are by the original text. It is easy to see, for example, why an obscure reading in the original might be clarified, but why would a clear reading be obscured?

After the internal evidence has been weighed, attention is turned to the **external evidence**. This is the attestation for a particular reading by various textual witnesses. To accomplish this evaluation, it is necessary to know the characteristics of the various text-types which exist. Then, the relative value of the different text-types must be considered. Because not every individual text witness to a given text-type is as consistent as every other, each individual witness has also to be considered. When all of these different witnesses and collections of witnesses have been assessed for a particular reading, then the same process must be undertaken for the next reading.

With the number of documents available to the text critic, it is not surprising to find that weighing the external evidence can be a difficult and time-consuming task. Today this work has been greatly facilitated because of the efforts of two 19th century Cambridge scholars, B. F. Westcott and F. A. Hort. Their textual theory, set forth in a volume explicating their principles and shown in practice in their critical edition of the Greek New Testament, provided a foundation for subsequent labors in textual criticism. In essence, their theory stated that an examination of the available documents revealed their pronounced tendency to fall into four distinct groups.

This insight has persisted to the present, though the exact names and descriptions for these groups has undergone revision and refinement. These groups (or **families**, or **text-types**) contain documents in agreement on a large number of variant readings. Sharing common variants indicates that the manuscripts in question shared a common source; they can be traced to some dependence on certain copies. Being thus related, they can be called "families." Scholars have also found that these families can be grouped according to their geographic origin. Of course, this makes sense: a copy circulating in a given area would be copied and those copies in turn circulated throughout the region. Today, the four groups bear the names of these geographical regions.

The text-type generally considered to be the "best" is the **Alexandrian** text. This text, most scholars believe, was prepared by scribes who had been trained in the expert ways of that famous city. Witnesses to this text-type date from the late second or early third century ($\mathfrak{p}^{66}$ and $\mathfrak{p}^{75}$), and the two most prominent witnesses to this text-type (B and ℵ) date from the middle of the fourth century. Scholars have found this text-type to generally afford the best approximation to the original text. It retains rough readings, those that appear more difficult at first sight, and when it errs it likely does so in grammatical niceties. It is still the case that where B (named Vaticanus) and ℵ (named Sinaiticus) agree on a reading, that reading is highly favored. The Alexandrian witnesses contain a number of papyri, uncials, minuscules, and other documents.

The **Western** text stands in sharp contrast to the Alexandrian. Many scholars believe it reflects a rather undisciplined manuscript tradition. Its readings are often unique among the text-types, especially in Acts. Like the Alexandrian text it can also be traced back to very early times, since Marcion, Tertullian, Irenaeus, and Cyprian all knew and used it. Its most important witnesses are D (codex Bezae), and the Old Latin (Itala) versions. Some have divided the Western text into three divisions: Codex Bezae, the Old Latin manuscripts k (Bobiensis) and e (Palatinus, Laudianus, Sangerman-ensis), and the Old Syriac (syr^S, named Sinaitic, and syr^C, named Curetonian). The Western text features additions and paraphrases, sometimes relatively long, and a fondness for substituting synonyms for single words. Once dismissed as "corrupt" by many scholars, the Western text, today acknowledged to have as early an origin as the second century, is reckoned more seriously by textual critics.

The **Caesarean** text blends Western and Alexandrian readings and may be said to lie somewhere between them. It is the most mixed (and hence least homogeneous) of the text-types. Often found with witnesses of the Alexandrian text, it also is commonly found with Western witnesses; yet, it sometimes stands alone. Its most important witnesses are the Ferrar Group, comprised of Codex 13 together with miniscules (13, 69, 124, 174, 230, 346, 543, 788, 826, 983, 1689), and the Lake Group, made of Codex 1 and accompanying miniscules (1, 118, 131, 209). These two groups are known, respectively, as family 13 (f^{13}), and family 1 (f^1).

The **Byzantine** text generally is regarded as relatively inferior to the other text-types. This does not mean that some good readings are not maintained, but on the whole the text seems to be late, and somewhat further distanced from the original. The text is characterized by smooth readings, with many changes serving to clarify a passage or round it out. A very common feature is harmonization, and conflation is not uncommon either. The Byzantine text has an abundance of witnesses. In addition to many uncials, most miniscules belong to this text-type. The most prominent of the Byzantine uncials is A (Alexandrinus); other uncials include E, F, G, H, K, P, S, V, and W.

An awareness of the text-types is incorporated into the formal process of evaluating the external evidence. Some basic principles employed are: 1) the Alexandrian text generally is the most reliable single text-type; 2) where both Vaticanus and Sinaiticus agree a reading looks particularly favorable; but, 3) a reading strongly supported by good witnesses from two or more text-types generally is preferable to the witness of any one text-type by itself. Specific witnesses also must be examined. Hence, 4) where manuscripts within a text-type disagree, the preferred reading (as the one best representative of the text-type) is the one generally most consonant with that text-type, and different from the other text-types. Support must be weighed for each variant, then considered together with the internal evidence.

When all this effort has been concluded a reasonable estimate of the original text can be set forward. Of course, it is easy to see that textual criticism is at least as much an art as it is a science, and often its principles and decisions have been questioned and criticized. But it appears that, at least for the moment, the work justifies itself as the best available method for determining the original reading of a manuscript.

The Critical Apparatus: An Example

Obviously, a working knowledge of New Testament Greek is a basic prerequisite to gaining much aid from a textual apparatus. Still, there is no better way to see how textual criticism works than to wrestle with an actual example. Let us, therefore, examine Jas. 1:3 which reads, "for you know that the testing of your faith produces steadfastness." The text of the United Bible Societies' **Greek New Testament** (3rd ed.) looks like this:

γινώσκοντες ὅτι τὸ δοκίμιον[1] ὑμῶν τῆς πίστεως κατεργάζεται ὑπομονήν·

The reader is alerted to the presence of a textual variant by the raised number following the appropriate word or words. At the bottom of the page the number can be located and the information read. This information appears as follows:

[1]3 {B} δοκίμιον ℵ A B C K P Ψ 049 056 0142 33 81 88 104 181 326 330 436 614 629 630 945 1505 1739 1877 2127 2412 2492 2495 *Byz Lect* it[ar, c, dem, div, ff, p, s, (t), z] vg arm // δόκιμον 110 431 1241

The variant's location is noted ("3" referring to verse 3). Then, in braces, is listed the relative degree of certainty given to the Greek reading adopted by the text ("B", on a scale where "A" represents certainty and "D" bewilderment). The reading adopted follows next, together with its manuscript support. This support is listed in a definite order. Any papyri are listed first (signified by 𝔭 and an accompanying number). Uncials follow, denoted by Hebrew letter (as in the case of Sinaiticus, ℵ), Greek capital (e.g., Ψ), capital letters (e.g., A, B, etc.), or numbers preceded by a zero (e.g., 049). Then come the miniscules, designated simply by numbers. Following these are abbreviations: *Byz* denotes Byzantine, and reflects the reading of the majority of Byzantine manuscripts; *Lect* denotes lectionaries, and reflects the majority of lectionaries in both the Synaxarion and Menologion (two lectionary formats), when they agree. More abbreviations follow, these reflecting the evidence from ancient versions. Hence, "it" stands for Itala (Old Latin), and the raised letters refer to various manuscripts of the Old Latin (in the study of James it [ff] , a manuscript named Corbeiensis, has had significant importance). The abbreviation "vg" stands for Vulgate, or "common" version, a Latin work from the fourth century; "arm" refers to Armenian, a version dating from the fourth or fifth century. A dividing mark (//) separates the support for the first reading from the listing of the next alternative and its manuscript support. In this example, there are listed only two variants, but in some instances there may be several variants. The entire system of the textual apparatus is explained carefully by the UBS committee in the introduction to the **Greek New Testament.**

It is obvious that there is overwhelming manuscript support, in terms of quantity, for the first reading (which is pronounced "dokimion," and is translated by the RSV as "testing"). But quantity is not the issue in textual criticism. To evaluate this external evidence it is necessary to follow the general guidelines discussed earlier. First, remembering that the Alexandrian text is generally the most reliable text-type, ask what support from this text-type is to be found for the reading. What immediately catches the eye is the agreement of the most prominent Alexandrian manuscripts, Sinaiticus ($\aleph$) and Vaticanus (B). But there are other Alexandrian uncials, too (A, which is Alexandrian, not Byzantine, in the Catholic Epistles; C, P, Ψ, 056, 0142), and also several miniscules (33, so reliable it is known fondly as "the Queen of the cursives"; 81, 104, 326, 1739).

The first reading is well supported by the Alexandrian text-type. The next direction to look is for corroboration by another text-type. This is represented by Byzantine support (designated by *Byz* ; the uncial K is also Byzantine). All the other miniscules listed "exhibit a significant degree of independence from the so-called Byzantine manuscript tradition" (UBS **Greek New Testament,** p. xix), and so further corroborate the dependability of the reading. As also is evident, the various ancient versions agree on this rendering as well (Itala, Vulgate, and Armenian).

Against this stands the alternative reading (pronounced "dokimon"; an adjective meaning "that which is approved or genuine"). Its support consists of a few miniscules, and perhaps a papyrus ($\mathfrak{p}^{74}$; a document listed in the **Textual Commentary,** published to complement the UBS **Greek New Testament).** It does not enjoy anywhere near the support that the adopted reading does. At least in terms of external evidence the first reading is preferable.

But what about the internal evidence? Here the matter becomes more interesting. The adopted reading is unusual; the term "dokimion" only occurs here and at 1 Pe. 1:7 (where the alternative, "dokimon," is again a textual variant). The word is a neuter noun and its rendering as "a means of testing," or simply, "testing," strikes some scholars as rather unsatisfactory. In fact, it is this sense of not quite being the most appropriate selection that may have given rise to the alternative reading (which can be viewed as a regularizing of the noun). A scribe conscious of style may have selected "dokimon" as an adjective used substantively to smooth the grammar and make plain the meaning. In light of this possibility, and other factors, it is apparent that the adopted reading is preferable on internal evidence. It is a somewhat harder reading and may be used to explain the choice of "dokimon" in its place.

However, enough doubt remained in the minds of the UBS committee to assign to the adopted choice a weight of "B," meaning they retained an element of doubt. This is not a strong suspicion, but a recognition that enough manuscript support and internal considerations can be mustered to cause a pause in determining the original text. The exact reasoning of the committee, explained in the companion volume, **Textual Commentary** (p. 679; cf. p. 687 on 1 Pe. 1:7), is similar to that given above.

Conclusion

The art and science of textual criticism is both complex and interesting. Like so many other scholarly research methods it embodies a history of theoretical development and a developing sophistication in actual practice. Learning to interpret the various symbols of the textual apparatus is somewhat like learning a foreign language. New and strange terms (like "uncial" and "miniscule") abound, and patience is required to sort through them.

But there is an excitement that comes with working with old manuscripts, with reasoning out why various changes take place in the readings of a manuscript tradition, and in puzzling through many alternatives to reconstruct the most likely look of the original text. This excitement starts with even a cursory look at textual criticism, and grows as one progresses in understanding the work. Even for those who never make a career out of such labors the rewards of mastering a rudimentary understanding of textual criticism are many and continuous. The study of the Bible and its meaning is enriched immeasurably, and an appreciation is gained for the many who so selflessly spent themselves preserving and transmitting the Scriptures. Even modern English translations take on new significance because the textual notes there now have meaning. With so much to gain, why delay appropriating the method?

Textual Criticism:
Simple Guidelines

The following guidelines are a summary of those given in the chapter, to provide an easy reference while doing the suggested exercises.

Making a decision between alternative readings means weighing two kinds of evidence. The more important kind is the *internal evidence*. It is that material within the reading that reflects the possibility of a scribal change. *External evidence* is the attestation for a particular reading by different manuscripts (called "textual witnesses"). These two kinds of evidence are weighed in three steps:

1) Evaluate the internal evidence according to two sets of probabilities:
   (1) *intrinsic probability:* the likelihood that a particular reading is what the author would have written; and,
   (2) *transcriptional probability:* the likelihood that a given reading is what it is because a scribe changed the original, either intentionally or be accident.
2) Evaluate the external evidence according to its attestation from different textual witnesses.
3) Reevaluate each alternative in light of both steps 1 and 2 considered together.

Use the following guidelines to help you evaluate the evidence:

1) *Internal evidence:*
   (1) Intrinsic probability (likelihood the author would have written a certain reading).
      a) Is the reading consonant with the style and vocabulary of the author as found throughout the document?
      b) Is the reading supported by the sense of the immediate context?
      c) Is the usage of the reading essentially like that employed elsewhere by the author?
      d) Does the reading seem explainable by the influence of the Christian community and tradition?
   (2) Transcriptional probability (likelihood the reading is due to scribal change).
      a) A shorter reading usually is preferred to a longer one (since intentional changes tend to add material, and unintentional changes either may add or delete material).
      b) A more difficult reading usually is preferred to an easier one (changes tend

to smooth the sense or style).

    c)   The reading least explainable in terms
of possible changes generally is preferred; also, the reading least explained
by the other readings generally is preferred (the original often is likely to be
adjusted for clarity; it aids us in understanding why and how later readings
came into being).

    d)   The reading which best explains the
others is most likely to be the original
(cf. the comment in "c" above).

2)   *External evidence:*

    (1) Assess witnesses according to these criteria:

       a)   The "best" text-type is the *Alexandrian*.
It generally affords the best approxima-
tion to the original. It retains rough
readings. Its witnesses include papyri,
uncials, miniscules, etc. Witnesses are
as early as 2nd/3rd century ($\mathfrak{p}^{66}$ and
$\mathfrak{p}^{75}$), and the two most prominent witnesses date from the middle of the 4th
century (B: Vaticanus, and ℵ: Sinaiticus).

       b)   The *Western* and *Caesarean* text-types
are next in importance. The Western is
represented by some very early witnesses; its most important witnesses are codex Bezae (D) and the Old Latin (Itala,
abbreviated "it" in the text apparatus).
The Caesarean lies between the Alexandrian and Western texts in that it is the
most mixed text-type. It can be found
alongside witnesses of either Western or
Alexandrian text, or alone. Its chief
witnesses are the Ferrar Group (013;
miniscules 13, 69, 124, 174, 230, 346,
543, 788, 826, 828, 983, 1689), and the
Lake Group (001; miniscules 1, 118, 131,
209). These two groups are designated,
respectively, as family 13 (f^{13}), and
family 1 (f^1).

       c)   The *Byzantine* text-type generally is
regarded as inferior to the others. A
common feature is smooth readings;
also very common are harmonization and
conflation. In addition to many uncials,
most miniscules belong to this text-type.
The most prominent uncial witness is A
(Alexandrinus); other uncials include E,
F, G, H, K, P, S, V, and W.

(2) Follow these basic principles:
a) Where ℵ and B agree, a reading looks especially favorable.
b) A reading supported by good witnesses from two or more text-types generally is preferable to the witness of any single text-type.
c) Where witnesses within a text-type disagree, prefer the one most generally consonant with its text-type and also different from the other text-types.

Supplement:
Manuscript Kinds and the Text Apparatus

The Greek New Testament has portions of itself preserved in different kinds of manuscripts. These include:

Papyri designated in the apparatus by 𝔭 and a raised number. These date from the 2nd through 7th centuries.
Uncials (text written in Greek capitals), designated by Hebrew letter (ℵ), Greek capitals (e.g., Δ, Π, Ψ), English capitals, or numbers preceded by 0. These date from the 4th through the 10th centuries.
Miniscules (text written in cursive), designated by numbers. These date from the 9th century through the 16th centuries.

In addition to the above, there are:

Lectionaries, designated by *Lect* when a reading is held by the majority of lectionaries; otherwise by *l* with a raised number.
Ancient Versions (see below).
Church Fathers, identified by name.

The principal abbreviations and dates for ancient versions:

Old Latin (Itala): cited by "it" with raised letters (2nd to 4th centuries).
Vulgate: cited by "vg" with raised letter (4th century).
Syriac: cited by "syr" with raised letter (2nd/3rd to 7th century).
Coptic: cited by "cop" with raised letter (3rd to 6th centuries).
Gothic: cited "goth" (4th century).
Armenian: cited "arm" (4th/5th century).
Ethiopic: cited "eth" with raised letter (6th century).
Georgian: cited "geo" with raised letter (5th century).
Nubian: cited "nub" (6th century).

Suggested Exercises

Below are two texts taken from English Bibles. When using more than one translation it occasionally can be seen that different decisions have been made with regard to the reading of the original text. Even with just a single translation, attention to footnotes or marginal notes sometimes may reveal the presence of alternate readings. The decisions made as to what should be printed as the correct reading of the text follow the guidelines of textual criticism. In each of the two exercises below the passages used are well known. They are listed with alternative readings for each. Which reading would you adopt, using the principles of textual criticism?

Exercise 1. Rom. 8:28. The passage may read:

We know that in all things God works for the good of those who love him, who have been called according to his purpose.

Text support: $\mathfrak{p}^{46}$ A B 81 cop^{sa} (eth) Origen

or the passage may read:

We know that all things work together for good to those who love God, who have been called according to his purpose.

Text support: א C D G K P Ψ 33 88 104 181 326 330 436 451 614 629 1241 1739 1877 1881 1962 1984 1985 2127 2492 2495 *Byz Lect* it$^{ar, d, dem, f, g, t,}$ it$^{x, z}$ vg syr$^{p, h}$ cop^{bo} arm Clement Origen$^{gr 3/5, lat}$ Eusebius Lucifer Cyril-Jerusalem Chrysostom Augustine Cyril Theodoret John-Damascus

Exercise 2. Mt. 6:13. The passage may read:

And lead us not into temptation, but deliver us from evil. For thine is the kingdom and the power and the glory, for ever. Amen.

Text support: K L W Δ Θ Π f^{13} 28 33 565 700 892 1009 1010 1071 1079 1195 1216 1230 1241 1242 1365 1546 1646 2174 *Byz Lect* it^{f} syr$^{h, pal}$ cop$^{bo mss}$ goth arm eth geo Diatessaron Apostolic Constitutions Chrysostum

or the passage may read:

And lead us not into temptation, but deliver us from evil.

Text support: א B D 0170 f^1 l^{547} it$^{a, aur, b, c, ff, h, l}$ vg^{ww} cop^{bo} Tertullian Origen Cyprian Hilary Caesarius-Nazianzus Gregory-Nyssa Chromatius Augustine mss$^{acc. to Peter-Laodicea}$ Maximus-Confessor

(The actual decisions of professional text critics can be found in any of several fine works. Among these is Bruce Metzger's *Textual Commentary on the Greek New Testament* (UBS, 1971).

10

Source Criticism

Definition and Purpose

Source criticism (or **source analysis**) is a manner of examining the documents of the Bible. It blossomed in the nineteenth century and helped bring into existence several subsequent analytical approaches, including form criticism (see next chapter). As the name suggests, the biblical documents are viewed under this method as composed of various written sources (which may or may not be "literary" in the strict sense of that term). A **source** is a written document foundational to subsequent writings. In the Bible are writings which rest on earlier materials. In fact, the existing documents of Scripture encompass, to a greater or lesser degree, the prior labors represented by various sources. The aim of source criticism is to recover these underlying sources and understand them in their chronological and literary relationships to one another and to the final production of the document. Thus, source criticism seeks both to delineate the sources and comprehend their functions.

Source criticism has undergone much refinement since its early days. To try to specify all these changes and describe the exact present state of source criticism would be impossible. Moreover, it would be foolish to make such an attempt divorced from an understanding of the early efforts at source analysis and the basic forces still at work in the method. All this chapter aims at is a rather modest introduction to source criticism. This means a brief review of its history, an examination of its presuppositions, and an indication of the basic features of its methodology. Thus, in the main, this is a presentation of classical source analysis. Any number of advanced articles or books can be consulted to see the number and kinds of changes which have come into existence and served to refine or to modify this classical approach. Such texts should also be used to acquire a fuller understanding of the extent and characteristics of the sources themselves.

History of Old Testament Source Criticism

Source criticism has been practiced in both Old Testament and New Testament research. In the Old Testament, where the method first reached prominence through the work of Julius

Wellhausen, source analysis focused on the Pentateuch. Today, it is Wellhausen's name which is most associated with source criticism because it was he who developed the theory fully and applied it most successfully. However, Wellhausen's work did not appear full-blown from nothing. For a long time rudimentary efforts had been ventured which prepared the way.

In the late seventeenth century a scholar named Campegius Vitringa had proposed the idea that Moses had access to ancient sources as he composed the first five books of the Bible. In 1753, Jean Astruc went further by suggesting that Moses had recourse to both oral and written sources. He concluded that written sources predominated and, while he defended Mosaic authorship, he believed that he could detect four distinct strands in Genesis. Among Astruc's important observations were the recognition of two different creation accounts, and the peculiar uses of the divine names "Elohim" and "Yahweh."

Some thirty years after Astruc, J. G. Eichhorn's **Introduction to the Old Testament (Einleitung in das Alte Testament,** 1780-1783) added more compelling evidence to the earlier findings. Eichhorn observed the importance of diverse literary styles and unique words or phrases for isolating supposed sources. Not long after, during the period 1792-1800, Alexander Gettes published a series on the first six books of the Bible (commonly known among scholars as the **Hexateuch),** which presented the idea that these works were a composite. He theorized that the various fragments, woven into a whole by a single compiler, were in some cases older than Moses. He dated the Pentateuch to Solomon's time.

In the early nineteenth century three other scholars continued to build upon some of these early ideas. In 1805, J. S. Vater's commentary on the Pentateuch placed the date of these books in the Exilic period, and sought to identify as many as forty different fragments. In 1807, W. M. L. DeWette identified Josiah's "Book of the Law" (2 Ki. 23; 2 Chr. 34) with the nucleus of Deuteronomy. He conceived of the Pentateuch as the product of separate editors (commonly called **redactors),** each utilizing independent fragmentary sources. In 1835, Wilhelm Vatke stood traditional thinking on its head by arguing that the Torah was the product of Israel rather than its founding basis. He, too, found various strands in the Pentateuch indicating works behind the finished document. With others, he identified the Elohistic strand as the foundation source of the Pentateuch, but unlike most he assigned to it a rather late date.

In 1853, Hermann Hupfield tried to show that what had been identified as the foundation document was, in fact, the result of two writers. One was the already named Elohist. But some of what had been attributed to the Elohist belonged to what Hupfield called the Priestly document. In 1865, K. H. Graf placed this Priestly document as the most recent source, not the most primitive. The so-called "Graf's Hypothesis," that the law of the Levites was produced in the post-Exilic age, had a major import on the study of ancient Israel's history. Now it appeared that Israel had undergone a long, gradual climb from simplicity to complexity of religious understanding and development. By placing the law near the end of ancient Israel's history, rather than at its beginning, much of what scholars had once found confusing became, quite suddenly, reasonable.

The Dutch scholar Abraham Kuenen was among the most enthusiastic in embracing this new chronology. In 1869-1870, just five years after the publication of Graf's work, he set out a history of Israel's religion based on an analysis of sources. He championed Graf's hypothesis and slightly refined it. He pointed out, for example, that assent to a post-Exilic origin for the Priestly Code did not rule out an earlier origin for some of its contents.

But it was in 1878, with Julius Wellhausen's publication of his **History of Israel** (the second edition of which is entitled **Prolegomena zur Geschichte Israels,** 1883, from which the English translation, **Prolegomena to the History of Ancient Israel,** is taken), that the new view began forcefully to gain ascendancy. Wellhausen popularized Graf's hypothesis. In his work was set out the JEDP hypothesis so well-known in the late nineteenth century, and still widely embraced today. In brief, this work identified four principal sources underlying the first books of the Bible. The earliest of these was the Yahwist ("J"), followed by the Elohist ("E"), the Deuteronomist ("D"), and the Priestly Code ("P"). The originality of Wellhausen's effort rested in the manner by which he wove together the earlier labors and applied their insights with vigor and confidence to a vast amount of biblical data.

Wellhausen's influence was pervasive. His work dominated Old Testament scholarship for a generation, though he himself turned his attention increasingly to applying source criticism to the New Testament. Analysis subsequent to Wellhausen tended to be quite technical as scholars sought to refine the boundaries of each source. More attention was brought upon the editorial processes by which the Old Testament took its form. Increasingly, the documents of the Pentateuch were broken into smaller and smaller bits. The general impression this created varied from a feeling that source analysis was hopelessly arbitrary and subjective, to the opinion that it was the Pentateuch itself that was impossibly complex. As source criticism found itself upon a treadmill of constant reexamination of the materials, with finer literary analysis but no significant historical insights, it took on an appearance of artificiality, sterility, and often superficiality.

A reaction set in, led by the most conservative scholars, who had never accepted the methodology on presuppositional grounds. Yet despite the many criticisms leveled against Well-

115

hausen's construction, it stood relatively firm. In the middle third of this century, Old Testament scholars started turning in large numbers to newer and creatively fresher approaches to the literature and the history of the biblical documents. Still, the critical approach adopted by early source analysis has remained in force as a kind of bedrock of the higher criticism of the Old Testament. Today, while source criticism generally is conceded to be past its position of preeminence, its gains are still acknowledged and built upon. While the source analysis done today remains troubled by its tendency to focus overmuch on detailed analysis of minutae, it has not been, and cannot be, set aside or dismissed. The debt that modern Old Testament research owes to source criticism is considerable. Nor is the debt any less substantial in the New Testament research of our time.

History of New Testament Source Criticism

The source analysis of the Bible generally is thought of in connection with two specific areas. In the Old Testament, source analysis has focused on what is known as the "Synoptic Problem." This problem concerns the relationship of the first three Gospels, and particularly their common dependence on certain sources.

Virtually as long as there have been the Gospels there has been comment about their often striking similarities. Tatian's **Diatessaron** (meaning "a harmony of four parts"), dating from the latter half of the second century, enjoyed widespread use and indicated an awareness by the Church of the likenesses and differences among the Gospels. Tatian's work reflected a popular desire to find the unity of the account of Jesus' life and ministry. But it was not until the eighteenth, and especially the nineteenth century, that the problem of origins and relationships gained prominence.

It takes very little examination to realize that John's Gospel is different from the other three. Nor is it hard to see that Matthew, Mark, and Luke resemble one another far too closely to be the product of chance. G. E. Lessing, in 1778, suggested as an explanation for the Gospels' origins that they were translations, perhaps only extracts, of an Aramaic "Gospel of the Nazarenes." He dated Matthew as the earliest of the four Gospels, with Mark written as an abbreviated form of Matthew. John's Gospel, he thought, was composed last, and with full knowledge of the other three, as well as of the Aramaic document. J. G. Eichhorn, writing in 1812, expanded this theory, postulating the existence of not only the original Aramaic Gospel, but some nine Gospels from it. The first three Gospels of our New Testament, the **Synoptics** (meaning "same, or common view"), he thought to be the final result of the literary process stemming from the original Aramaic Gospel.

J. J. Griesbach, in 1789, championed the cause of literary dependency among the Gospels. He dated both Matthew and

Luke as earlier than Mark, but Mark as a summarizer of Matthew's message. Variations on the idea of literary dependency have been popular ever since, with some placing Luke earliest, others Mark, and in different instances supposing different lines of dependence. In 1835, a philosopher named Karl Lachmann, following the earlier ideas of J. B. Koppe (1782) and G. C. Storr (1786), proposed the sequence Mark, Matthew, and Luke. The priority of Mark over the other Synoptics, together with their dependence upon Mark, has become the hallmark of modern conclusions on the Synoptic question. (It must be added, in fairness, that there has been a revival in recent years of Griesbach's hypothesis, though it still has not persuaded a substantial number of today's scholars.)

With Lachmann's work the way was prepared for the "two-source" theory commonly maintained over the last century. In 1838, two scholars working independently of one another demonstrated the viability of viewing Mark as a common source for Matthew and Luke. One of these scholars, C. H. Weisse, added the suggestion that a common collection of sayings about Jesus was also used by Matthew and Luke. This "sayings collection" is called Q (from the German Quelle, "source," which in turn is short for Redenquelle, "sayings source"). The source Q has not survived apart from our knowledge of it in the Gospels. Its existence as a real, originally independent document is hypothesized, but on rather solid grounds: the amount of verbal agreement in non-Markan materials shared by Matthew and Luke, and an order to this material which suggests not only a common source, but quite possibly a written one. Together, Mark and Q are viewed as the two sources of the two-source hypothesis.

In 1924, the two-source hypothesis was expanded by B. H. Streeter to a four-source hypothesis. Simply put, he accepted Q and Mark as sources, but he limited Q as a source to only that material common to Matthew and Luke. This was a simplification of the use of Q, which had been called forth increasingly as a label for materials beyond those obviously shared by Matthew and Luke. So Matthew's Gospel had as its basic sources Mark, Q, and sayings unique to the Gospel (symbolized by M). Luke had the two basic sources and sayings unique to him (symbolized by L). These four sources found acceptance by many scholars, though Streeter's attempt to associate these sources with geographical areas met with less agreement.

Despite the general acceptance of the idea of literary dependency among the Gospels, and an avowal of some kind of source hypothesis, the use of source criticism in the New Testament has gone much the same way that such analysis did in the Old Testament. Having contributed a major and creative solution to an important problem, it has since been eclipsed as a method of study by more recent tools, notably form criticism, then redaction criticism. What source analysis that has been done, and still is done, has focused on the Gospels and Acts. Much less attention has been given to the epistles, especially the Pauline corpus. Still, as with Old Testament scholarship, it is not possible to dismiss the ideas and gains of source analysis. If its application is limited today, it yet remains a profitable method for the student to examine and try.

Presuppositions

To be able to practice source criticism requires more than a brief survey of its history. The presuppositions undergirding source analysis must be specified. Some basic assumptions are:

1) Ancient documents frequently make use of earlier (written) sources.
2) These sources are often only infrequently acknowledged. This means that their presence in many cases must be inferred.
3) Where sources **are** acknowledged they may not be accurately named, or correctly quoted.
4) Though sources remain unacknowledged they still leave clues by which they may be uncovered and identified.
5) The identification of sources (or the proper identification of an acknowledged source), and their description, rests upon the utilization of certain specific features which best can be explained only by the hypothesis that a source is present, and it is exerting an effect upon the material.

The application of these assumptions to principles for doing source analysis is in some instances easy; in other cases, rather difficult. But, once it has been granted that a work has made use of earlier material, then, whether easy or difficult, the challenge to uncover the sources used becomes irresistible. Like most research, the analysis of sources involves a strong dose of detective work. The clues are irregularities in the style or substance of the document being studied, or perhaps a formulaic introduction to a saying that the author has taken from an earlier work. As the document is analyzed it is broken into its constituent parts in order better to understand it in itself, and also to achieve a better picture of its place in a literary history. This history, in the case of the biblical documents, is also a history of God's acts and involvements with individuals and with nations. Every document and every source has a vital role in that history.

Principles

Two general principles, or guidelines, are basic to source analysis. First, **watch for the presence of factors indicating the use of a source.** A list of such factors should include:

1) Open acknowledgement of dependence on a known source (e.g., "As the prophet Isaiah said"). This can be called a **statement of obligation.**
2) **Allusion** to a known source (e.g., "spoken by the prophet" in Mt. 1:22f.).
3) **Allusion** to an unknown source.
4) **Citation** of a known source without acknowledgment (e.g., the quotation found in Mt. 1:23).
5) **Stylistic differences** in the text.
6) The presence of **formulaic introductions** (e.g., "It is written").
7) **Interruptions** in the text indicating insertions.
8) **Unusual vocabulary** (and/or different linguistic usage).
9) **Different perspectives** on the same matters.
10) **Common material** shared between documents.
11) Texts, or fragments of texts, appearing in different locations with distinct **alterations.**
12) Use of a source discernible by **context.**
13) Use of **traditional forms** (e.g., hymns, doctrinal summaries, catechetical formulations, etc.).
14) **Logical hiatus or digression.**
15) Materials **anachronistic** to the document.

All of these can be placed in one or the other of two general categories. The first, which I call **statements of obligation,** contains direct and indirect acknowledgments of a source by citation or allusion. These tend more obviously to be artificial in their inclusion in the text, and are often easily observable. They are self-contained references, and so easier to delineate and less susceptible to substantial alteration. The second category I term **statements of influence.** These include all those factors displaying an effect on the text's style and/or content. Such factors are more debatable in analysis. Determining the presence of a source by its effect or influence also is much simpler than delineating its extent and nature. Yet source analysis often must content itself with working with this kind of factor.

As indicated above, some factors are more reliable than others. A clear citation, for instance, is more trustworthy than unusual vocabulary usage to indicate the utilization of a source. In indicating the possible use of a source it is wise to keep in mind the relative weight that can be attached to any given factor. Moreover, the reliability of any factor can vary with a particular document depending on the care with which an author used his sources.

The second general principle is, **when once a source has been identified or inferred, there are two fundamental queries that must be put to it: What does it say? What relationship does it have to the document at hand?** The more basic of these questions is the first. As an examination of the history of source criticism discloses, this is not an easy question to answer. Sources may be mixed together in such a complex fashion that trying to uncover the original contents of each source in a given location becomes a matter of artful conjecture.

The latter question, which can be recast as, "What is the present document's relationship to the source?", may make answering the first question easier. If the author has made an exact copy of his source, as through direct quotation, then specifying what the source says is simple and obvious. But what if the author has changed his source, perhaps even misunderstanding its original intent? In such cases the recovery of what the source itself actually says may be beyond reach. It is little wonder, then, that the specification of sources (e.g., JEDP, or Q) is not only tedious and difficult, but controversial as well.

Methodology

The way has now been laid to enumerate the three steps, or stages, in source analysis. These are comprised by applying the principles in an orderly fashion to any ancient document. These stages are:

1) Determine if a source is present.
2) Determine the **nature** of the source.
3) Determine the **use** of the source.

First, **determine if a source is present.** There are many different kinds of sources the analyst must be prepared to recognize. These include:

1) **Secular documents:**
   (1) Lists
   (2) Receipts
   (3) Business documents
   (4) Administrative documents
2) **Personal documents** (notably letters)
3) **Juridical documents:**
   (1) Court records
   (2) Contracts
   (3) Law collections
4) **State documents:**
   (1) Letters of state
   (2) Royal lists and records
   (3) Covenants/treaties
5) **Scholarly documents:**
   (1) Scribal aids (e.g., alphabets, dictionaries)
   (2) Histories
   (3) Medical documents
   (4) Astrological and astronomical materials
   (5) Natural histories and other scientific works
6) **Literature:**
   (1) Rhetoric
   (2) Poetic works
   (3) Narrative works
7) **Religious documents:**

120

        (1) Cultic documents
        (2) Theologies
        (3) Wisdom literature
        (4) Poetry (e.g., psalms)
        (5) Musical materials (e.g., hymns)
        (6) Educational materials (e.g., catechisms)
   8) **Inscriptions:**
        (1) On coins, medals, royal seals, etc.
        (2) On buildings
        (3) On gravestones and tombs

Even such a partial list discloses how many sources there are to contend with in source analysis. Still, the task hardly is impossible. Sources leave clues when they are used, and that is decisive. But to perceive these clues requires some idea of the characteristics of the sources. Just as critical is an awareness of the kinds of clues, such as those specified under principle one. What, though, should be done when one or more factors become visible? The following list should help answer this question:

   1) **Enumerate** the factors in an orderly fashion, as they occur.
   2) Weigh each as to its **reliability**. This includes:
      (1) An evaluation of the **writer/editor** of the document using the source.
         a) An awareness of how this editor generally uses his sources is important. Is he usually trustworthy in his handling of sources?
         b) To check a writer's reliability, look for the consistency with which he handles his sources. Do you observe any regularities in his use of his sources (e.g., a preference for statements of obligation, or, within such factors, a preference for direct citation over allusion)?
         c) Be particularly careful to see how he handles the most obvious manifestations of a source, i.e., his actual citations. Does he quote accurately and fully? In the New Testament it might be worth determining if the citation is drawn from the Hebrew Old Testament, or from the Septuagint.
      (2) An evaluation of the **document** itself.
         a) This, of course, is related closely to the evaluation of the editor. But where that is broad enough to examine that writer's entire corpus, this concerns itself only with the internal consistency of this document's use of sources.
         b) Even though a writer may have a good

121

reputation for handling material in one fashion, within this document he might pursue an uncharacteristic course. So, the document as a whole, and in its constituent parts, must be examined carefully. This is especially important where a document (e.g., Genesis) is a complex compilation of skillfully interwoven sources.

    c) Do not neglect the possibility that any source may contain the remnants of an even earlier source. The detection of a source-within-a-source can be as taxing as it is exciting.

(3) An evaluation of the **intrinsic reliability** of each of the factors.

    a) Some factors are more reliable indicators of the presence of a source (refer back to the discussion under principle one). Reliability tends to run from the very reliable (e.g., an acknowledged direct citation) to the unreliable (e.g., moderately different vocabulary usage).

    b) Ask: Is this factor a clear and consistent indicator of source usage?

Obviously, the more one knows about a writer, or about ancient sources, or about the factors indicating a source, the better he or she is able to state that a source is present, and such and such evidence says so. But, as has been stated before, the presence of these factors usually only can establish the probability that a source has been used (the obvious exception is a citation known from its existing source).

3) Remember that both **quality** and **quantity** of evidence is important. However, quality is relatively more important than quantity. One highly reliable factor is worth more than several unreliable factors in determining the presence of a source.

The goal in stage one is the ability to state confidently that a significantly higher probability exists that a source stands behind a given passage than that one does not. The analyst bears the burden of establishing the presence of the source.

Stage two: determine the nature of the source. By "nature" I mean the source's native content and meaning. This can be a difficult task; sometimes, it is an impossible one. In rough order of ascending difficulty to answer are the following questions:

122

1) Does the source exist as an **independently known document?**
   (1) If it does, then the source's content is established so that it is a relatively simple task to view how the document being examined uses the source.
   (2) If it does not, determining content, intent, and the meaning of the source likely may prove impossible, at least in any final sense. What is left, then, are only the existing fragments, which may or may not reflect accurately the general nature of the full, original source.
2) **Where** is this source most likely to occur?
   (1) Certain sources show up regularly in certain contexts. This is because any source has its own distinctive interests. When a document considers the same subject it is likely to draw upon a source noted for its interest in and contribution to this subject.
   (2) Learn the logic of analogous usage, which permits prediction. Knowing where a source already has been established may lead to predicting where else it might be found.
3) What **relation** to other sources can be observed?
   (1) Does a source itself reveal dependency on yet earlier materials?
   (2) Does a source parallel other materials?
4) What knowledge of this source can be garnered from its **use in other documents?**
   (1) How many documents display evidence of this source?
   (2) Which documents display such evidence?
   (3) What is the pattern of the evidence gathered from these different documents about the source?
   (4) On the basis of the usage of the source by these different documents, can a rounded picture of the source be drawn?
5) What are the characteristic **literary and thematic features** of the source?
   (1) The vocabulary of the source is a very basic starting point. The writer/editor of document may prefer certain words (e.g., a particular name of God), and the source may prefer others. Of course, the editor may not follow the source's usage but regularize it by alteration so that the source follows his convention. But the editor may choose to follow the source and so provide us with important glimpses of the source's

123

vocabulary.

(2) The style of the source must also be considered. In Col. 1:15-20, for example, many scholars believe a hymn has been preserved. The evidence lies in large part in the stylistic structure of the passage. But style also refers to characteristic modes of expression. A source may preserve stylistic features which stand out from their place in the document being studied.

(3) The substance of the source, in terms of themes, ideology, and the like also must be examined. This probably is harder to describe and to discern. We can generally suppose that an editor will select from a source material he believes to be compatible with his own views. But occasionally, he misunderstands his source and faithfully records a perspective different than his own. Then we can see most clearly the source's own distinct viewpoint, at least for a moment.

6) What was the **original content** (message) of the source?

(1) Outline the points of the message contained by each source fragment. When all these have been gathered, attempt to sketch the content of the source.

(2) Attempt to reconstruct the actual wording of the source. Such an exercise is speculative, and may seem both superficial and subjective. Yet it also may lead to valid insights into the source.

7) What was the **original intent and meaning** of the source?

(1) From what you have been able to reconstruct of the source, has any dominant interest of the material emerged? Perhaps a particular situation, a problem, or an idea prompted the source's production. Do you have enough material to estimate what it was?

(2) What did the source mean to its original audience? To answer this requires hazarding the placement of the source in a particular time and place. The setting of the source has thus become your concern. By addressing such matters the source is fit into a literary history.

This second stage is quite important. To more fully elucidate each of the seven questions listed above requires further

124

discussion.

Does the source exist as an independently known document? In the source analysis of the Synoptic Gospels two important sources that have been identified are Q and Mark. The former of these is unknown to us as an independent document, although it may have circulated once in such a form. Mark, however, we possess. Our exact knowledge of Mark makes it easier to identify it as a source in both Matthew and Luke. In fact, as seen from the history of the source analysis of the Synoptics, it was the presence of the Markan material in Matthew and Luke that furnished the key to the hypothesis that a literary dependence exists among these Gospels. Where the source exists independently of its use in a given document it is much easier to understand the processes being used by an author/editor depending on that source. The editor's use can be checked against the original formulation. On the other hand, where a source is only known through its use by other documents, it is a difficult task to specify the nature of that source. We cannot know if all of Q (if indeed it is a genuine source document) is retained in the Synoptics. Where Luke and Matthew vary in their use of material taken from Q it cannot be known for certain which reflects the original source, if either do.

Where is this source most likely to occur? Sources are not used indiscriminately. The way in which they are used reflects on their nature. This, in turn, allows a certain ability to predict where else the source might be found. If investigation in those places turns up factors indicating the use of a source, then it becomes a better bet that the source is there and that it is the same, or of the same kind, as was found elsewhere. In other words, asking this question prompts a kind of extension of logic designed to seek out a given source in other places, and so develop a better picture of it. For instance, prophetic material may be quoted that clearly indicates its source. The location of this prophetic material in a context where it is used to support some claim about Jesus suggests that in similar situations a similar use of prophetic materials might be expected. Thus, it is profitable to examine other such passages, seeking sources the same or similar to those already found. So an author may use Isaiah several times, or perhaps only prophets from a certain time period, or maybe a wide variety. Whatever may be the case, a valuable amount of information has been gathered about both the way in which the author uses sources and about the nature of the sources used.

What relation to other sources can be observed? A proper understanding of the nature of a given source can be immeasurably enhanced by knowing how it stands in relation to other sources. This is a matter not just of chronology, although that is important, but also of viewpoint (ideology) and dependency. Is a source being used itself depending upon another source (a source-within-a-source)? Or, does a source somehow show awareness of another source's existence (e.g., 1 Ki. 11:41, and many other places in the historical books of the Old Testament)? In either of these instances the source can at best be contemporaneous with these other sources, and probably is later in origin. By asking the question of what relation to other sources can be observed, and then forming answers, the nature of the source can be illuminated in ways that other means may neglect. Perhaps a source shows a tendency to modify or to extend the language or thought of another, earlier source. Only by working to discover what relationships exist between sources can the importance of such an observation be known.

What knowledge of this source has been garnered from its use in other documents? Without asking this question a source might never be identified. For instance, if we did not have Luke's Gospel, would Q have been hypothesized? The nature of Q has been worked out from a constant comparison and contrast of materials from both Luke and Matthew. In a like fashion, the characteristics by which the Old Testament sources JEDP are known today were not all gathered from one document but compiled from several documents. To best know a given source where that source has no independent existence it must be known from the totality of its occurrences in all the documents in which it may be used. Perhaps that seems too obvious an observation to merit much attention. But when studying the sources of Genesis it would be foolish to ignore entirely the sources that Genesis has in common with other Old Testament books. To know the sources of Genesis as fully as possible demands recognizing that some knowledge of them can be gained outside of Genesis.

What are the characteristic literary and thematic features of the source? This is the question most immediately associated with the idea of the nature of a source. It is also the question that gives itself most readily to the minute analysis of a text for which source analysis became nearly infamous. But it is at the heart of source analysis to want to know what the source behind a passage itself looks like, and how its composers thought. A passage in the Bible might carry more than one message. In the shape it has today it carries the meaning intended by its author/editor. But if that author/editor used sources, and those sources themselves had meaning they intended to convey, then recovering those sources may give to us those meanings as well (at least in part). Such information is both of historical interest and theological significance. The more precisely a source can be known as to its vocabulary, style, and thought, the more exactly we can recover the meaning intended by those earlier writers. The goal of accomplishing this, though obstructed by many difficulties, is a laudable one.

What was the original content (message) of the source? The determination of this is generally quite problematic. What frustrates the answer to this question is the incomplete nature

126

of the evidence. Whenever a source is not known to us as an independently existing document there remains a degree of uncertainty as to the extent of it which we presently possess. Still, the attempt to outline what we do possess may lead to some insight into what is missing. In other words, the idea of prediction again enters in. The gaps in the outline may suggest the kind of material that was originally present, though today remains unknown. Thus matters of context, thought progression, and internal hints may lead us to conclude that certain kinds of material once existed but were not preserved.

What was the original intent and meaning of the source? The attempt to answer this question suffers all the same obstacles that the preceding query does. Yet it might be that all of the surviving material displays in one manner after another a single dominant concern. It is only logical, then, to hypothesize that the source as a whole had this concern as either its main theme or one of its principal themes. Intent, though, is easier to estimate than meaning. Although it may seem a rather straightforward exegetical matter to determine the meaning of what survives from a source, this is hardly as simple a task as it appears. The writer using the source has chosen some material, left out more, and perhaps has altered what he has used. But even if the writer has been careful to preserve his source to the degree that he has lifted out a distinct unit of text and cited it exactly, it has still been removed from its original context. That one fact alone can seriously diminish our ability to state with confidence the original meaning of the particular passage from the source.

Stage three: determine the use of the source. In practical benefit for understanding our canonical literature, the third stage receives preeiminence. The use made of sources is imoprtant to understanding the mind of the biblical writer before us. When we turn our attention in this direction we come close to—if we do not actually enter into—the concerns of a discipline such as redaction criticism. Of course, in practice the tasks and methods of source, form, and redaction criticism intermingle. My placement of certain matters in the sphere of source criticism is not intended as a critique of any other research methodology. Instead, I wish simply to call attention to certain concerns that can be closely connected to the evaluation of sources.

The following points are basic:
1) Once the sources have been **separated from the writer's own unique contributions**, both the sources and the unique contributions will stand in stark relief and better illuminate important facets of the writer's mind and style. This point embraces two distinct sub-points:
(1) Viewing the source as used and shaped by the writer-as-editor. (Depending on focus, this may concern mostly the writer or the

source or the interaction between them.)

    (2) Viewing the writer's own processes and products. (This is more properly the domain of redaction criticism.)

2) The usage a source receives indicates its **valuation**.

    (1) The valuation placed upon the source by history (i.e., the editor's predecessors) is important. Observing the treatment of a source through time may indicate its importance, gift for relevance, and continuing impact on the present. Matters like these are sure to bear on such concerns as the care with which a source has been preserved.

    (2) The valuation of the source by the writer-as-editor also can affect our understanding of the source (as well, of course, as our understanding of the author using it). We should ask:

        a) Is there evidence that the author uses this source frequently?

        b) In what connection does he use it?

        c) For what purpose does he use it?

    All of these reflect in some way on the likelihood that the writer-as-editor has preserved the source either accurately or completely. He will if it is in his interest to do so.

    (3) The valuation of the source by the community to which the writer belongs matters, too. The same questions asked of the writer-as-editor can be put to his community (which is most possible when we possess more than one example of the use of a source by a community).

3) The usage a source receives indicates its likely **function within the community** to which the editor belongs. The use to which a source is put by a community will also affect the manner in which it is preserved in the writings of that community.

4) The **interpretation** of a source sheds light on the source, the writer who uses it, and the writer's community. This point is related closely to the preceding ones. Whenever we can find not merely the use of a source, but evidence as to its interpretation, we can learn much.

    (1) Actual commentary on the source (e.g., a Church Father on a Scripture text) tells us how the commentator esteems it, views it,

and applies it.

(2) Alterations of the source itself are particularly important. When we know a source has been altered we both can deduce things about the editor and about the source.

5) The source **selected** and those **shunned** may indicate the tradition to which the writer-as-editor belongs, and so explain his usage of the source. Where the writer's tradition is known but the source's is not, then perhaps a guess can be hazarded as to the source's tradition.

These interrelated concerns are important to more than source criticism. For source analysis care should be given to maintaining a focus on the source itself. Now, let us examine each point again.

The **separation of sources from the writer's own unique contributions** is a natural goal of source criticism. It is also a natural goal of redaction criticism, and the two methods stand as close here as at any other point. In an ideal situation, where every source has been clearly identified and exactly separated from the writer's own creative product, that product could be scrutinized to maximum benefit. So, too, could the source selections. Of course, ideal situations are all too rare. In practice we often find it frustratingly difficult to determine where a source begins or leaves off. Writers-as-editors can be remarkably skillful! So, one does the best that one can. In identifying as far as possible the author's own contributions we are able to know his mind better, see his style more clearly, and focus upon his distinctive interests. At the same time, the use the writer makes of his sources, particularly in the way he shapes them to fit his own framework and program, is crucial, too, for understanding his mind. Thus, with regard to the author, two ideas surface: seeing the writer's own products **and** seeing the writer at work as an editor of other writers' products. However, in this second idea a focus can be set upon the sources as selected, shaped, and used by the writer. Speculation as to how the editor's usage affects our ability to delineate the nature of the source is very helpful. It encourages caution without stymieing creative reflection.

The second and third points may be treated together. The **valuation** and the **function** a source receives in a document probably reflect those same qualities in the community of which the writer is a part. This makes sense, since it is highly unlikely any community will bother to preserve a work which does not share or contribute to its essential needs and perspective. (This is true even where a source seems manifestly at odds with the community; its preservation is accomplished by creative interpretation of its contents so that it is relevant to the community, **or**, in rare cases, the work may become part of the nucleus of a new community and tradition.) If a document shows that it highly values certain sources, then it also can be supposed that so does the community behind that document. Likewise, if the document uses a source in a particular or distinctive way, then it may be guessed reasonably that the community did as well. This need not strip the writer-as-editor of all creativity, or even limit unduly his creativity. This observation merely recognizes that editors of sources were members of communities which shaped them. Thus, these matters reflect on our comprehension of the sources, the writers, and their communities. The interrelation of all three spheres suggests that, while not impossible for an editor to haved used his sources in a previously unknown manner, it is far more probable that he used them, and valued them, much like those around him.

The fourth point is naturally critical. The **interpretation** of a source reflects on several important matters simultaneously. First, it reflects on the source itself. Has the writer accurately understood the message, the intent, and the meaning of the source? Or, has his interpretation missed the point, whether intentionally or unconsciously? Second, the interpretation reflects the writer. Why does the writer offer this particular understanding of his source? Is it to bring out a special portion of the meaning of the source? Is it to add a new or different slant to the meaning already present in the source? Perhaps the writer-as-editor himself only knows the source in part. The interpretation might reflect that. Or, it may display his tradition, training, or some other factor of particular import. Finally, the interpretation reflects on the community. Why does this community receive this interpretation? Is it what should be expected for this community? Has the community somehow shaped this interpretation, and if so, how? Might it be that this interpretation has shaped the community? Some of these questions bridge the gap between the concerns peripheral to a source analyst and those central to other scholars. Such questions again reflect the overlapping common in research, especially in research practice.

The **selection** of sources (or the **shunning** of them), in addition to what such selecting says about the valuation of the sources, also reflects upon the tradition to which a writer and his community belong. Certain traditions are more esteemed than others by a given community (and often precisely because it was those traditions that called the community into being, and shaped its life). This is true in any culture. Those documents which best reflect that tradition are those that will be best known, most used, and most carefully preserved. Hence, a writer-as-editor likely will make most prominent use of the sources associated with that tradition to which he belongs (e.g., the use of the Old Testament by the early Christians). Thus, historical insights into traditions can be gained from source analysis even though the study of those traditions belongs properly to other research endeavors.

The three stages of source criticism can be used in a

self-contained study, or as preparatory work to a more comprehensive kind of research project. Some source analysis studies involve one or two of the stages, and some only part of a single stage. But the method itself is flexible enough to entail, at its broadest, all of the stages and work enumerated here.

Sources

All that remains to complete our treatment of source analysis is briefly to discuss five of the most famous sources which have been identified. As might be guessed, the existence of these sources can be, and has been, disputed. The precise extent and the characteristics of each still are subject to debate. Accordingly, what is presented here should not be taken as assured fact (an observation that pertains, too, to the appendix on this subject at the book's end). What this material below represents is as general and helpful an illustration of hypothesized sources as is practical in a confined space. The first four sources are JEDP, and the fifth is Q. (It should be noted that, properly, something would be said about Mark as a source, and about the characteristics of that special material unique to Matthew and to Luke. But I have left these aside since an understanding of them is relatively less critical to beginning source critical work, and because any good New Testament introduction or commentary on the Synoptic material will cover these quite adequately. The goal in this section is purely illustrative.)

Source J, the **Yahwist**, is perhaps most famous for the creation account of Gen. 2:4b-3:24 ("Creation, temptation, and fall"). The source derives its name from its preference for "Yahweh" in naming God (the J is from the German spelling, **Jahve**); this term appears in English as "LORD" in many translations (e.g., KJV, RSV, NASB, NIV). The Yahwist was dated by Wellhausen back to the ninth century B.C. Today most scholars agree with this general figure, placing the J source in the tenth or ninth centuries and hypothesizing its origin from ancient folk traditions. Considered the oldest of the sources, it is most frequent in Genesis and Exodus, though not unknown in Numbers and, perhaps, in Deuteronomy. The Yahwist pictures God as intimate with man. In his activity God is very personal and even human-like. Israel's history, and especially her well-being, is pictured as directly connected to God's promises to Abraham (cf. Gen. 12:1-4a, 7). The Yahwist language about God is simple, even "childlike," though the ideas are profound. Yahweh is the Creator, and man is the focus of creation. The whole source as it is known to us has the style and substance of an epic narrative. Gerhard Von Rad, a prominent Old Testament theologian in this century, thought the Yahwist's theme is woven around God's response to the growing power of sin, culminating in the divine election of the patriarch, Abraham.

Source E, the **Elohist**, also has derived its name from the use of that name of God which it prefers: "Elohim," commonly translated "God." Wellhausen dated this source to the eighth century B.C. Today it is dated in the ninth or eighth century. Unlike J, which is thought to have originated in Judah (perhaps in Solomon's time), E is considered to have come from the northern kingdom, after the ministry of Elijah, but reflecting much older traditions. Of the four sources, it tends to be the most difficult to ascertain, though it is frequently located in passages from Genesis, Exodus, and Numbers. It is found most often in Genesis, and since it often is difficult to delienate precisely, and frequently occurs closely joined to J, the Elohist is considered by some scholars to be a redactor's supplement to the Yahwist. The Elohist refrains from picturing God in human shape, preferring to use visions and angels. God appears to be a more powerful being than in J, and man appears to be portrayed more sympathetically and humanely than in J. The "fear of God" seems to be emphasized, and the idea that God's power can be glimpsed in his tendency to make man's choices for him appears occasionally. The covenant receives a somewhat nationalistic interpretation (cf. Ex. 19:5-6), and the sacred mountain is called Horeb, rather than Sinai (cf. Ex. 3:12).

Source D, the **Deuteronomist,** generally is dated more precisely than the other three sources. Some scholars identify the Deuteronomic Code (cf. Deut. 12-26) with the "Book of the Law" found in the Temple in Josiah's reign (621 B.C.; cf. 2 Ki. 22-23). Few would argue with a general date of 640/39-609 B.C. (i.e., seventh century). The name means "second law," and the source consists essentially of the book which bears that name (mainly excepting chapters 32 and 33). The source not only presupposes that revisions in the Law are necessary, but that changes can be made legitimately. Thus the Elohistic idea that sacrifice properly may be offered at any of many places is revised and restricted by the Deuteronomist. The style of the source employs stereotyped phrases and definite formulas. It is strongly homiletical (i.e., it preaches; the book of Deuteronomy is very like an extended sermon), with repetitions and exhortations. While it seriously considers the problem of "unjust suffering," it emphasizes the theme of rewards: the just are rewarded while the unrighteous are punished. Another emphasis is on God's sovereign, electing purpose for his people, and his solitary position as the one and only God of Israel.

Source P, the **Priestly Code,** may be the easiest of the four sources to recognize. Dated to the fifth century B.C., this source has a relatively well-defined vocabulary and a quite recognizable style. It is solemn in tone, even striking some observers as rather pompous in places. It makes full use of cultic ideas and terms (i.e., things pertaining to the rituals, worship, and institutions of Israel's religion). To it belongs the stylish creation account of Gen. 1:1-2:4a. But it can be found in many places, including especially Leviticus, as well as portions of all of the other four books of the Pentateuch. The history of the Priestly account is rich and full, reaching from creation through the settlement of the Promised Land. Even matters that some might find mundane, like genealogies and measurements, find their way into this source's account. Today some view this source as principally a narrative into which various legal material has been introduced. Regardless, the themes of the Priestly source are clear: they are the ideas especially important to the Hebrew priests. Thus God's actions are viewed as planned and orderly. God can act merely by speaking; nothing more concrete or physical is necessary. God's foreknowledge, his divine plan, and the universality of his goodness are all present in this source. God meets with his people, but on his terms, and those terms are exact and orderly. Accordingly, special emphasis is given to matters such as the hallowing of the Sabbath.

These four sources are not always unmixed. Nor, as was mentioned before, are they always easily discernible. Yet, as can be seen from these brief descriptions, they do seem to be distinct sources, each with its own style, dominant themes, and perspective. Using these sources to account for various things in the Pentateuch (or Hexateuch) has proven helpful to many scholars and laypeople in coming to a better understanding of these ancient books.

Source Q, or **Quelle,** has also been a helpful tool for New Testament students. Found principally in Matthew and Luke (the presence of Q in Mark is debated), this source has been instrumental in the framing of the two-source hypothesis. The outstanding characteristic of this source is that it embodies sayings. While no universal agreement exists about the date or circumstances of its origin, some scholars hold that it predates Mark, was originally in Aramaic (a few think at the hand of Matthew)', and may have been designed to serve as an instructional handbook in the primitive Church. The probability is that it was extent in Greek when Matthew and Luke made use of it. Luke's order, and generally his wording, is preferred by most scholars as being closer to the original of Q than that found in Matthew. Accordingly, most reconstructions of the source follow Luke. Using only the material from these two Gospels this amounts to some 250 verses. The kinds of material encompassed by this source include the preparation of Jesus, his sayings on various matters, and at least one parable (the mustard seed: Lk. 13:18-21 and Mt. 13:31-33). Oddly enough, it does not seem to have contained any passion narrative. Given the nature of the source, it probably is misleading to think of it as possessing themes as such. Rather, it was probably a collection designed for the many uses appropriate to instructing Christians in their faith.

These five sources are the most famous in the history of source analysis. Of course, there have been many minor sources detected as well. Still, the analyses of these five are paradigmatic for what takes place in source criticism.

Conclusion

Given the multitude of modern research methodologies in vogue today it may seem odd, even inappropriate, to give so much attention to source analysis. Yet the attention seems justifiable to me given the admitted importance the method has had, and its foundational place in relation to so many newer and more popular techniques. A study of source analysis is a good way to be introduced to the so-called "higher criticism." Source criticism has its limitations, but it also has definite advantages, and is more robust than some credit. Moreover, it is a method that can be mastered very quickly to the extent that a student may employ it in its broadest and most general form. Through it a valuable "hands on" experience with the biblical materials can be gained.

Suggested Exercises

Excercise 1

Can you identify the following sources (JEDP) from their characteristics in each of these Pentateuchal texts?

Genesis 1:1-3

In the beginning God created the heavens and the earth. The earth was without form and void, and darkness was upon the face of the deep; and the Spirit of God was moving over the face of the waters. And God said, "Let there be light"; and there was light.

Genesis 2:4b-7

In the day that the LORD God made the earth and the heavens, when no plant of the field was yet in the earth and no herb of the field had yet sprung up—for the LORD God had not caused it to rain upon the earth, and there was no man to till the ground—then the LORD God formed man of dust from the ground, and breathed into his nostrils the breath of life; and man became a living being.

(Can you identify where this text is from?)

"Hear, O Israel: The LORD our God is one LORD; and you shall love the LORD your God with all your heart, and with all your soul, and with all your might. And these words which I command you this day shall be upon your heart . . . ."

Genesis 22:10-12

Then Abraham put forth his hand, and took the knife to slay his son. But the angel of the LORD called to him from heaven, and said, "Abraham, Abraham!" And he said, "Here am I." He said, "Do not lay your hand on the lad or do anything to him; for now I know that you fear God, seeing you have not withheld your son, your only son, from me."

Genesis 28:10-14 (Be warned: there are two sources here!)

Jacob left Beersheba, and went toward Haran. And he came to a certain place, and stay there that night, because the sun had set. Taking one of the stones of the place, he put it under his head and lay down in that place to sleep. And he dreamed that there was a ladder set upon the earth, and the top of it reached to heaven; and behold, the angels of God were ascending and descending on it! And behold, the LORD stood above it and said, "I am the LORD, the God of Abraham your father and the God of Isaac; the land on which you lie I will give to you and to your descendants; and your descendants shall be like the dust of the earth, and you shall spread to the west and to the east and to the north and to the south; and by you and your descendants shall all the families of the earth bless themselves."

Answers: Genesis 1:1-3, "D"; Genesis 2:4b-7, "J"; Deuteronomy 6:4, "D"; Genesis 22:10-12, "E"; Genesis 28:10-14, "E" through the exclamation mark, "J" after it.

135

Exercise 2

Can you identify the sources in these texts? Start with Matthew and try to specify what comes from Mark, what is shared with Luke (Q), and what is unique to Matthew. Outline the passage to show the mixture of the sources, e.g.: Mt. 10:16a, Q; Mt. 10:16b, M (i.e., belonging to Matthew alone). Next, follow the same procedure with the Luke texts. (See a following page for a suggested outline.)

Mk. 6:7-13; 13:9-13

7 And he called to him the twelve, and began to send them out two by two, and gave them authority over the unclean spirits. 8 He charged them to take nothing for their journey except a staff; no bread, no bag, no money in their belts; 9 but to wear sandals and not put on two tunics. 10 And he said to them, "Where you enter a house, stay there until you leave the place. 11 And if any place will not receive you and they refuse to hear you, when you leave, shake off the dust that is on your feet for a testimony against them." 12 So they went out and preached that men should repent. 13 And they cast out many demons, and anointed with oil many that were sick and healed them.

13:9 "For nation will rise up against nation, and kingdom against kingdom; there will be earthquakes in

Mt. 10:5-23

5 These twelve Jesus sent out, charging them, "Go nowhere among the Gentiles, and enter no town of the Samaritans, 6 but go rather to the lost sheep of the house of Israel. 7 And preach as you go, saying, 'The kingdom of heaven is at hand.' 8 Heal the sick, raise the dead, cleanse lepers, cast out demons. You received without paying, give without pay. 9 Take no gold, nor silver, nor copper in your belts, 10 no bag for your journey, nor two tunics, nor sandals, nor a staff; for the laborer deserves his food. 11 And whatever town or village you enter, find out who is worthy in it, and stay with him until you depart. 12 As you enter the house, salute it. 13 And if the house is worthy, let your peace come upon it; but if it is not worthy, let your peace return to you. 14 And if any one will not

Lk. 10:1-12; 21:10-19

1 After this the Lord appointed seventy others, and sent them on ahead of him, two by two, into every town and place where he himself was about to come. 2 And he said to them, "The harvest is plentiful, but the laborers are few; pray therefore the Lord of the harvest to send out laborers into his harvest. 3 Go your way; behold, I send you out as lambs in the midst of wolves. 4 Carry no purse, no bag, no sandals; and salute no one on the road. 5 Whatever house you enter, first say, 'Peace be to this house.' 6 And if a son of peace is there, your peace shall rest upon him; but if not, it shall return to you. 7 And remain in the same house, eating and drinking what they provide, for the laborer deserves his wages; do not go from house to house. 8 Whenever you enter a town and they receive you, eat what is set before you; 9 heal the sick in it and say to them, 'The

kingdom of God has come near to you.' 10 But whenever you enter a town and they do not receive you, go into its streets and say, 11'Even the dust of your town that clings to our feet, we wipe off against you; nevertheless know this, that the kingdom of God has come near.' 12 I tell you, it shall be more tolerable on that day for Sodom than for that town."

21:10 Then he said to them, "Nation will rise against nation, and kingdom against kingdom; 11 there will be great earthquakes, and in various places famines and pestilences; and there will be terrors and great signs from heaven. 12 But before all this they will lay their hands on you and persecute you, delivering you up to the synagogues and prisons, and you will be brought before kings and governors for my name's sake. 13 This will be a time for you to bear testimony. 14 Settle it therefore in your minds, not to meditate beforehand how to answer; 15 for I will give you a mouth and wisdom, which none of your adversaries will be able to withstand or contradict. 16 You will be delivered up even

receive you or listen to your words, shake off the dust from your feet as you leave that house or town. 15 Truly, I say to you, it shall be more tolerable on the day of judgment for the land of Sodom and Gomorrah than for that town.

16 Behold, I send you out as sheep in the midst of wolves; so be wise as serpents and innocent as doves. 17 Beware of men; for they will deliver you up to councils, and flog you in their synagogues, 18 and you will be dragged before governors and kings for my sake, to bear testimony before them and the Gentiles. 19 When they deliver you up, do not be anxious how you are to speak or what you are to say; for what you are to say will be given to you in that hour; 20 for it is not you who speak, but the Spirit of your Father speaking through you. 21 Brother will deliver up brother to death, and the father his child, and children will rise against parents and have them put to death; 22 and you will be hated by all for my name's sake. But he who endures to the end

various places, there will be famines; this is but the beginning of the sufferings. 9 "But take heed to yourselves; for they will deliver you up to councils; and you will be beaten in synagogues; and you will stand before governors and kings for my sake, to bear testimony before them. 10 And the gospel must first be preached to all nations. 11 And when they bring you to trial and deliver you up, do not be anxious beforehand what you are to say; but say whatever is given you in that hour, for it is not you who speak, but the Holy Spirit. 12 And brother will deliver up brother to death, and the father his child, and children will rise against parents and have them put to death; 13 and you will be hated by all for my name's sake. But he who endures to the end will be saved."

by parents and brothers and kins-men and friends, and some of you they will put to death; [17] you will be hated by all for my name's sake. [18] But not a hair of your head will perish. [19] By your endurance you will gain your lives."

will be saved. [23]When they persecute you in one town, flee to the next; for truly, I say to you, you will not have gone through all the towns of Israel, before the Son of man comes."

For Matthew, the following outline is suggested:

Matthew 10:5-8   M (unique to Matthew; "special Matthew")
     :9-13   M + Mk. + Q
        :9   Mk. (cf. Mk. 6:8b)
        :10   Q   (cf. Mk. 6:8, 9 and Lk. 10:7. It seems likely that Mark, like Matthew and Luke, used Q here. However, other alternatives cannot be dismissed.)
        :11   Mk. (cf. Mk. 6:10)
        :12   Q   (cf. Lk. 10:4b-5)
        :13   Q   (cf. Lk. 10:5-6)
      :14-15   Q (cf. Lk. 10:11-12)
      :16a   Q (cf. Lk. 10:3)
      :16b   M
      :17-22   Mk. (cf. 13:8-13) Note Matthew's adaptations as uses his source.
      :23   M

For Luke, the following outline is suggested:

Luke 10:1   L + Mk. (cf. Mk. 6:7b)
    :2   L
    :3   Q (cf. Mt. 10:16)
    :4a   Mk. (cf. Mk. 6:8)
    :4b   L
    :5-6   L
    :7   Q (cf. Mt. 10:10 and Mk. 6:8,9)
    :8-9   L (but cf. Mk. 6:12)
    :10-11   L + Mk. (cf. Mk. 6:11) Note carefully Luke's reworking.
    :12   Q (cf. Mt. 10:15)

Luke 21:10-11a   Mk. (cf. Mk. 13:8)
    :11b   L
    :12-17   L + Mk. (cf. Mk. 13:9-13) This is an interesting and involved passage. Compare, for example, Lk. 21:15 with Mk. 13:11b.
    :18   L
    :19   Mk. (cf. Mk. 13:13)

(This passage in Luke should also be compared to the text of Mt. 24:4-14.)

Remember that source identification is not always easy, and that the exact delineations for sources may differ from one scholar to the next. Do not be discouraged by this. Instead, labor to gain as much understanding as you can from the process of working through the texts. Afterwards, compare your efforts with those of others.

11

Form Criticism

Definition and Purpose

Form criticism logically follows source criticism. This is true both because form criticism largely owes its origin to source criticism and because in many respects form criticism can be viewed as a supplement to source analysis. Form criticism, as the name indicates, is the **study of literary forms.** But, whereas source criticism seeks the written materials behind a document (thus assuming the preeminence of written materials), form criticism seeks "forms," a much broader concept. These forms are linguistic expressions which are often oral, or pre-literary, rather than strictly the written creations of an individual. Thus, form criticism is a method of study, applicable to any literature, which attempts both to classify the linguistic structures underlying a document and to reconstruct the process by which these structures assumed their present state.

The German term for this research approach, **Form-geschichte,** meaning "history of form" (or, "Form-history"), captures the essential aim. Like source criticism, form criticism desires to move behind the documents. But form criticism, addressing some of the perceived limitations of source analysis, conceives its task more broadly. Though a literary method, it is also vitally concerned with history, especially the pre-literary history of the literary materials we possess. This means that form criticism is, inevitably, more speculative than source analysis. Those disinclined to accept the plausibility of source criticism are even less likely to approve form criticism.

While form criticism is thus closely tied to source analysis, its rise can also be attached in part to another important factor. As source analysis came to be more and more restricted in its focus, it raised acutely the problem of the broader situation of any text. The need to place documents in their historical context, or "life situation" (**Sitz im Leben**), became stronger as the modern passion for historical study blossomed. Source analysis proved inadequate to the task when it showed much interest in it at all. Although, as it was suggested in the previous chapter, source analysis **can** be extended to address broader concerns, the fact is that it has been form criticism that has actually done so.

The modern interest in history naturally raised some very specific questions for both Old and New Testament scholars. Yet, because of the different natures of the two Testaments, form criticism developed along different lines in each discipline. Of course, this is especially understandable when we remember that the Old Testament is much larger, having many more forms, and covering a much greater span of time. So it is needful to treat briefly the history of form analysis in each area separately.

History of Old Testament Form Criticism

Even as source criticism in Old Testament studies is most closely associated with the name of Julius Wellhausen, so form criticism is linked to Hermann Gunkel. Although he termed his research **Gattungsgeschichte**, meaning "the history of literary types," his work set forth the basic principles of what would later be known as form criticism. Gunkel started with the results of source analysis. But he recognized that the identification and the description of the sources, and even their placement in Israel's history, could not recover a vital matter: the period of the events recounted by the sources. Some new approach was needed to breach the gap between the time of the sources and the time of the events they depict.

To accomplish a new approach it was necessary to adopt new assumptions concerning the sources. Whereas the source critics were disposed to view the sources as the products of individual writers, Gunkel conceived J and E as collectors of pre-literary materials. If the sources used earlier materials to shape their work, then certain implications could be drawn that would be helpful to further research. First, the dependence of the sources on older, pre-literary materials meant that if these materials could be detected, then they could be traced, too. Second, their existence suggested that communities and their traditions were a more important factor in producing the biblical literature than had been credited by the source critics. Third, it would be natural to assume that the longer stories circulated in their pre-literary state the more susceptible they would become to change as each new generation, or different community, shaped their form to best fit the particular situation at hand.

But how could the literary history be pushed back beyond the sources? Gunkel seized on the idea that this task could be accomplished by an analysis of the literary forms embedded in the documents. He reckoned that these various forms offered clues to the oral tradition that lay behind them. This meant that literary materials should be treated as individual units, recognizing that such units originally existed not in their present state but in oral form. Since the history of the materials was so intimately bound up with the communities that preserved them, Gunkel also focused on determining the specific life-situations associated with the various literary types. His hypothesis was that a literary type was a formal expression of the religious experience of a community.

Gunkel aimed at nothing less than producing a history of the Old Testament literature. He insisted that such a history could show how the literature came into existence from the people's own history, as an expression of their religious experience in history. Working first with Genesis, Gunkel divided the narrative material into separate literary units. He argued that these reflected a pre-literary stage when they circulated among the people and, over the course of time, came to be grouped in certain cycles of stories (e.g., the Joseph cycle of collected stories about the patriarch, found at the end of Genesis). He classified the stories in terms of their purposes. He named various kinds of literary types (e.g., ethnological and etymological legends). He tried to trace the history of these types by minute analysis, maintaining that changes in the material's history are indicated in the material itself. So the additions or the omissions, whether slight or extensive, that can be glimpsed in the form provide clues to the development of the material.

Gunkel's work on Genesis was published in 1901; later, he added significant analyses of the Psalms, in works stretching over a quarter of a century, from 1904-1933. Other Old Testament students followed in Gunkel's footsteps. In 1910, Hugo Gressmann used the new method to study Exodus and Numbers. In recent years the most famous of the Old Testament form critics have been Gerhard Von Rad and Martin Noth. Their work, not only in the Pentateuch (where each wrote significant commentaries), but elsewhere as well, led a surge in form critical studies. Form analysis became the most prominent methodology. The early passion for minute analysis gradually came to be balanced by a healthy interest in using the method for the constructive purpose of better understanding the process of literary composition. So form criticism should be seen as interested not only in moving back in time from the documents it studies, but also moving forward from the oral forms to the composition of the literary forms. While the nearly unbridled enthusiasm for form criticism once common has waned, the method continues to be employed widely in Old Testament research.

History of New Testament Form Criticism

While more people probably associate Rudolph Bultmann with New Testament form criticism than any other name, the pioneering work in New Testament studies was not accomplished by him alone. In the brief span from 1919-1921, three scholars independently applied form critical methods to the study of the Gospels. The earlier of these were K. L. Schmidt and Martin Dibelius. Schmidt's 1919 study, **Der Rahmen der Geschichte Jesu** ("The Framework of the Story of Jesus"), built upon the earlier source analysis of the Gospels. But he pushed beyond that analysis, examining the whole Gospel tradition, and concluded that the Markan framework was not itself original. He saw that the Gospels consist of short episodes, linked together, and set alongside the passion narrative. Schmidt used form criticism to analyze the Gospel framework, commenting on the origin and nature of different literary units.

Dibelius was the first to use form criticism to move back into the oral stage of the Synoptic tradition. His work, **Die Formgeschichte des Evangeliums** (translated as **From Tradition to Gospel**), also appeared in 1919. Dibelius, in fact, gave the still young research method its name in the title of his book. His aim was to penetrate to the origin of the tradition about Jesus, and so move back in history from the written Gospels. Dibelius offered clear and formal distinctions between different literary types. He went on to trace these forms to definite kinds of people and communities. His approach, which may be termed the **constructive** approach, reconstructs the history of the Synoptic tradition from a study of the community, rather than the text. This is not to suggest, however, that Dibelius did not analyze the text. He did, with great vigor. His 1935 work, **Die Botschaft von Jesus Christus** (translated as **The Message of Jesus Christ**), presents Dibelius' conclusions as to the "old tradition, restored." There may be found the texts of tradition, organized according to literary forms. Dibelius' approach emphasizes the idea that the tradition is the product of the Church and serves its needs.

Easily the most influential of the early works was Bultmann's 1921 study, **Geschichte der synoptischen Tradition** (translated as **History of the Synoptic Tradition**). Bultmann followed a different avenue from Dibelius. More detailed, his is an **analytical** approach, which begins with the text rather than the community. This approach emphasizes the forms themselves. But Bultmann's goal is still a familiar one: to trace the origin and formation of the material of the Synoptic tradition from its oral stage to its written form. What distinguishes Bultmann's work from the others, however, is his radical skepticism. As a researcher, he is about as conservative as it is possible to be in his reluctance to draw conclusions that other form critics have thought quite reasonable. What Bultmann was willing to admit could be known certainly about Jesus historically from the Synoptic tradition is very little. It is for this that his form critical work is often (and rather unfairly) remembered.

In the years after these three books were published a substantial number of things appeared explaining or applying form critical principles. Among works in English an early and influential treatment was provided by Vincent Taylor's **The Formation of the Gospel Tradition** (1933). German scholars were quicker to embrace the new methodology, and to employ it with greater trust than either British or American scholars. R. H. Lightfoot, in England, became a prominent defender of the method, and C. H. Dodd put it to landmark use in his study of the parables (as did Joachim Jeremias on the Continent). The study of the parables, and a renewed hope in the possibility and legitimacy of a new quest for the historical Jesus, owe much of their present status and shape to form critics. It is no understatement to say that modern New Testament conclusions cannot be understood apart from the influence of form criticism.

Presuppositions

Form criticism in both Testaments embraces common assumptions and methodological procedures, though the actual practice of the method varies widely. The articulation of assumptions, the relative weight given to one or another, the particular focus of a given study, or the individual refinement of the procedures all can create variations. For the sake of clarity, then, the terminology and the specifications given in the discussion to follow proceed along the lines of New Testament form criticism, especially that of the Synoptic tradition. The main exception to this rule is found in the listing of various Old Testament forms found in the Analytic Method section. A basic understanding of work in the tradition will prepare the student to extend his or her understanding into the particulars of form critical study in other portions of the canon.

The presuppositions undergirding form criticism can be set out in an orderly sequence of reasoning, as follows:

1) Behind the written documents of the Bible is a history; this history is of a written and, especially, an oral tradition.

2) Differences in literary material reflect, at least in part, the influence of oral transmission; but they also reflect, at least in part, the presence of definite and distinguishable sources (e.g., JEDP in the Old Testament hexateuch; the two—source hypothesis in the Synoptics).

3) The literary materials of the tradition in the documents we possess consist of individual literary forms which have been joined together through the labor of editors (redactors).

4) These literary expressions, whether in their written form or in a pre-literary oral shape, make use of more or less fixed types, which have their own laws of style.

5) Thus, these laws, discoverable by biblical glimpses of the early Church and its forms, by discerning 'laws of tradition' from the modifications of the editors, through the study of comparable literature, and by other means, govern the further shaping of the material.

6) Once deduced, these laws of style and the laws of tradition may be projected back in time to uncover the shaping of the tradition and, ultimately, its original shape and substance.

7) All of these literary forms belong to communities, and the shaping of tradition, along with the use

145

of various forms, is the result of these communities seeking to satisfy their needs.

8) Forms, therefore, reflect communities; different forms represent different communities (though not exclusively) in their origin and transmission.

9) It is a natural task, then, to seek to uncover the **Sitz im Leben** of these communities.

10) Knowledge of the **Sitz im Leben** is appropriate to refining an understanding of the communities.

11) Those forms representative of the earliest communities stand closest to the bedrock of tradition.

12) The form, content, and function of tradition are all related to one another, but in varied and robust ways.

These assumptions, of course, can be challenged. What they accomplish at their best is the establishment of a conceptual framework that permits a certain kind of scholarly approach to the documents of the Bible. This approach stresses the possibility of access to the history and tradition **behind** the documents themselves. Certain presuppositions can be read as prompting more than one manner of approach to the task. So the statement in 10, above, reflects the possibility of either a constructive or an analytical approach.

Now let us apply these presuppositions to the Synoptics. The result is a series of statements that establish an assumptive backdrop for form critical analysis of the Synoptic tradition. These might be as follows: "The Synoptic Gospels are a 'popular' production, writings by and for the people. They were not written with the intention of being 'art' or 'literature.' In fact, the community of believers plays a more important role in the production of the Gospels than do even the actual editors of the material. The communities of disciples contributed all kinds of traditions; the editors merely selected from these, adapted and joined them, and added minor connections to hold the whole together. At first, the traditions existed and circulated in oral form. Later, when these traditions were set down in writing, it was as individual units of material, which were then linked to one another by an editor's hand. These individual units (commonly called **pericopes**) display a limited number of forms, which are identifiable by their characteristic features. The origin, or at least the shaping, of these forms occurred in real, concrete life-situations. Their preservation, as well as their prominence, reflects the manner in which they proved relevant and useful for believers. Thus, an analysis of the forms and traditions can supply us with important information, perhaps about the historical Jesus, but also often about the early Church."

Obviously, all of these presuppositions together reveal the specific ideas central to form criticism. These include the prominence of the role of the community in shaping the tradition, the conception of certain 'laws' at work that make discoveries reliable, and the utility of literary forms as critical indicators of tradition. At the same time, these presuppositions indicate areas that actually have proven to be relative 'blind spots.' Thus the lack of importance and corresponding inattention given to the thought and setting of the Gospel writers themselves was a major source of dissatisfaction, and helped give rise to **redaction criticism.**

Methodology

Despite its establishment among the important critical tools used in the study of the Bible, form criticism still suffers from such rather fundamental problems as a lack of terminological clarity, and substantial agreement as to its exact investigative course. Form critics still debate among themselves the precise categorization of forms and their names. They continue to vary in their methodological steps, though not generally in its broadest outline. They do disagree over the ability of form criticism to provide valid knowledge in different arenas, and about its reliability as a methodological tool. Yet, they use it, because it is useful. Some form critics employ the method cautiously and restrict its applicability. Others use it boldly, pushing its scope, attendant assumptions, and discoveries to their speculative limits.

This situation makes it difficult at best to outline the methodology of form analysis. What follows as an attempt to do this may be called folly by some and futile by others. But even though debate about various particulars is inevitable, the reward of such an endeavor is a working tool which can make viable those first awkward steps in actually practicing form criticism. The ability to try form criticism as a research model starts with understanding the method's assumptions and processes. The following illustration of the method is only one possible model. But it is a simple one that has proven effective in preparing students to actually undertake basic form critical exercises such as those found at the end of this chapter. This model follows the analytical approach, though indication is given as to how it might be converted to the constructive approach.

Analytic Model

Note: To convert to the **Constructive Model**, place step 5 first.

Step 1 **Analyze the structure of the text.**
In essence, this means establishing what were the original individual units of material so that these may be analyzed.
1) **Outline the text.** What individual units can be detected? Is there more than one form present? (The kinds of forms are indicated below, in Step 2.)

2) Detect and describe the pattern of the text. How are the forms arranged?

3) Specify the schema of the genres. What characteristics of style are visible in the text? In the forms?

4) Delineate the formal features of the introductions and conclusions in the text. How does the text begin? How does it end? Why do these indicate an individual unit, or do they?

5) Look for any conventional patterns. Are there any expected or familiar patterns? These should be noted. Is the text structured in a manner characteristic of a particular source?

This step should be viewed as preparatory to the work most characteristic of form criticism. It not only embodies a stage of analysis essential to the method, but also incorporates basic skills of literary research. Attention to particulars at this stage will avoid waste in later steps.

In this first step, concentrate on acquiring an overview of the features of the text. Thus an outline of the text should indicate the presence of every apparent individual pericope. Of course, it is helpful not to seize on to too large a body of material to begin with. If you discover that your passage contains five units with several obviously different kinds of forms (which, at this point, you need not name), then you have taken too large a text to use in an introductory analysis. Instead, use a paragraph by paragraph approach until you feel relatively comfortable with the model. Then you can tackle a chapter.

In completing points 2-5, above, aim at being sufficient without being exhaustive. The goal is to see how the passage has been put together. This means looking at its constituent parts (e.g., its beginning and ending), and its pattern (how the text progresses; whether it follows a highly stylized pattern of composition, etc.). Again, aim at acquiring an overview of the material as a starting point.

Step 2. Classify the literary forms.

Once the individual units have been identified, the forms embodied by these units can be identified, analyzed, and classified.

1) In deciding upon a classification, cite the supporting evidence and indicate any anomalies. It is not enough to assert the pres-

ence of a form. It must be established carefully by stating the stylistic laws governing the form. At the same time, any evidence contrary to, or outside these laws should be noted. Later, such anomalies may prove critical in tracing the tradition.

2) Consult the following list and descriptions of literary forms. Note that the classification of forms already has been prepared for by the work of Step 1. The list of forms, which is not intended to be exhaustive, focuses upon forms common to the Synoptic Gospels.

Old Testament forms

Prose forms:

Myths: stories of the gods.

Legends: stories of men, i.e., of individuals (see below).

Folk tales: stories of people (collectively, i.e., of groups).

Romances: imaginative, fanciful stories or visionary fabrications.

Historical narrative: factual recording of actual events.

Prayers: addresses to deity or deities.

There are, naturally, subdivisions of the above. Thus, prayers might be intercessory or petitionary in shape. An example of subdivisions follows:

Legends (a prose form):

Aetiological: general; explain the origin and meaning of things.

Ethnological: focus on explaining tribal relations.

Etymological: explain the origin and meaning of names.

Ceremonial: explain the origin and meaning of rites, ceremonies.

Geological: explain the origin and meaning of places.

Historical: (sagas); accounts of men's actions which have a basis in fact.

Mixed: combine features of various of the above into a single legend.

What is not prose is, broadly speaking, poetry. The various poetic forms comprise the second major division.

Poetry forms:

Apocalyptic: revelatory of hidden matters; generally utilizing cryptic lan-

guage and imaginative images.
Eschatological psalms: psalms focused on future events.
Hymns: musical in character, commonly of praise or thanksgiving.
Prophetic oracles: addresses purporting to be from a deity.
Secular lyric poetry: nonreligious poetry.
Thanksgivings: characteristically, psalms or prayers of gratitude.
Wisdom oracles: proverbs, wise sayings.
The above examples are only that: examples. The Old Testament has many forms, and these may cross the lines drawn above.

New Testament forms

While a substantial variety of forms could be listed here, such as epistle, pseudo-epistle, paraenesis, apocalyptic, etc. (including forms in both the broadest and the narrowest senses), only principal forms of pertinence to studying the Synoptic Gospels are discussed below. This is in the interest of simplifying the task the beginner faces in doing form analysis.

It might be of interest to note that a broad distinction can and has been made between **narrative** and **sayings** material in the Synoptics. Thus, H. C. Kee, in his **Jesus in History** (1977), classifies material as follows:

Sayings Tradition	Narrative Tradition
Aphorisms	Anecdotes
Parables	Aphoristic Narratives
Sayings Clusters	Legends (cult and biographical)
	Passion Narrative
	Wonder Stories

The order of the following forms is not arranged along these lines. Instead, they follow a rough order according to length. So, generally speaking, the formulas are the shortest, and the Passion Narrative the longest, of the forms.

1. **Formulas**

Definition: A short phrase, or perhaps a brief sentence, used to introduce a longer piece of material.

Characteristics: 1) They are very brief. 2) They are not independent per se, but are attached to a unit which is independent. 3) They introduce an independent unit, or perhaps some constituent part of it. 4) Formulas are

150

established by usage; any phrase or sentence regularly used to introduce an action or style of discourse is formulaic.

Types: There are many kinds of formulas. Some of these are: 1) Liturgical: introducing rites of worship. Both eucharistic and baptismal formulas are liturgical in nature. 2) Quotation: introducing a citation. "As it is written," is an example. 3) Asseveration: introducing a statement with an earnest affirmation. The most famous example is, "Truly, truly I say to you." 4) Prophetic: introducing a word of the Lord God. "Thus says the Lord," is a familiar example. 5) Accusation: introducing a complaint against someone or something. 6) Greeting: introducing oneself, or perhaps one's written product, as in the greeting of a letter. 7) Catechetical: introducing material intended for instruction. Each formulation is of like construction for ease of memory. By such constructions forms can be mutated in transmission (e.g., polemic into rules). 8) Geographical: introducing an episode by reference to place. In such a manner an editor could link episodes into a connected narrative. 9) Temporal: introducing an episode by reference to time. This also served editorial needs to link episodes. 10) End: a stylized conclusion used to recount the impression, or effect, made by some teaching or deed.

2. **Apothegms**
(Apophtegms)/Paradigms/Pronouncement Stories
Note: The various designations reflect differences among, respectively, Bultmann, Dibelius, and V. Taylor. Each uses these terms to designate roughly the same form.

Definition: short stories which quickly reach their climax in a saying of Jesus.

Characteristics: 1) The narrative has more in common with discourse than actual narration since the narrative exists to serve the saying it encompasses. Apothegms belong to the "sayings" rather than to the "narrative" material. They are not, properly speaking, stories at all, although it is easy to see them as such. 2) There is a sparing use of detail. 3) No portrait of the persons is attempted. Personal characteristics, when given, are set forth indirectly. As a rule, the figures are types (e.g., Pharisees or disciples, rather than a specific individual; even individuals, thinks Bultmann, are often types in essence). 4) A minimal account of the situation is given. Time and place, as well as other details, are incidental compared to the importance of the saying. Specific indications of such things, then, are likely to be secondary additions. 5) Generally, a question put to Jesus is utilized as the occasion of his saying. 6) The response may be shaped as a counter question, a pointed ethical or religious precept, or a parable. 7) The story may end with the saying, or with a brief statement of its effect. 8) It may have a formulaic introduction or conclusion. 9) The general style reinforces its utility as a teaching tool. 10) It may serve as an example in a sermon, and its ending may be a word, thought, or act of particular usefulness for preaching.

Types: 1) Controversy apothegms (**Streitsgespräche**): the dialog is initiated by Jesus' enemies. 2) Inquiry apothegms, also known as "school sayings" (**Schulgespräche**): the dialog is initiated by friendly questioners. 3) Biographical apothegm (**biographischen**): the dialog is precipitated by an incident. The narrative element generally is larger here than in other types of apothegm, a situation which has caused some Gospel materials to be classed here by some critics and as "Stories about Jesus" by other critics. 4) Chria: this is a more general designation for a sharply pointed saying connected to a particular situation and person. (Chria is distinguished from Gnome, which is a maxim , or aphorism, and which also delivers a saying of general significance but devoid of the connections to person and situation. It is worth noting, too, that some prefer the term "anecdote" for this form.)

3. **Sayings of Jesus**

   Definition: independent words ascribed to Jesus.

   Characteristics: 1) Variable in length, they are frequently shorter than apothegms. 2) They do not exist as an essential part of the story as direct speech. 3) They commonly display a hortatory or paraenetic character. 4) certain "ornamental motifs" (Bultmann's designation) are common. These include simile, metaphor, paradox, hyperbole, and parallelism (synthetic and antithetic alike). Rhythm and rhyme also are to be listed here. 5) Sayings often are grouped together by an artifical arrangement: by content, or formal relationship (i.e., instances of a

152

type collected together, as, for example, parables in close proximity), or by catchword (i.e., a word shared by two or more independent units forming the connection between or among the units). 6) Three "constitutive motifs," of particular importance for the logia, have been identified by Bultmann. These are treated under logia (below).

Types: 1) Logia, or wisdom sayings: maxims and aphorisms might be placed here, but the constitutive motifs are:

    (1) Principles, which are of four kinds:

        a) those where some material thing is the subject;

        b) those where a person (or type of person, e.g., a woman) is the subject;

        c) blessings (which also are placed under the next type); and,

        d) arguments (e.g., Mt. 10:29f.).

    Principles constitute the declarative form of the logia.

    (2) Exhortations (imperative form of the logia).

    (3) Questions (interrogative form).

2) Prophetic and apocalyptic sayings: these are characterized by brevity and vigor, and focus upon eschatology. Such sayings encompass a diverse group, which Bultmann separates into:

    (1) The preaching of salvation, which includes the Beatitudes ("blessings," known also as Makarisms);

    (2) Minatory sayings, which include woes, prophetic threats (**Drohwerte**), and warnings;

    (3) Admonitions (e.g., to be watchful); and,

    (4) Apocalyptic predictions, which range from short words to the 'Little Apocalypse' of Mark (13:5-27).

In this type can be located also the report of a vision (e.g., Lk. 10:18), and the 'eschatological correlative' (cf. Lk. 17:22-37).

3) Law words and community rules (or, as they are also known, "Legal sayings and Church rules"): these sayings include the following:

    (1) Sayings focusing upon the Law, such as those concerned with marriage and divorce, with purity, with prayer and fasting;

    (2) Citations of the Old Testament;

(3) Community rules, which include rules of discipline (e.g., Mt. 18:15-22), and instructions for the Christian mission. These sayings serve to distinguish the followers of Jesus from other people. Both short and extended commandments can be found here; and,

(4) Confessional sayings, so-called because they reflect the Church's faith in the person, work, and fate of Jesus. These are sayings put by the Church on the lips of Jesus (according to Bultmann and many others). Examples may be found at Mk. 8:31, 9:31, 45.

4) "I" sayings: words that direct attention to Jesus' own person or ministry (e.g., Mt. 5:17).

5) Parables: the material here is almost surprisingly diverse. It includes:

(1) Similitudes: simple metaphors elaborated by details;

(2) Illustrative stories: where the moral lies in the narrative itself; and,

(3) Parables: concise and simple stories which aim at a single, striking point of comparison. They are often grouped.

At this point should be mentioned also Allegory. Its characteristics include: (1) that the largest feasible number of details are accorded a hidden significance; (2) that it is not necessarily tied to the concrete reality of this world or everyday life; (3) that it may be founded upon a parable; and, (4) that it generally reflects a secondary interest and formulation (i.e., it is more likely to be a product of the Church than original with Jesus).

A word should be said, too, about Catechesis. Not uncommonly, sayings were grouped together for catechetical (instructional) purposes. This process, obviously a late dvelopment, caused changes in the original shape and/or tone of the material (cf. formulas, type 7).

4. **Miracle Stories/Tales (Novellen)**

Definition: narratives with a focus on a miraculous occurrence.

Characteristics: 1) A broader portrayal of setting exists than is found in an apothegm. 2) Greater detail is found than in an apothegm. 3) The story typically follows a three-fold pattern:

(1) The condition or situation is described (as of a sick person). This introduction commonly stresses the seriousness of the

situation or the inherent problems attendant to its correction.

(2) The miracle occurs (which, on occasion, is not directly witnessed). Typically, this is instantaneous in occurrence, and often prompted by a word and/or gesture.

(3) The reaction is described, accompanied perhaps by a clear demonstration of effect (as in a healed person proving the fact).

4) Miracle stories, when collected together, are known as an Aretalogy. 5) It has been suggested by V. Taylor that the longer of these stories are most likely genuine, since the tendency of oral transmission is toward abbreviation. 6) Miracle stories probably were told to substantiate Jesus' Messiahship and divinity, and to demonstrate his power and goodness.

Types: 1) Healing: in which demons are cast out, physical ailments made well, or the dead raised. 2) Nature: in which natural elements are altered in unexpected and atypical ways.

5. **Stories about Jesus/Historical Stories and Legends**
    Definition: narrative accounts of Jesus and his works.

    Characteristics: 1) Generally longer than other forms (except for the Passion Narrative, which is a special case in several respects). 2) Most are isolated or self-contained. 3) All are tied closely to the life and the interests of the early Church. 4) They share no common structural form as do, for example, apothegms. This must caution us to be especially careful to treat each story in its own right. 5) They describe divine acts. 6) Some appear to be put together from fragments of the tradition so that the perspective is not that of an eyewitness but of a later time. 7) Other stories are less 'literary' and more 'popular.' These bear less evidence of editorial change, appearing to be set down essentially as the writer received them. 8) Other stories seem to be 'personal,' that is, received from individuals involved in the story's situation or account. 9) Occasionally, stories will display a transference of details. Distinctly different stories may share certain details. 10) A single story may be used to focus many incidents of the same kind. It is thus a 'representative' story. 11) Often the stories are used to communicate ideas important to the community and/or writer. They are, to some degree, 'symbolic' stories. 12) The stories commonly are simple and direct, showing signs of having been shortened and/or rounded out. 13) The precise outline of the story is often difficult to delineate (cf. #4 above). 14) Very frequently Jesus occupies the center stage to such an extent that the other characters are neither named nor described. 15) Conversations generally involve just two parties (e.g., two individuals, or an individual and a group). 16) Though a practical aim predominates in shaping the stories (i.e., the religious and educational motives of the community), they may indicate clearly their basis in historical fact (even though the determination of that historical event may not be possible to specify).

Types: The kinds of stories are quite varied, and not all can be named here. A convenient rule of thumb is this: include here all those narratives which are not miracle stories nor belong to the Passion Narrative. Representative examples include: 1) Birth and infancy accounts. 2) The preaching of John the Baptist and his relation to Jesus. 3) The Baptism accounts. 4) Jesus' relation to others (e.g., children, non-Jewish persons, etc.). 5) Ministry accounts (e.g., the calling of the disciples). 6) Conflict stories; the larger controversy apothegms (such as Lk. 11:14-23) are sometimes classed under this form. 7) The Transfiguration accounts. 8) The triumphal entry accounts.

6. **Passion Narrative**

Definition: connected narrative(s) concerning the 'Passion' of Jesus (i.e., roughly from the plotting of Jesus' death by the Sanhedrin to Easter).

Characteristics: 1) A continuous narrative, it is the longest form (and commonly thought to be the first form of the tradition to gain the shape of a continuous story). In this fact a certain logic of the primitive Church's situation can be viewed. Early Christians needed a simple and connected account of these most important events. 2) The detection of separate stories within the narrative is difficult; only the anointing of Jesus in Bethany can be immediately separated from the rest (according to a consensus of form critics). 3) The Passion Narrative enjoys the highest degree of agreement among the Gos-

pels.   4) The sequence of events is tightly told,
with gravity and realism.   5) The exact scope of
the narrative is indeterminable.   6) Eyewitnesses
are named in the narrative, often with detail
added.   7) Jesus is relatively more silent than
might be expected given the length of the material.   8) The events themselves have preeminence.
9) Old Testament ideas prefiguring the Passion
are interwoven in the narrative without direct
citation.   10) Closely linked with the above,
proof from prophecy of Jesus' Messiahship is a
critical motive in the narrative. 11) An apologetic motive is at work, too, especially in such
places as the relative guilt affixed to the Romans
and the Jews in Jesus' condemnation and death
(cf. Mt. 27:24-25).   12) Sensational story details
can be detected at various points, which height-
en the drama (e.g., Mt. 27:51-53; Mk. 15:6-15).
Bultmann calls these "pure novelistic motifs."
13) Bultmann indicates, too, the presence of
"incidental paraenetic" material (e.g., Mt.
26:52).   14) The idea that Jesus suffered and
died as the Messiah is obviously of the first
rank in importance (a fact to which Bultmann
calls attention in describing both the "dogmatic"
and "cult" interests found in the narrative).

Types: The form is continuous, embodying
elements that take their full meaning and import
only from their context in the narrative. Different Gospels add individual elements, and some
parts may seem more recent than others, but the
Passion Narrative should be conceived as one
form.

The suggestions as to which portions of the
narrative are most independent of context reveal the
difficulty in making such determinations with this
material. Consider the following estimations:

K. L. Schmidt:
the anointing, the priests' plot, Judas'
treachery.

M. Dibelius:
the anointing, Gethsemane, Jesus before
the High Priest, the selection of a room
for the Last Supper.

R. Bultmann:
the anointing, the prophecy of the
betrayal, the Last Supper, Gethsemane,
Peter's denial.

V. Taylor:
the anointing, the Weeping Women (Lk.
23:27-31), the penitent thief on the

cross, Herod and Jesus, and, perhaps, the discourses after the Last Supper.

Once the forms have been identified and classified, each form must be taken through the remaining steps.

Step 3 **Trace the history of the form.**

This is where the task of going behind the existing documents is begun in earnest.

Note: in what follows, the order of treatment is first the Sayings material (the shorter forms), and then the Narrative material (the longer forms).

1) Use the following tools in detecting stages in the form history:

(1) Literary and source criticism provide basic data.

(2) The **use of earlier sources** by later ones may reveal laws governing the shaping of the tradition. The tradition then may be projected back from one stage to another in order ultimately to move behind the earliest written sources we possess. (The use of earlier sources by later ones is exemplified by the use of Mark and Q by Matthew and Luke.)

(3) Be alert for instances of forms preserved as **examples** by the biblical literature itself (e.g., sermons in Acts), as well as examples of community settings, practices, etc.

(4) Use comparative literature studies (paralleling New Testament forms with those in contemporaneous Judaism and Hellenism).

2) Note these general tendencies of the Sayings tradition:

(1) Sayings originally circulated in independent units. Traces of the original form should be sought.

(2) Sayings already in circulation may occasion the rise of an **analogous formulation** (cf. Lk. 16:10-12).

(3) Secondary expansions may be detected where an incomplete saying only makes sense in the **context**, i.e., in view of what precedes it. When sayings are expanded at their beginning it is because of the context. These, then, are changes in the written tradition, made by the editor.

(4) Changes in sayings generally reflect particular **motives**. These might be

linguistic (or stylistic), or ideological in origin and nature.

(5) Alterations in a saying may be due to its **insertion** into a context that necessitates some change.

(6) Jewish material may be taken over and **reformulated** by Jesus and/or the Church (as in the prophetic and apocalyptic material, or wisdom sayings).

(7) **Additions and expansions** of material are common. These reflect Christian editing of earlier material. Such editing is most typical of the transmission of the written tradition.

3) Note these principles operative in the collection of material then composed into speeches:

(1) At the earliest stage, oral tradition is put into writing by a simple **serializing** of sayings without reference to their context. Thus, sayings may occur in series connected to one another only by a particle or by the simplest of phrases (e.g., "and he said"; "truly I say to you").

(2) But there are other possible principles that may guide the serialization of sayings:

  a) The ordering of material according to **content** (e.g., sayings about the Baptist).

  b) Association of sayings by **formal relationship** (e.g., similitudes in Mk. 4:1-32).

  c) Association of sayings by **catchword**.

4) Note also how speech material is inserted into the narratives by the various sources. Keep these general ideas in mind.

(1) Sayings derive their meaning from their **context**. If a saying has been placed in a context by the early community we may not be able to determine its original meaning (cf. Lk. 12:3//Mt. 10:27; Mk. 8:27//Mt. 16:13; Mk. 3:28//Lk. 12:10 and Mt. 12:32).

(2) There is a tendency in the tradition to **combine statements** that, though different, bear some similarity to each other.

(3) The **arrangement of grouped sayings** is important. An obviously **artificial** scheme probably indicates the Church's selection of the sayings from a collection

of sayings. But a **natural** scheme may reflect the work of an original mind. (As an example of the former: Mt. 11:12f. and 5:18, 32; as an example of the latter: Lk. 6:27-38).

(4) The insertion of material commonly occasions the **addition of a formal editorial introduction** to the saying.

(5) Occasionally, **transitional passages** by the editor are needed when sayings material is inserted.

(6) Sayings material may have been first grouped **topically**; this motif (ideal for instruction) then gave way to the broader demands of a **chronological** succession of the materials of tradition.

(7) Some **situation in the life of Jesus** was necessary for the proper location of each saying or collection of sayings.

5) Consider these special notes on Saying material:

(1) **Apothegms:**
   a) Developed from the union of independent sayings to situations;
   b) Were easiest to insert into a narrative framework;
   c) Should be considered in the light of Rabbinic material (as, indeed, it is profitable to examine all sayings material in this light although any idea of dependency or even true parallelism must be advanced with extreme caution);
   d) Must be distinguished carefully between those where the framework and saying are so closely related that one cannot be told without the other, and those where the framework and saying share only a loose connection;
   e) Bultmann believes the controversy dialogs are all "imaginary scenes," as are (probably) many of the school sayings;
   f) Those with formulaic introductions are probably Hellenistic; biographical apothegms are mostly the creation of the early Church.

(2) **Sayings about Jesus:**
   a) **Logia** are related closely to the Jewish **mashal** (a form close to that

of a New Testament parable, but susceptible to referring to anything from a proverb to an allegory to a discourse).

b) Some **logia** are enlarged from a mashalic shape by the addition of an illustration (e.g., Mt. 6:19-21).

c) The **logia** are the least guaranteed of the words of Jesus to be authentic. The majority have parallels in Jewish wisdom literature.

d) Most **logia** appear in contexts where their application provides them explicit significance.

e) The **prophetic and apocalyptic** sayings ascribed to Jesus contain many authentic sayings.

f) The **prophetic and apocalyptic** sayings are brief and vigorous, tend to parallel ancient prophecy rather than apocalyptic, and often are supplemented by Church formulations.

g) Among the **law words and community rules**, most of the words of Jesus which cite the Old Testament are suspected of originating in the early Church (and used for apologetical, polemical, or other purposes).

h) The **law sayings** themselves are likely to be authentic.

i) **Law sayings** also often parallel ancient prophecy, but frequently with additions setting forward the regulations of the primitive Church.

j) **Community rules** utilize material that often originated in the Church's earliest debates with 'outsiders.'

k) References to Jesus in the "I" **sayings** are commonly secondary introductions added in order to adapt the saying to a particular context. Such references may be marked by additions or alterations in the saying.

l) **Parables** circulated singly or in pairs before being collected.

m) There is a tendency to add to **parables** sayings of a similar nature. Likewise, introductions often were added.

161

n) **Allegorical expansions** of parabolic material occur in a few instances (cf. Mt. 22:11-14 and Lk. 12:35-38).

o) The formal characteristics of all sayings should be noted carefully. The presence, for example, of synonymous or antithetical or synthetic parallelism points to the Jewish character of a saying.

6) Look for the evidence of the 'laws' governing the formation of popular narrative and tradition. These are basic ones:

(1) Narrators do not provide long, unified accounts but rather **small, single pictures**, individual scenes which are narrated with great simplicity. The **conciseness** of the story is a fundamental trait of the tradition.

(2) The **simplicity of focus** results in a "scenic duality" (Bultmann), where more complex episodes of narrative are set forth through simpler successive scenes. Where several individuals or groups are present, only one or two participate meaningfully in the scene.

(3) The accounts always occupy a **brief space of time** (generally hours, rarely days).

(4) Only two, or occasionally three **characters** appear in the scenes.

(5) The **motives and feelings** of participants typically are not expressed.

(6) Where **groups** or crowds are present, they are **treated as a unity**.

(7) The use of **repetition** is common; such is a characteristic tool of popular story telling.

(8) The utilization of **numbers** (2, 3, 40, 70, etc.) is a popular device.

(9) There is a tendency toward **differentiation and individualization** (e.g., persons not distinguished in the primitive stage are so in the later stage). See the next 'law' for elaboration.

10) While in both oral and written transmission the fundamental character of the accounts remains the same, the **details are subject to change** (usually in the direction of becoming more explicit; a novelistic' tendency). Elaboration is often sparked by imagination. Three rules

162

for this tendency are:

a)   Later tradition supplies **names** to previously unknown characters (an especially marked tendency of the Apocryphal material). However, this is true principally for written transmission; in oral transmission the reverse tendency commonly is seen.

b)   Later tradition prefers **direct discourse** to the source's indirect. Again, this tendency holds most true for written transmission; in oral transmission the opposite is common (and, indeed, that this opposite is not unknown in written tradition, cf. Lk. 8:29, 31f. with Mk. 5:8, 12).

c)   Later tradition is inclined to impose what has been called a "schematic idea" (Bultmann) about Jesus' activity. In other words, items are fitted to a schema, a **structured framework**.

7)   Watch for these characteristics reflective of **oral tradition** (described by V. Taylor), and compare to the rules above (in 3.6.a-c).

(1) Items of an **explanatory or inferential** character tend to be **added**.

(2) At the same time, accounts tend to become **shorter**.

(3) Direct speech tends to be replaced by **indirect speech**.

(4) Personal and place **names** tend to be **deleted**.

(5) The further along in transmission, the **more rounded and less detailed** the account becomes.

(6) In great measure the **substance remains the same**.

8)   Be guided by an awareness of which forms have been found to correspond to the various communities. A short guide is as follows:

(1) Palestinian Church:

a)   Apothegms (most);

b)   Sayings: Logia (most), prophetic and apocalyptic (most), law words (most), "I" sayings (few), parables (some);

c)   Miracle Stories (some: Mk. 1:40-45;

4:35-41; 6:34-44; 8:1-9);
- d) Stories about Jesus (some).
- (2) **Hellenistic Church:**
  - a) Apothegms (some; those with formulaic introductions, e.g., "When he was demanded of the Pharisees . . . .");
  - b) Sayings: logia (not likely), prophetic and apocalyptic (few), law words (some, especially Church regulations), "I" sayings (most), parables (some);
  - c) Miracle Stories (most);
  - d) Stories about Jesus (most);
- 9) Having analyzed each form according to the above guidelines, now describe in detail the probable history of the material being studied. This entails:
  - (1) Notations on differences between the record of the material as found in its various places in the Synoptics (e.g., how Luke and Matthew vary from Mark and from each other).
  - (2) Hypotheses as to why such differences would arise. What explains the alterations, additions, etc.?
  - 3) Observations about what 'laws' and/or tendencies of tradition appear to be at work.
  - (4) Observations, too, about the editorial work that might be evident.

  The goal here is as complete an analysis of the form as it exists in a given setting and its parellels in order to trace its development and return to the situation which gave it its origin and/or shape in transmission.

Step 4. **Describe, if possible, the original form.**
- 1) Recognize that in many instances this is not possible. If it is not possible for a given text, so state.
- 2) Where possible, recreate the original form by stating the text without its existing additions, alterations, etc.
- 3) Does the original form suggest a different meaning than the one it has attained in the course of tradition? If so, state it and reflect upon the significance both of the change and the recovery of the original intent.

Step 5. **Establish the setting (Sitz im Leben).**
- 1) Reason from the form to the community that

created it. Ask questions like:
(1) Why would such a form arise and become popular? Why in this setting?
(2) To what purpose(s) does such a form lend itself?
(3) What does the form tell us about the community? This may be answered, in part, by asking:
    a)   Who is speaking the form?
    b)   Who are the listeners?
    c)   What is the setting?
    d)   What effect is aimed at?

2)   Make free and generous use of the help provided above in Step 3.8. But be wary of following blindly suggestive guides as though they were firm laws.

3)   Consider the possible communities, taking into account their characteristic features and interests. (For our purposes, these communities have been divided into only two.)

(1) **Palestinian Church:**
    a)   This was the earliest community of Christian believers, Jewish in composition, with Aramaic their principal language (a fact accounting for many matters).
    b)   It was not, however, a totally homogenous community. One segment of it, at least, was influenced strongly by Oriental speculations.
    c)   The Old Testament was their Scripture and they were thoroughly Jewish in their outlook on matters pertaining to theology and ethics.
    d)   However, under the impetus of Jesus, this community reshaped its Jewish heritage. Its apocalypticism, for instance, is not identical with its Jewish background.
    e)   More importantly, its conception of the Messiah is different from that of the contemporary Judaism. The Palestinain Church was centered in a 'Son of Man' faith.
    f)   It adopted an acute eschatological perspective toward the world and people.
    g)   It assessed the Law in a new way and maintained a 'deep and

165

fundamental' cleavage with Pharisaic scribism.
h) It was poor.
i) It was within this community that the Easter accounts first circulated.
The sources Q and **Urmarcus** (the primitive source that many suppose the editor of Mark to have used) belong to this community. It is important to remember that the translation of Aramaic sayings, etc., into Greek often helps explain variants, changes in form, and the like.
(2) **Hellenistic Church:**
a) No radical discontinuity should be sought between Palestinian and Hellenistic Christianity. Both personal and doctrinal connections existed.
b) Sometimes a distinction is made between the pre-Pauline and Pauline Hellenistic Church.
c) Greek, not Aramaic, was the principal language. Hellenistic Jews and Gentiles were the constituency. Thus, this segment of the Church abandoned any sense of Jewish particularism in favor of a universalistic outlook.
d) The idea of "Messiahship" came to be replaced by that of "Lordship," a concept more readily understandable in the Hellenistic world.
e) One part of the Hellenistic community maintained a close relationship with Hellenistic piety.
f) This community deemphasized eschatology (as futuristic eschatology), and stressed a present, already accomplished salvation.
g) Accordingly, it accented the person and work of the Holy Spirit.
h) It also began to practice a wider social outlook as the Church expanded into a diverse world.
i) Of particular interest to this community were both bodily healing and spiritual enthusiasm.
j) Another critical tendency to observe is toward the veneration of the first Christian 'heroes.' Of these, Peter

166

is the most obviously important. The initiation of the Petrine tradition belongs to this community.

Matthew and Luke belong to this community. (Matthew, though, has been linked, too, with a later Palestinian-Syrian stage.) A Hellenistic editing of Q also can be placed here. Forms familiar to Hellenism mostly belong here as well: biographical apothegms, miracle stories, illustrative stories, and non-historical stories.

Step 6 **State the intention of the text.**
(Note: This is linked closely with Step 5.)
1) Remember that forms served the needs of the communities that utilized them. Thus form and intent are linked intimately.
2) Consider each of the following (as well as other ideas that may come to mind) as possible needs served by this text in its present form:
   (1) **Apologetic:** Are the practices, beliefs, or worship of the Church being defended?
   (2) **Polemical:** Is the Church engaged in debate?
   (3) **Dogmatic:** Is the Church trying to convey a theological point?
   (4) **Catechetical** (instructional): Is the Church seeking to lay down precepts for worship, practice, education, etc.?
   (5) **Paraenetic** (hortatory): Is the Church trying to bolster the hope of the community of believers? Is it offering practical advice, encouragement, or admonition?
   (6) **Proclamatory:** Is the Church presenting its witness in order to persuade others?
3) Various forms appear particularly suited to certain needs. Thus:
   (1) **Apothegms** work wonderfully as sermonic material.
   (2) **Miracle Stories** function both as popular accounts and as instructional tools.
   (3) **Stories about Jesus** afford portraits of the Lord which serve both to acquaint believers with the Master and also to explain and defend his followers' beliefs and practices.
   Be wary of making too much of such generalizations. Treat each case separately.
4) State as clearly as possible the intent of

the text. In so doing show how the form is appropriate to such an intent. If possible, explain the effect of changes in the tradition leading to this final product, and point to any earlier and/or different intents that may have existed.

Step 7 **Present conclusions.**
1) Has a form critical study mattered? Try to demonstrate the value of such work in understanding the text.
2) Briefly comment on how an understanding of the text would be changed if form critical work was neglected.
3) State the limitations of the study.
4) Suggest any reasonable alternative explanations that have not been discussed already but which have bearing on the study.
5) Indicate the main conclusions of the study.
6) Point to areas requiring further study, if any.

Conclusion

The above model owes much to the early giants of form criticism (and especially to Bultmann's **History of the Synoptic Tradition**), but a model is only as good as its utility, no matter its lineage or claims. The giants of form criticism grew to their stature only by continuous effort. We must follow their example (even where we may not follow their conclusions), not being too quick to move past them. We need to pause and walk awhile in their footsteps before moving on to the more recent refinements of methodology.

This chapter, like all of the others in Part Two, has tried to present an overview of the history and ideas of an important research methodology. Also like the other chapters, though in relatively greater detail, it has provided a specific course of action by which this scholarly methodology can be attempted. Obviously, the more one knows already about the materials being studied (e.g., a competency in Greek, or a mastery of the Synoptics), the easier the application of the method will be, and the greater the return. But even the beginning student of the biblical materials, perhaps confined to the use of a single English translation, can venture the rudimentary steps of form criticism (especially the identifying of different forms). To do so is to step into a new way of seeing the contents of Scripture and the history behind them. Step boldly, or move timidly, but take that first step!

The methodology presented in the chapter on form criticism is fairly extensive. It probably appears bewildering in its complexity. The purpose of these exercises is to test that methodology using the English Bible (the author worked through it using the RSV). The various exercises will provide initial training in:

1) Recognizing various literary forms;
2) Viewing the differences in the handling of tradition by Mark, Matthew, and Luke;
3) Attempting to analyze larger texts in terms of their component parts;
4) Recognizing the role of community concerns in the shaping of tradition; and,
5) Discerning distinct stages in the tradition.

Because the methodology presented is so detailed, focus first on learning to identify the various literary forms (Step 2 of the method). Later you can work at the other steps as well. If a form is not obviously present, then do not invent its presence. Work only to see what is really there, and have your supporting reasons ready at hand. Remember that the editorial hand of the book's writer is active, too. Watch for editorial formulations of various kinds (such as summaries, or transitional passages). Let the experience of the exercises be both profitable and enjoyable.

Before engaging in the main exercise, it might prove helpful to utilize the following "warm up" exercises:

1) Examine Mark 2:13-14 (//Matthew 9:9 and Luke 5:27, 28). This is a *biographical apothegm* to which has been attached a setting and editorial elaboration, as follows:

2:13a   Setting
 :13b   Editorial elaboration
 :14   Apothegm

Note the changes in tradition as exemplified by the parallels. How many can you specify?

2) Examine the *apothegms* in these texts:
Luke 13:1-5
Mark 2:23-28 (//Matthew 12:1-8 and Luke 6:1-5)
Mark 3:1-6 (//Matthew 12:9-14 and Luke 6:6-11)
What features make these identifiable as apothegms? What differences, if any, exist between the Markan texts and their parallels?

3) Examine the *law sayings* in these texts:
Matthew 5:17-19 (//Luke 16:17)
Matthew 23:23-24 (//Luke 11:42)
What features make these identifiable as law sayings? What are the differences, if any, between Matthew and Luke? Can the text of Q be reconstructed from these parallels? If so, how does it read? Which of the Gospel texts seems

to have preserved *Q* more accurately? What evidence
supports your contention?

4) Examine the *collection of sayings* in these texts:
Luke 6: 27-38 (//Matthew 5: 43-48)
Matthew 11: 2-19 (//Luke 7: 18-35)
What features make these identifiable as sayings collections?
The first text (luke 6) has been said to enjoy a "natural
arrangement" while the latter text (Matthew 11) has been
called an "artificial arrangement." Can you see any evidence for these designations? Focus a moment on Matthew
11:11-12. Compare it to Luke 7:28 and 16:16. What do
you observe?

The above are designed to show literary forms in various texts
of the Synoptic Gospels. By examining these passages and asking
questions like those posed, the researcher becomes familiar with different forms and their structures. Use the methodological outline to
guide the examination of the texts.

Now, take the English text of Mark. Look at chapter one. Do
the following exercise:

1) Break the text into its major parts. Outline it so that each
unit is obvious.
2) Determine the parallels in Matthew and Luke to the text
parts of Mark.
3) Identify the form of each part.
4) Examine how the parallels treat the tradition differently.
5) Look for any editorial formulations introduced into the
framework of the accounts.
6) Hazard an estimate of the community which might be represented.
7) Add any special notes about the material, its structure,
etc., that you wish to remember.

(On the following page can be found a very simple outline
written as one response to this exercise. It should not be viewed
as an answer sheet; it is quite incomplete. Instead, see it as what
it more truly is: another researcher's attempt to do a rudimentary
form analysis of the chapter as preparatory to further work.)

Mark 1:1-8 (//Matthew 3:1-12; Luke 3:2-17)
Story about Jesus
In Mark the text seems to break down as follows:
1:1   Editorial introduction
1:2-3   Conflation of Old Testament texts (Ex. 23:20a;
         Mal. 3:1; Isa. 40:3). Perhaps this reading came
         from a collection of prooftexts in use by the early
         Church. Some have thought this material did not
         originate with Mark but was added later from the
         influence of Matthew. Mark's introduction of John
         the Baptist *follows* the quotation whereas Matthew
         and Luke agree in *preceding* the quote with John's
         appearance.
1:4-8   John the Baptist in relation to Jesus. A comparison
         of Mark with the parallels reveals different hand-
         lings of the tradition. As an example of how Luke
         and Matthew treat Q differently:
         Matthew 3:11   Q + Mark
         Luke 3:16   Q
         At least 1:7-8 is probably from the Palestinian
         Church.

Mark 1:9-11 (//Matthew 3:13-17; Luke 3:21-22)
Story about Jesus
Bultmann classifies this as a *legend*, though he does not
dispute the historicity of Jesus' baptism by John. He calls
this a *faith legend*.
The story is likely Hellenistic in origin. Mark 1:9 gives
the historical basis of the tradition. Perhaps Mark 1:11 is
derived from the Palestinian tradition.
Matthew replaces Mark's "in those days" (1:9) with a
simple "then." Matthew also deletes the reference to Naz-
areth (Mk. 1:9). But see how abbreviated Luke's account
is compared to Matthew. The significance of the difference
between Mark's "and he was baptized," and Matthew's "in
order to be baptized" needs further investigation.

Mark 1:12-13 (//Matthew 4:1-11; Luke 4:1-13)
Story about Jesus
This story would have made an interesting independent
unit in early circulation. Its expansion by Matthew and by
Luke is striking. But Mark's account looks very like just
a summary. Perhaps he has taken a more elaborate tradition and simplified it. In 1:13 "tempted by Satan" may be
an editorial addition.
Matthew's account, though taken mainly from Q, is
shaped by Mark. He omits Mark's reference to wild beasts,
as does Luke. But both of them have much more material
than Mark, material detailing the temptations. However,

171

they vary the order of the temptations.

Mark 1:14-15 (//Matthew 4:12-17; Luke 4:14-15)

Prophetic and Apocalyptic saying

Mark uses these words as an editorial summarizing which he prefixes to his account of Jesus' ministry. The structure is simple enough:

1:14 Markan redaction

1:15 Saying

In Matthew the tradition has been reworked, with some importance evident in his shaping of the topographical framework (Mt. 4:12-13). Matthew 4:12-16 is an extended backdrop to the saying in verse 17. Luke substitutes indirect discourse (or, more exactly, a report) for the direct discourse of Mark and Matthew. The brevity of Luke 4:14 compared to Matthew 4:12-13 displays clearly the different interests of these Gospels. Matthew 4:12 is taken from Mark, but 4:13, 17 are editorial.

Mark 1:16-20 (//Matthew 4:18-22; Luke 5:1-11)

Double Biographical Apothegm

Mark's structure looks like:

1:16-18 Apothegm 1: the calling of Simon and Andrew

1:19-20 Apothegm 2: the calling of James and John

It is easy to see why these apothegms were joined together. The tradition comes from the Hellenistic Church.

The changes in Matthew are minor, most noticeably in the addition of Simon's identification as Peter.

But look at Luke! Suddenly the apothegm is replaced by a *miracle story*. Its structure looks like this:

5:1-5 The situation: Simon has fished all night without success.

5:6-7 The miracle, occasioned by Jesus' word (and the act of Peter, which can hardly be ignored here).

5:8-10a The response: Simon, James, and John are all astonished (note the lack of reference to Andrew and the characterization of James and John as Simon's partners).

5:10b The saying.

5:11 The response.

This story originated in the Hellenistic Church. Perhaps by examining the tradition it is possible to say that a word uttered by Jesus about becoming "fishers of men" prompted both the apothegm and miracle story. Both forms preserve the saying prominently.

Mark 1:21-28 (//Luke 4:31-37)

Miracle Story

Mark's introduction in 1:21f. sets the story in its context. The three typical aspects are present:

1) The condition and situation: a demon-possessed man in the synagogue (1:23-24).

2) The miracle, following Jesus' rebuke (1:25-26).

3) The response: "they were amazed" (1:27) and Jesus'

fame spread (1:28).

The larger context is Mark 1:16-39, or perhaps 1:21-39, where a "typical" picture of Jesus' ministry is provided. It is not merely 1:21 which shows an editorial hand; so, too, do 1:22 (which has the character of an insertion), and 1:28 (the editorial conclusion).

Noticeable by its absence is any parallel in Matthew. In Luke's account are variations of detail (e.g., the addition of "a city of Galilee" to further locate the place; the deletion of the phrase, "and not as the scribes"; elaboration of the demoniac's words; the alteration of the account of the seizure).

Mark 1:29-31 (//Matthew 8:14-15; Luke 4:38-41)
Miracle Story

Mark's introduction in 1:29a sets the story in its context. The story unfolds typically:
1) The condition: Peter's mother-in-law is sick with a fever (1:30a).
2) The miracle, accompanied by Jesus' touch (1:30b-31b).
3) The effect and response: the fever leaves her and she serves them (1:31c).

Again note the similarity between accounts. The handling of names is particularly interesting. Mark names Andrew and Simon, James and John (1:29); Matthew and Luke name only Simon (whom Matthew calls Peter). The Markan division of attention is alleviated by Matthew and Luke in a concentrated focus on Jesus alone.

The story is from the Hellenistic community.

Mark 1:32-34 (//Matthew 8:16-17; Luke 4:40-41)
Editorial formulation and linking Summary

Jesus' healing activity is summarily depicted here, linking the previous miracle story with the account of Jesus' ministry. Luke, especially, follows Mark's account, but adds dialog ("You are the Son of God!" in 4:41). Matthew adds a quote from the Old Testament (Isa. 53:4).

Mark 1:35-39 (//Luke 4:42-44)
Editorial formulation and Summary introducing the account of Jesus' ministry

This is not the easiest passage to analyze. Probably reflecting Hellenistic tradition, it might be broken down as follows:

1:35-37 or 38   Tradition material
1:37 or 38-39   Editorial addition

It is difficult to determine whether verse 38 belongs to the material that precedes it or was also added by Mark. The "I" saying enclosed (1:38) cannot likely be traced back to a primitive tradition.

Mark 1:40-45 (//Matthew 8:1-4; Luke 5:12-16)
Miracle Story

This is another healing, this time of a leper. The typical structure unfolds as follows:

1) The condition: leprosy (1:40).
2) The miracle, accompanied by Jesus' touch (1:41-42).
3) The effect: the cleansed man's response despite Jesus' "stern" admonition (1:45; 1:43-44 is characteristically strong in Mark compared with the parallels).

The structure can be also examined as follows:

1:40-42 Tradition

1:43   Markan addition (compare parallels)

1:44   Possible addition by Mark of "See that you say nothing to anyone"

1:45   Markan end formulation

Matthew begins with two phrases not found in the parallels of Mark and Luke: "when he came down from the mountain" and "great crowds followed him" (8:1). Mark lacks any special indication of setting, but Luke states, "in one of the cities" (5:12). Mark's "moved with pity" (1:41, a rare indication of feeling) drops out of both Matthew and Luke, as does the emphasis on Jesus' stern charge to be silent. Matthew omits the response to (effect of) the healing; Mark and Luke vary somewhat in their reporting of it.

As you can see, this outline was built with New Testament texts in view, and using the methodology of the chapter as a guide. Yet no effort was made to be exhaustive or to attempt in any complete fashion to accomplish all of the steps. The result is a brief outline (despite its size, it is brief).

It is not essential that your own effort look like this one. You may see much less— or more! You may agree or disagree about some details. What matters is if, and to what extent, you are able to see that different forms exist, what they are, and how they change.

Remember, this is an exercise, not a test!

12

Bible Study

Foreword

Why should Bible study be discussed at this point? The customary order would be to begin with Bible study, then go on to discuss such particulars as translation, text criticism, and the other "more sophisticated" approaches to the Bible. Two problems connected with that order has prompted the placement of Bible study at this point and not earlier. First, the specific hermeneutical conceptions and exegetical practices considered in this chapter are logically the ultimate research practices for the Church as the Bible is studied. Valuable as they are, such things as source and form criticism remain penultimate ways of studying the Bible. In and by themselves they cannot take the place of what most Christians consider good, old, basic "Bible study." In fact, rather than being visualized as afterthoughts in the study of Scripture, a kind of scholarly appendix that adds esoteric but unnecessary information, the research models already considered ought to be seen as vital operations that can precede or stand alongside biblical exegesis.

The second problem stems directly from the first. Because of faulty thinking there is shoddy practice. On the one hand, Bible study is all too often regarded as an inferior means of scholarly research. Some people are so concerned to get others to read their Bibles regularly that they establish programs of Bible study that have little to do with the Bible and nothing to do with study. A common misconception is that little should be conceived or required in Bible study. Even exegesis at the college and seminary levels is too often reduced to a process that has little, if any, resemblance to research. No wonder we disparage the widespread ignorance of the Bible! The other side of this situation is reflected in the ordinary order of treating approaches to the study of Scripture. By placing Bible study or exegesis first, and demanding little in its practice, the idea is communicated that Bible study (or exegesis) is not really a scholarly matter as such—but quite a sufficient and self-contained approach all the same. Those "other" approaches are ones for "the experts." The end result is quite predictable. No one gets around to reading about or trying out such methods as source analysis or form criticism (or any of a host of other valuable research approaches). By

175

placing Bible study after some of these other research approaches, and adding this foreword, I hope to stimulate some reflection on how all these things relate to one another. I also hope to avoid the reader who thinks it profitable to "check out" this chapter but merely "skim through" the preceding ones.

Definitions

To understand this chapter, and the relation in which it stands to what has been discussed in other chapters, it is essential to clarify some terminology. The key terms here are "hermeneutics" and "exegesis." The former is more basic and merits first consideration. **Hermeneutics** is the study of the methodological principles of interpretation. At least, that is one possible definition; it has had various definitions over the years and today may mean different things to different people. But historically, hermeneutics has been interested in the interpretation of written texts, and has focused upon setting forth the correct principles and steps of interpretation. It is in this sense that it is used here.

Exegesis is the name given to various systematic or methodical approaches to interpreting (or explaining) a written document. Broadly conceived, then, exegesis can refer to the many methods of **biblical criticism**, including those methods examined in other chapters. Exegesis often has a narrower meaning, too. It is used to designate an **inductive study** of the text as opposed to **eisegesis**, which refers to reading into a text a meaning self-imposed by the interpreter. For many people the term exegesis has actually come to be popularly opposed to the methods of biblical criticism. Where biblical criticism denotes ungodly approaches to the sacred text, exegesis is invoked as the simplest and purest literary, historical, and theological interpretation of the Bible. Although such usage is misinformed, it does point out that there is a widespread popular understanding that pits Bible study against biblical criticism.

In this chapter, exegesis retains its broad meaning but the narrow sense is the focus. In other words, exegesis is used here to designate a systematic and inductive study of the Bible. I resist the ideas that exegesis should be conceived in a complete divorce from biblical criticism, or that Bible study can be truly complete apart from bringing to bear all the methods and tools at the student's disposal. At the same time, I also resist the snobbery that suggests that Bible study is insufficient unless it immediately occupies itself with every facet of research that exists. A good research study is always a sufficient examination of something, but rarely an exhaustive examination of it. Thus, most research is incomplete without also being insufficient.

This means that it is possible, even appropriate, to discuss Bible study as exegetical in character in the narrow sense, whether it is also exegetical in the broader sense. As long as

176

the Church can maintain a consciousness that Bible study is at heart a fundamental and ongoing enterprise, one that here involves a little inductive study of the text and there a full range of biblical criticism, then false ideas that separate limited studies from more comprehensive ones, and assign value to one and damnation to the other, can be avoided. Exegesis in its narrow and in its broad senses is still exegesis.

By focusing on the narrow sense of exegesis, and laying aside the methods of biblical criticism for the moment, I wish to discuss those ideas and methodological steps that will aid in the inductive study of the Bible regardless of whether one has yet attained a competency in the biblical languages or in the forms of biblical criticism. In simpler terms, this chapter sets out "basic Bible study." While recognizing the relationship of hermeneutics to other matters, here the discussion of it is to establish certain fundamental ideas useful for inductive Bible study. By calling such inductive Bible study by the name "exegesis," I wish to remind both that Bible study is genuine research and that it cannot be exempted from the demands of research or isolated from the aid of other research endeavors.

The Interpretive Process

Broadly portrayed, the interpretive process can be said to have four distinct phases. While all four are vital to the proper understanding of the Bible, and are closely interrelated, the study of the text stands forth as the one phase most closely identified with research. This is an important preliminary point, because no one should acquire the idea that biblical research in and of itself is all that is needed in a Christian posture toward the Bible. It is just one aspect, although one integral to a holistic approach to the Bible.

The Church has acknowledged the Bible as "Canon," that is, its rule or standard. Moreover, in its place **under** the Bible, the Church is faced with decisions placed before it by the Scriptures. Part of the interpretive response to this demand is met by faithful and creative research. Bible study is truly a basic facet of a Christian stance toward the Bible. But it is not the **only** proper stance. Likewise, it cannot be excluded from such a stance, and it is **always** intertwined with the other elements of a Christian stance.

The four phases of the interpretive process are:
1) Approach the text.
2) Hear the text.
3) Study the text.
4) Apply the text.

In that the interpretive process is dependent on the **text**, it is the text that unites and intertwines the process. This means that approaching the text in practice already involves the interpreter in hearing it; hearing the text already necessitates some study of it; and, studying the text is already pointing to its application. To approach the text involves the interpreter

177

in a venture which draws it seriousness from the fact that it is God who beckons. The interpreter's response creates a situation. To approach the text involves the interpreter in presuppositions. Hearing the text involves the interpreter in translation and decision. Studying the text means participating in exegesis, in either the narrow or the broad sense described earlier. Finally, applying the text means proclaiming and practicing biblical meaning and its corresponding injunctions. The interpretive process starts with the Bible confronting the reader, continues with an unyielding demand for decisions about the text, and concludes with the reader's response.

In discussing exegesis and describing Bible study, it is unavoidable that the other facets of the interpretive process be mentioned in different connections with it. So in the material to follow, while **study** remains the focus, it will become clear how and to what extent it is related to, and affected by, the other elements of this process.

Presuppositions and Problems

At different times in different places many alternative presuppositions have been advanced for the interpretation of the Bible. In large part this has been because of problems associated with the Bible. These problems have been of theological, literary, historical, and ecclesiastical natures. Specifically, such problems have included questions about the unity of the Bible, the canonicity of certain books, whether one principle for interpretation should enjoy a preeminence, and whether all parts of the Bible should be considered binding on the thought and practices of modern Christians. So many important questions of this kind could be mentioned that a very large book would be needed to satisfactorily address them.

According to the response given to the questions asked, any number of presuppositions with regard to the Bible's nature and message, or to the proper attitude and ideology of the interpreter are possible. This situation has caused some to abandon the quest for any set of hermeneutical assumptions other than those specific ones brought by the individual interpreter. Others have sought to limit the presuppositions to ones so basic and universal that most interpreters can give assent to them. Still others have tried to produce radically new hermeneutical assumptions based on modern conceptions. It is very difficult to state with any great confidence a list of inarguable assumptions for interpretation.

Within conservative circles there is probably relatively more agreement on presuppositions and principles. Yet some ideas cherished by one group are strongly rejected by other groups. Thus, the idea that the Bible conforms to the so-called **law of noncontradiction** (an assertion of fact and its opposite cannot both be true), a notion that is set amidst a set of interdependent ideas, can be accepted as a logical extension of other assumptions by one group but rejected by another as an

178

unwarranted extra conceptual step. **Progressive revelation** is another such assumption, as is **propositional revelation.** These ideas posit a certain understanding of the nature of revelation which not all are willing to embrace. So even within conservative circles there are so many variations on whatever can be called a basic set of hermeneutical ideas that it is next to impossible to make a list that will satisfy everyone.

Taking all of these considerations together it may well seem that interpreting the Bible is a hopeless task. Without any basis for agreement, how can interpreters have any common discourse? Is the Church left with nothing more than the personal opinions of bickering scholars? In all honesty, sometimes it certainly seems that the Church is plagued by confusion and argument. But there is a positive aspect that is very important. Research, which is always a **human** endeavor, does the best with what it has. In interpreting the Bible it recognizes its own limitations but does not despair because diligent study can facilitate understanding. A multitude of understandings in genuine respectful dialog can, and often has, served the Church well.

Moreover, there are a few presuppositions that today are universally accepted. These are:

1) The Bible **can** be understood, however partially and imperfectly.
2) The Bible is comprised of literary documents that can be studied as such.
3) The Bible assists in its own interpretation (**Scriptura sui ipsius interpres:** "Scripture interprets itself").

The first of these assumptions must be granted if study of the Bible is to have any validity or meaning. The second stems from a recognition that if it is nothing else the Bible is at least literary. The third assumption takes into account the composite character of the Bible, and the interaction of its constituent witnesses. These three assumptions are fundamental to interpretive research of the Scriptures.

But where are any theological assumptions? Does not the proper explanation of the Scriptures require other presuppositions in addition to those just given? The answer to these questions rests in what is conceived as a **proper** interpretation. It can hardly be denied that anyone can study the Bible. But the Church has rather steadfastly denied that anyone can properly understand the Bible without certain things being true. Some of the most common theological presuppositions are:

1) The Bible is the Word of God (or, more exactly, the third form of the Word of God, together with Jesus Christ and proclamation).
2) As God's Word to man it presents Jesus Christ as the central message.
3) To properly receive this message and properly respond to it requires the assistance of God's

Holy Spirit and the existence of faith.

Biblical interpretation rests on the fundamental conviction that in these documents God himself addresses mankind. The person of Christ, and all that is represented by him, gains a preeminence in the explanation of the Bible. God himself assists the interpreter, who must exercise faith alongside reason to gain the full meaning. Thus the proper study of the Bible means research guided and completed by the Holy Spirit.

Perhaps it might seem nice to wish that Bible study could proceed without presuppositions. But that is impossible by the very nature of human beings. So it is better by far to recognize what our assumptions are. Where we find them to be undesirable and unnecessary, they should be consciously set aside as far as possible. Fundamental and desirable presuppositions should be examined and embraced. From them will stem certain attitudes and practices beneficial to Bible study. Then, as the research of other students of the Bible is reviewed, care should be given to identifying their guiding assumptions. How are they the same, or different? Recognizing these assumptions, respecting them as far as they can be respected, and establishing a dialog with their proponents can lead to increased insights and fruitful communion within the Church. There are no compelling reasons for Christians to ignore each other as they are engaged in the same great labor of seeking to understand God's Word.

Principles of Interpretation

The presuppositions and principles of interpretation are so closely associated that they are often discussed virtually interchangeably. The distinction between them is this: presuppositions are those fundamental ideas undergirding the conception of a process; principles are those basic ideas comprising the process itself, though without definite methodological shape. Presuppositions, then, are more basic than principles, which are more basic than methodology.

The extent and nature of interpretive principles are always influenced by the interpreter's assumptions. An interpreter who assumes the unity of the Bible's message is much more likely to state that the text should be understood in light of the whole Bible than is one who doubts this unity. This again means some caution in advancing any general set of principles. Still, some are reasonably fundamental and enjoy widespread acceptance. Among them are:

1) The **literal** sense (or **ordinary** sense) of a text is the one an interpreter should first uncover.

2) The **intended** sense of the writer of the text is the meaning the interpreter is chiefly concerned with.

3) The **literary** elements of the text must be treated by literary tools.

4) The **historical** elements of the text must be

180

treated by historical tools.

5) The **theological** elements of the text must be treated in their literary and historical settings as well as dogmatically.

These principles are not difficult to envision as assumptions. Yet they are properly principles because they suggest a process of working with the text so as to explain it. These five principles are as broadly stated as possible. The specific sub-principles and all of the attendant tools are not named by them. This is because the choice of such sub-principles and tools can vary so widely. Some very particular notions are developed by each of the two methodological models of Bible study which follow.

Models of Bible Study

It is no exaggeration to say that **the** exegetical method does not exist. This should not be surprising; **the** research method does not exist either. All of the methods examined in this book are practiced relatively differently by different people. They are identifiable as particular methods only because basic features retain their identity in broad prospectus. Some methods are more exact and closely defined than others, but all methods have certain essential and characteristic features as well as a degree of flexibility.

In exegesis the principal features are these:
1) The method is **inductive**.
2) The method is **critical**.
3) The method is **systematic**.
4) The method is **purposeful**.

Many possible Bible study methods exist which contain these broad features. Some are quite simple in design and scope. Others are quite complex and far-reaching. But they all can adhere to these features. To be **inductive** they must start with the text and draw out from the text its distinctive features and meaning. To be **critical** these models must engage in judicious evaluation and decisions. To be **systematic** they must entail a plan which is followed carefully, with exactitude and logic. Finally, and most importantly, they must be **purposeful**, which means that the interpreter has clearly in mind what exegesis is all about and has determined to accomplish that end. Since the purpose of exegesis is to explain the text, the feature of purposefulness is also that of working always toward the end of understanding what the text means.

Two different exegetical models follow. Both share the features just described. Additionally, they share certain particulars common to many, if not most kinds of exegesis. Yet the first model is very simple while the second is much more demanding and involved. While both are relatively easy to outline and describe, the practice of either can tax the student of the Bible. A method, remember, is what is made of it. The best tools in the world are only as good as the one who wields them.

Model 1: Basic Questions

This model derives its name from the heart of its organization. The six common questions: who? what? where? when? why? and how? provide the structure, or system, of this approach. The method can be set out in four steps which place it squarely in the interpretive process:

1) Select a text. Review the presuppositions behind your approach to this text.
2) Read the text and "hear" the Word of God.
3) **Seek to understand the text as the author intended by asking questions.**
4) After determining the meaning, apply it and proclaim it.

It is with step three that the model assumes its own distinctive form. This step is the exegetical step. In this model it incorporates the six basic questions, and it can do so in two slightly different formats according to the needs or interests of the interpreter. In one format the questions can be divided into three areas as follows:

Historical work: Who? When? Where? Why? What?

    1) Who wrote the text? (Author or source.)
    2) When was it written? (Date.)
    3) To whom was it written? (Audience.)
    4) What was the audience's life-situation? (**Sitz im leben.**)
    5) Where is the action situated? (Place and/or geography.)
    6) Who are the main and the lesser characters? (Actors.)
    7) When is the action taking place? (Time and/or chronology.)
    8) What is happening? (Action.)
    9) Why was the text written? (Purpose.)

There are other questions of this nature that might be asked according to the nature of the text and the imagination of the interpreter. These questions, because they are put to documents, are also of a somewhat literary nature; i.e., they cannot assume historicity in every text but must take literary features into account. Yet in their very nature these questions are interested in historical matters.

Literary work: What? How? Why?

    1) What is said? (Content.) Some subpoints that might help:
       (1) Paraphrase the message; put it into a shortened summary, but without personal opinions. Simply try to say what the text says, but in a personal way, that

is, using your own words.

(2) Determine the theme and main points of the message. Try to see the forest without getting lost in the trees. Too often it is easy to get caught up so much in interesting particulars that the main point is lost. Find it as early as possible.

2) How is it said? (Structure.) Some more sub-points:

(1) Outline the text. This can help gain a sense of perspective that permits seeing relationships and direction. Avoid making the outline too detailed, at least at first. It is best to create several outlines, becoming more exact and detailed with successive ones. This approach avoids errors and helps a progressive growth in understanding the text.

(2) Identify the literary genre. Is the text poetry or prose? Is it a narrative? What kind of story is it if it is a story? Initially, all Bible students are limited in what they are able to see. But with practice and training an increased ability to discriminate between kinds of literature can be gained.

(3) Look for the writer's style. This kind of exercise will not only aid in the development of literary sense but may be employed in many different aspects of scholarly study, like determining the authenticity of certain letters attributed to Paul, or identifying different literary sources, or helping to uncover the unknown writer of a text.

3) Why was the text written in this particular fashion? (Motive.) If the last book of the Bible was written in apocalyptic form, there must have been a reason. But this is true for all texts and their forms. Sometimes the reason is unknown or not too important. Other times it is a critical factor. Two complementary questions to be asked are:

(1) How does the literary form affect the meaning?

(2) How does it change the way it might be heard, received, passed down, and interpreted, especially in contrast to other literary forms?

The questions concerned with literary features

can as easily be asked before those concerned with history as after. Within this section itself, the question of structure can be treated before that of content. There is a flexibility to the model that makes it adaptable to many research studies of the Bible.

Theological work: What? Why?
1) What did this text mean to the people to whom it was addressed?
2) What has it meant to its later readers?
3) What does it mean to us?

This triad of questions involves historical and literary work but builds upon them while also focusing them. Here the intent is to ask what is the meaning of the text and how has its interpretation proceeded through time. The aim behind this intent is a theological one: what is God trying to communicate here?

A related set of questions ask:
1) Why is this text important?
2) Why should I, or anyone else, listen to, and obey, this text?

Here the theological concern is with the relevancy of the meaning of the text for today. These kinds of questions engage the interpreter in dogmatics, where the concern is to address a modern audience in a faithful but relevant manner. All persons have a right to ask such questions and to receive reasonable responses.

The benefit of this format is in allowing a clear focus on the different kinds of work involved in Bible study. Each area is considered separately, though all remain interrelated. The basic questions are put to use in each area and help guide the study. The disadvantages of this model are that the relationship between the various areas might be forgotten because of the scheme, and the limitations of the system might be neglected. The principal limitation of this model lies in its inability to make plain how a given text stands in relation to its larger context, or to other texts. In other words, it is best at focusing close scrutiny on one text at a time. The second format provides for a wider focus. It can be used to study a book, a chapter, or a smaller portion of text, and to see it in relation to other relevant material. It can be outlined as follows:

Book context: Who? When? Where? Why? How?
What? Questions of an introductory character include those of a literary, historical, and theological interest. These include:
1) Who wrote (or edited) the document? (Authorship)
2) To whom was it written, and what was their situation? (Audience and Sitz im Leben)

3) When was the document written? (**Date**)
4) Why was the document written? (**Purpose**)
5) How was the document written? (**Literary structure, etc.**)
6) What is the document's message and meaning? (**Content and meaning**)

It is immediately obvious that both formats ask these questions but the organization that provides when they are asked, and in what connection, can vary. Here the questions are addressed to an entire book.

Chapter, paragraph, or other shorter division: Who? When? Where? Why? What? How?

Assuming now that the study is focusing on a short section but wishes to retain connection* to the broader context, all of the questions asked about the document as a whole can be rephrased and asked about the specific text. Then the two sets of answers can be compared. First, the questions:

1) Who is responsible for this text? (Is it the work of the author/editor, or does it come from an older source?)
2) With whom is this text principally interested? (Is a part of the document's whole audience singled out? If so, who are those particularly addressed by this text?)
3) When was this text written? (Should it be assumed that this portion came into existence when the document as a whole did? Might it be earlier in origin? Could it have been added after the document was first written, like Mark 16:9-20 probably was?)
4) Why was this text included? (What particular purpose is disclosed by this text? Does it show some need in the audience, or a special interest by the author?)
5) How is this text written? (Is it different in structure or form from what might be expected by the character of the rest of the book?)
6) What does the text mean? (Does it agree with the meaning of the whole document?)

The observation bears repeating: both formats ask basic questions but in differing connections. They produce different kinds of exegetical studies and can actually be considered two models in some respects. They can also be joined and modified. Thus, the second format could easily retain its present form and then add the first format with its narrow focus. The questions, too, can be mixed and varied. Questions tend to be only as valuable as the insights they produce. The more creative and acute the questioner the more information questions

185

are likely to produce. Of course, implicit in this idea is that the questions will be appropriate. Their appropriateness comes from their being prompted by close attention to the text. Because exegesis is inductive, the questions should be suggested by the text itself. Then they are normal questions to ask, or natural ones, not artificial or superficial.

The Basic Questions Model simply capitalizes on a feature prominent in any research: interrogation. A scholar studies something because of a need or desire to know. To elicit information from it, a researcher puts questions to it. This approach can be profitably applied to Bible study. But remember: once the questions have been asked and suitable answers accumulated, they must be applied in proclamation and practice. Study that leads only to information is incomplete.

Model 2: Canonical-Historical

There exists an approach to the study of the Bible known as **canonical criticism**. It is a method formulated and defended by Brevard Childs and others. It would not have been inappropriate to discuss this method in a separate chapter. But it is alluded to here because it lends itself admirably to a Bible study design that is as simple as it is rigorous. Without detailing all of the ideology behind the approach, or attempting to encompass all its possible points, its essential concerns are given here in a model for a comprehensive Bible study which anyone can undertake.

First, let us locate it in the context of the interpretive process:

1) Select a text. Review the presuppositions behind your approach to this text.
2) Read the text and "hear" the Word of God.
3) **Seek to understand the text in its canonical context and in its history.**
4) After determining the meaning, apply it and proclaim it.

This outline should be compared with that given for the place of the Basic Questions Model in the interpretive process. It will be seen that the Canonical-Historical Model also wants to understand the text but in much more sweeping terms than is possible by the other model. Five specific stages are entailed in this model's system:

1) Determine the intra-Testamental contexts.
2) Review the inter-Testamental relationships.
3) Perceive the canonical conversation.
4) Trace the history of interpretation.
5) Focus on relevant theological reflections.

These five stages vary a bit according to whether the text selected comes from the Old Testament or the New Testament. This is because the relationship between the two is looked at differently depending on the direction from which the interpreter comes. In moving from an Old Testament text to a

New Testament treatment the interpreter is interested in seeing how or if the text in question was quoted, interpreted, or applied in the New Testament. If the starting point is in the New Testament, it is likely the interpreter will look back for any "shadows" or "prefigurings" or "origins" relevant to the New Testament text.

The differences may be more apparent by seeing the model in outline form:

The Intra-Testamental Contexts:

1) For either an Old Testament or New Testament text the same contextual circles must be identified:

   (1) The Broad context: this is generally the document in which a text is located. In identifying this context it is helpful to provide a brief **survey** of the book including:

      a) Introductory concerns (authorship, audience, date, purpose;

      b) Literary characteristics (genre, style, principal actors, principal actions, themes, etc.);

      c) A broad outline of the contents.

It is important to remember to keep this short. Include only the significant material. Try to start as general as possible but lead quickly to the next context.

   (2) The Narrow context: this is the relevant material immediately surrounding the text which is the focus of the study. It receives a similar treatment to that given the Broad context. Again a survey is used, including:

      a) A brief outline of the material;

      b) A specification of the kind of literature and its most important characteristics;

      c) A statement of its dominant ideas or theme;

      d) A summary of its principal actors and actions.

This, too, should be kept short. It is a transitional portion between the Broad context and the most focused context.

   (3) The Specific context: this is what the study wishes to focus upon. It is, in fact, the text itself. This text should not be too large. It can be as small as a single thought, or better, a unit like a paragraph.

The study of the text here can incorporate the first format of the Basic Questions Model. The aim is to get at the meaning intended by the writer and to understand it as a contemporary of the text would have.

Among the many things that can help in this exegetical focus are the following:

a) Notice common literary devices like comparisons, contrasts, repetitions, and quotations; ask why they are used, and what purpose they serve.

b) Consider common conceptual devices like questions to focus attention, logical relationships, and generalizations; ask why they are used and what they do in shaping the meaning.

c) Particularly watch to see if any direction in the text is evident. Is the material just a list, or a calculated story or argument? Where is it headed and why?

d) Check words that seem particularly important. Use a reference tool (e.g., Bible dictionary, word study volume, lexicon, or concordance) to find their meaning and use. It might be valuable to check some cross-references too, but be wary of overindulging in this.

e) Consult other translations, or if working with the original, compare your translation with others. This can help avoid errors like placing too much emphasis on a term that has been mistranslated or carries a shade of meaning different than you thought.

f) Use appropriate tools like commentaries, articles, and specialized studies to learn more about the historical setting.

In short, use whatever is available that might help in getting at the meaning. However, one caution should be added: never let someone else do your thinking or your research for you. First get out of a text all that you can on your own. Then use tools to help you grow in your abilities as well as your understanding of the text. This means not accepting unquestioningly all that you hear or read, but examining it as research to be evaluated and decided upon. Questioning the experts means healthy progress toward becoming one in your own right.

It is important to remember not to waste words (or time and effort). Be selective, reporting the most pertinent observations. Have the courage to face obscurity and difficulties in the text and to be honest about them. A good Bible

study is honest with the text.
2) The contexts identified and analyzed, the study should turn to any treatment of the text (or its ideas) found within the rest of that Testament. Specific treatment of the text by way of direct quotation is unlikely, but allusions may exist or the same ideas interacted with elsewhere. This material should be handled briefly along the lines suggested for the Narrow context.

The Inter-Testamental Relationships

1) This varies according to whether the specific text under study is found in the Old Testament or the New Testament. If the specific text is from the Old Testament, the New Testament relationship might be seen in:

(1) Direct uses of the Old Testament text. Is it quoted? Is it quoted accurately? How is it used?

(2) Indirect uses of the Old Testament text. What indicates this text is in view? Are there allusions? How is it used?

(3) Christological considerations. Does the New Testament give to this text a specific christological interpretation? If so, why?

It should be obvious that the concern is to see how the first Christians viewed the Old Testament. What were their favorite texts? Why were some so important? How were they used?

If a given Old Testament text is not mentioned in the New Testament, its ideas might be. Then the different treatments of the same ideas can be compared. If no relationship at all is apparent, do not create one! Simply remark on the fact with a brief comment and move on.

If the specific text is from the New Testament the work becomes a bit more difficult (unless, of course, the New Testament text is a quote from the Old Testament). But the relationship might be seen in:

(1) The meaning of the Old Testament passage from which a quote is taken or an idea has its origin. Even though a New Testament text may not quote from the Old Testament, it might owe its idea or form or terminology to something its writer found there.

(2) The Old Testament historical background, broader than any specific Old Testament text, might be what is in view by a New Testament text. How has this history influenced the New Testament passage?

189

It is all too easy to read too much into the
other testament as we look for relationships
between them. But the goal here is to carefully
and inductively examine the actual use a New
Testament text makes of the Old Testament or
the background of the Old Testament appropriate
to understanding fully a New Testament passage.
2) In considering the relationship between the Testaments in this stage it is important to remember
that it is only being examined uni-directionally.
That means that either it is being viewed from
the Old Testament forward to the New, or
backward from the New Testament to the Old.
The conversation at this point is really more a
monologue.

The Canonical Conversation
1) Having examined the text within its Testament
and in light of the other Testament, it must now
be viewed in its place in the entire canon. This
means that the use of the text, but more
importantly its ideas and message, must:
(1) Be viewed in their Old Testament
development and articulation as used by the
New Testament, and;
(2) Be viewed in their New Testament development and articulation as used in the Old
Testament.
This is differentiated from the second stage
by the concern to interrelate the Testaments and
see the movement back and forth between them
(and not just uni-directionally).
2) This finds concrete expression ultimately in a
summary statement issued by the interpreter in
answer to the query: What does the whole canon
say about the meaning found in this text?
While this stage may not be easy at first to
grasp, it is worth the effort to understand it.
Try to remember that the aim is to recognize the
canon as the ultimate context for any text.
Therefore, the meaning of the text stands within
the meaning given by the whole canon in regard
to the specific ideas of that text.

The History of Interpretation
1) Trace the history of the interpretation of this
text in Judaism, both ancient and modern.
Several reference aids can help in this (like
Encyclopedia Judaica). Especially worth
consulting, if it is possible to gain access to it,
is the Talmud. Careful searching will almost
certainly turn up commentaries by Jewish
scholars on Old Testament books (and sometimes

on New Testament concerns, too).

2) Trace the history of the interpretation of this text in **Catholicism**, both ancient and modern. As with Judaism, there are sets of encyclopedias and commentaries that can provide this information. The Church Fathers, the scholars of the Middle Ages and of the Reformation, all are worth looking at. Generally, it will be Roman Catholicism that is meant here, but those who have access to the writings of the Eastern Ortho-dox Church will profit immensely from exposure to that perspective.

3) Trace the history of the interpretation of this text in **Protestantism**, both old and modern. Both Luther and Calvin write extensively about the Bible, often offering many comments on the same passage in different works. Other reform-ers and scholars since also have contributed a wealth of material about virtually every text of the Bible.

In tracing the history of interpretation it is not necessary to spend a lifetime and write a library. The idea is to keep being exposed to the research tradition and its diversity, and most importantly, grow in an understanding of the text. The often striking way in which interpretation of a text has changed in different times and places offers great instruction.

Theological Reflection

After all the prior labor is concluded the interpreter must ask again, "What does the text mean?" But in this asking, the interpreter now consciously addresses the text personally, feeling its weight and its demand. The question becomes, "What does the text mean for me, for my Church, and for my world?" This means real wrestling and dogmatic reflection, not idle speculation. This step does not seek to reduce interpretation to subjectiv-ity, but to involve the interpreter and the inter-preter's own audience in a meaningful and decisive manner.

The Canonical-Historical Model, it is readily seen, is much more involved than the Basic Questions Model. Its rewards are proportionately greater, however. It may seem that to accom-plish this model a book of some size would have to be written each time it is used. But it is entirely possible to do such a study and report it in a 10-15 page paper. Remember that the emphasis belongs on the particular text. A reasonable distri-bution of space might be as follows:

Analyzing the contexts: 3-4 pages
Reviewing inter-testamental relationships: 1-2 pages
Summarizing the canonical dialog: 1-2 pages
Tracing the history of interpretation: 2-3 pages
Theological reflections: 3-4 pages
This yields a lower limit of 10 pages and an upper one of 15, with at least half the paper directly involved with the biblical material. Naturally, there is often good reason for giving more attention to one or another of the parts or the whole. But the point is this: even such a model as this one can be managed by anyone who tries. Patience and diligence are their own reward, but the results produced by them are nice, too!

Conclusion

The study of the Bible, though variously conceived and conducted, is not outside the reach of anyone. Any person can study the Bible in a responsible fashion, regardless of inexperience, lack of resources, or advanced training. After all, every person has to start at the beginning before advancing through enough steps to become an "expert." God has given the Bible to us and we can, and should, study it. We should do so with diligence and with faith.

As advancement is made in the study of the Bible, exegesis will almost inevitably progress from its narrow sense to its broad sense. More and more methods and tools will be sought, tried, and mastered. All this is to the good of the researcher and the Church. Yet the scholar remains one who still receives the Scriptures as a gift of grace, a Word given to benefit all people. While study always is involved in the Christian scholar's stance toward the Bible, so too is gratitude and joy. When these things are brought together, the interpretation of the Bible brings life and hope, meaning and promise.

Each of the models suggested in this chapter should be tried. Use the first format of the Basic Questions Model to focus on a very specific text, such as a paragraph in the Bible. Then try the second format of that model, using a broader context, such as the chapter in which the paragraph you used is found.

Exercise 1. Take Mk. 1:1-8 for study using format one of the Basic Questions Model. Do the historical work first, then the literary work, and finally the theological work.

Ask each question in order. If the text does not provide an answer, do not invent one. Let the text guide the study. Some texts will provide more information of an historical nature than will others. Thus, the historical work may take very little time in one study, but much time in another. In Mk. 1:1-8, some of the questions asked under the section on historical work plainly are unanswerable. But answer those which can be answered. The literary questions inevitably will require more space. Take the time to do an adequate job of paraphrasing and outlining. Be exact as possible about the kind of literature. In Mk. 1:2-3 is a quote. Track it down and find how close it fits to what is written in Isaiah. Ask, "Does Mark use more than Isaiah as a source here?"

Exercise 2. Use Mark chapter one as the text for the second format of the Basic Questions Model. Remember, though, that this format starts with a brief overview of the entire book.

Because the focus of the study is Mark 1, not the entire Gospel, use whatever aids you can to move relatively quickly through the questions concerning the book context. A good study Bible will suggest answers, as might a commentary or New Testament introduction. Check several different books on the issues involved. Do not neglect to use your own familiarity with Mark to answer the questions of the model. Although you are not spending a lot of time on this part, and are using aids, the answers to the questions are still *your* responsibility, and they should reflect your best effort under the constraints of time and ability.

Spend an hour in Mark 1. Wrestle with the questions, and use the tools you have acquired for scholarly study (such as source criticism). When you have finished, write a three page report including your answers and the reasons behind them.

Having worked through both formats of the Basic Questions Model, turn your attention to the Canonical-Historical Model. As noted in the chapter, this model derives its inspiration from the ideas of Brevard Childs. It would be profitable to take time to examine his book *Biblical Theology in Crisis* (Phila.: Westminster, 1970). Especially observe the model in chapter 9, "Psalm 8 in the Context of the Christian Canon" (pp. 151-163), in order to see the similarities and differences between his work and the model proposed here.

Exercise 3. Do a study using the Canonical-Historical approach with Jeremiah 31:31-34 as your text. Be sure to follow the order, deleting no steps. Use whatever tools are necessary to accomplish your task, but remember the aim is to make *you* the competent student of the text. Try not to rely overmuch on the aid provided by others.

When you reach the specific context part of the study, set aside all tools. Do this with only your own mind and skills. After you have done the very best that you can, then turn back to your resources. See to what degree you have grown in experience and skill, and test your findings against those of other researchers.

Give yourself plenty of time to do an adequate job. The study will almost certainly lead you to the library, especially as you pursue the history of the interpretation of the text. Your research may require four to six hours of examination, reflection, and consultation of resources. The time will be well spent, so do not begrudge it. Afterwards, write your report following the suggested guidlines for space allocation offered in the chapter.

Exercise 4. Once again using the Canonical-Historical Model, study Heb. 5:5-10. Keep in mind what was said above. Remember that the goal of this model is comprehensive. It aims at seeing what the entire canon has to say with regard to the message of the specific text you are studying. It helps prepare us to truthfully claim, "The Bible says . . ." about what we are studying.

13

Historical Research

Definition and Value

Historical research is a broad designation, encompassing many ideas and techniques. In general, it may be thought of as the investigation of past events. Compared to such research models as those provided by source or form criticism, historical research is very wide in its breadth of concerns and relatively more versatile in its methods. To express this somewhat differently, it is possible to conceive many research models as tools serving the particular ends of historical study. Thus, while form criticism is primarily a kind of literary research, it provides material of vital interest to historians and can be used by them. So, unlike some other methods or models, historical research cannot be easily narrowed down to one set of precepts (and it may be asked fairly if any other method really can either).

Historical research has been around as long or longer than any other kind of research. It has seen a multitude of conceptions as to its proper course. Different approaches to historical study have fallen in and out of favor. Even today the manner in which such study is undertaken is subject to widely different interpretations. This means, then, that the discussion offered in this chapter, and the model set forth by it, ought not to be casually accepted as the way of doing historical research. But it is a way to conceive and carry out the task.

Despite the debates historical study engenders, no one seriously takes the position that such research should not take place. It has been universally recognized that historical study is an essential component to the gaining and passing on of knowledge. The values perceived in historical research are as important as they are numerous. First, the study of the history of any field of human endeavor or knowledge is the primary and fundamental step in acquiring competency in that field. But this rather formal educational function barely strikes the surface of the general educational function history provides. Virtually every person has a strong interest in the past of someone or something. The idea that knowledge of this past is both interesting and beneficial spurs on investigation, whether systematic or haphazard.

Second, a knowledge of the past preserves it. Every human being wants to be remembered. Whether an individual's share in history is little or great, the preservation of that share by someone is cherished by each of us.

Third, the study of the past helps ensure continuity and progress. Whether or not there is any kind of inevitable evolution or progress has been, and still is, vigorously disputed. But widespread attention to the past certainly does make progress possible. Each generation does not have to reinvent the wheel. Additionally, the continuity of the present with the past encourages those of the present to believe they can make meaningful contact with those of the past.

Fourth, historical study promises the ability, ultimately, to present us not just with information, but with understanding as well. In fact, it has often been an aim of such study to go beyond even mere understanding and also acquire the "wisdom of the ancients." Modern man can hardly afford the presumption of superiority over previous generations in the getting and dispensing of wisdom.

Finally, but by no means least valuable, historical research can yield a genuine sense of consolation and hope. Modern man is all too often and too easily tempted to despair. When the world and the society in which we dwell is examined, it seems preposterous to take an optimistic stance. Evil everywhere appears in triumph. Yet, while the study of history shows how common the lot of man has been across the ages, while it displays no less starkly the victories of evil, it also reveals that evil has never in any place or time proven to be the final word. "This too shall pass." A certain sense of equableness, without apathy or depression, can adhere over time to the one who dwells in the midst of history. Particularly for the Christian, whose hope has been birthed by the Gospel, the study of history provides a continuing supply of nourishment for hope and consolation.

Difficulties

Such a glowing tribute to the study of history should be quite inspiring. Unfortunately, mere inspiration is unlikely to carry one very far. The study of the past is hindered by many difficulties. In fact, the appearance of so many different ways to research the past is in part a natural response to the existence of many problems. Some of these problems are more basic than others, but at the very least they can all prove to be annoying nuisances.

Many of the problems can be grouped, thus producing a list of eight general kinds of problems. Four of these are relatively more general, the others relatively more methodological. All eight, however, contain aspects that are problems on two ends: they perplex present historians, and they are tied concretely to decisions and acts shrouded by the past. Here is the first half of the list:

196

1) **The objective meaning of history:** is there any?
2) **The perceived pattern of history:** what is that conceived by the historian? What was conceived by the past being studied?
3) **Personal perspective:** what was the personal involvement in the history set down by the historian of the past, and what involvement does the historian of the present have in it?
4) **Theological concerns:** is there a separate "holy" (or "redemptive") history? If so, what relation does it have to the rest of history?

This list may raise the question why there must be problems on two ends, for the past and the present historian. After all, is not the study of history the simple uncovering of the past? In answer, two matters come quickly to mind. First, the delicate effort of uncovering the past is not simple. Second, the meaningful uncovering of the past means not only understanding the past as it understood itself, but also interacting with that understanding in light of our present understanding and perspective. A modern historian cannot escape his or her own viewpoint, and should not try. Instead, like any good researcher, this viewpoint is disciplined and harnassed for the stage in the study to which it belongs.

Accordingly, it is vitally important to recognize and own up to the conceptions of the present. The ideas of the past about the nature and meaning of history matter, and so do ours. What we perceive about the pattern of history (e.g., cyclical, linear) is important, just as is the understanding of the past. Historical research is maximized by a disciplined and fruitful interchange between present and past, not by the stamping of one upon the other. Thus, we are twentieth century people, not first or sixteenth century people; we can no more permit their perspectives to govern us than we can expect to project our own views and still understand them on their own terms.

Now let us examine the other half of the list:
5) **Authenticity:** are the historical records genuine?
6) **Credibility:** are the historical witnesses believable?
7) **Relationships:** what relationships do these records and witnesses have to one another?
8) **Judgment:** how shall information be selected, arranged, emphasized, interpreted, and used for prediction?

One researching the past must sit in a position where he has to make decisions about the historians and records of the past. Of course, the historians of the time being studied, the ones who made the records (whether for purposefully historical reasons or not), also had to make decisions. In all this decision making some confusion, controversy, and misunderstanding are inescapable.

All eight problems are very real ones. While they are

197

only acknowledged here, in the material on analysis and methodology which is to follow they are addressed along definite lines. What is necessary at this point is merely some honesty. Historical research, it must be confessed, can be as hard and irritating as it is educational and exhilarating. Problems of a two-sided nature abound and often actually seem to proliferate as the study progresses. But careful research can yield satisfactory ways of handling these problems and producing helpful studies of the past.

The Science and Art of Historical Research

By now it should be easy to see that historical research by the nature of its task and problems is as much art as it is science. This situation should not be disparaged. No one has ever conclusively demonstrated that only knowledge gained by science is credible! All research, because it is a human endeavor, has an artistic element. Science itself incorporates "art," and art incorporates "science."

Sometimes a distinction is made between these two elements of historical research as follows. The methodological analysis of the past is conducted along scientific lines. But the interpretation and report of that analysis is conducted along artistic lines. So **scientific analysis** means a systematic investigation of the past, following a structured methodology, and striving for the possibility of replication by other historians using the same materials and method. The **art of historiography** means an openness and flexibility of approach, a degree of creativity in treatment, and a writing of history that has both flavor and fact.

The distinction between art and science may be more real than the distance between them. In actual practice, science and art are skillfully blended. Good history is interesting fact interestingly interpreted and reported. Both science and art have to be brought to bear on historical difficulties. Both can contribute to the satisfactory resolution of these difficulties.

Presuppositions

It is time to begin stating how historical research can be done. The first step is the enumeration of certain assumptions that undergird historical study:

1) Historical study is **possible.**
2) Historical study can be **valid.**
3) Historical study can be **reliable.**
4) Historical study can attain access to **facts.**
5) Historical study can detect **relationships.**
6) Historical study can uncover **meaning.**
7) Historical study can (and should) render **judgments.**

Undoubtedly, other assumptions might be set forth. But the above are certainly basic. In fact, the first may seem so basic it hardly bears mention. But it needs to be looked at carefully for a moment. Such an assumption should raise the question, "**Why** is it possible?" The more immediate answers are focused in the existence of materials from the past. These answers build themselves logically, as follows. First, historical study is possible because past events have been recorded. Second, these recorded events have been preserved, at least in part. Third, the records have meaning. Finally, fourth, the meaning of these records can, at least in part, be determined.

A more remote answer to the question raised by the first presupposition is provided by the support substantiating the second assumption. Historical study is possible because such research can be valid, that is, it can see what is really there. Historical study would not be possible if we had records but could not gain valid insights and information from them. In a like manner, the qualities named in the other presuppositions all indirectly state why historical research is possible: it is possible because it can be reliable, unearthing facts and meaning, finding relationships, and speaking intelligibly to our own time.

The **validity** of historical research stems from two preeminent considerations. First, human nature is relatively constant. No one should undersell the real differences that do exist between times and cultures. But whatever it is that makes people **people** has persisted. Second, the human experiences of the past have their parallels in the human experiences of the present. Human senses have remained constant though the interpretations of what those senses have perceived vary. It is this idea of the **analogy of experience** which is basic to believing that modern people can understand historical records. Without such a presupposition it would be difficult to see how such research could be valid.

Historical study can also be **reliable**, meaning that what one historian sees, others can see, too. But this is true only and whenever certain conditions are operating. Where a multiplicity of witnesses to an event exist the researcher has greater confidence that the event took place and, when the accounts agree substantially, their reliability increases. Likewise, where a number of historians find themselves in agreement about the history of an event or subject, there is a feeling that their understanding is more reliable than if only one or two scholars come to that conclusion. Of course, sheer numbers does not guarantee truth, but where sound methods yield comparable results, those results are reliable. When events can be verified by independent, non-historical means (e.g., by extrapolation of scientific data to verify an extraterrestrial phenomenon seen in the past), then this corroboration increases reliability. The reliability of records themselves vary, as any historian can attest. Some ancient records were carelessly put together, others gave great attention to accuracy and detail. Obviously the latter is more valuable than the former. It is reliable in being a dependable record and also in being subject to verifiability. Researchers prefer materials that can be tested; as they yield the same results each time, as they enjoy outside confirmation, they grow in the researcher's esteem and are credited as very reliable.

Facts, relationships, and **meanings** are all aimed at by historical study and it must be assumed they can be attained or such study is quite fruitless. What might be called a "sense of fact" is indispensable to success in research of any kind. Not every thing that purports to be a fact, or first appears to be a fact, finally proves out as such. Yet facts can be found, and the relationships among them determined. These relationships between facts, between records, and between historical witnesses, can be described and analyzed. They often serve as the basis for inferences and predictions. Since facts about a given event tend to cluster, as one would expect, their relation to one another may point to the existence of further, but initially unknown facts. Thus knowing certain things allows a researcher to infer other things. The presence of some thing may lead to predict the presence of another thing. In all this activity, meaning is the end result at which the historian aims. This meaning is first of all that intended by the record. Historians want to understand past events as the contemporaries of those events (or ideas, or people) did. But they also want to uncover meaning for their own time. All history is, finally, **applied** history. Put in another fashion, history is a dialog meant to enrich our understanding of both past and present.

To accomplish meaning in this sense, the historian must be able to render **judgments.** Historical study assumes not just the possibility for doing such, but the actual obligation to do such. Naturally, there are judgments, and there are judgments. Some are decisions of a methodological nature: what evidence to select, how to arrange it, what to emphasize. Other judgments are philosophical: why is this important, what does it mean to us? Some judgments are actually judicial: this is right; this is wrong; this is irrelevant. It may seem bold to make some of these judgments, or it may seem inappropriate, or even immoral. What right have we to pass judgment on the past? The answer is inevitable: we have the right of the present, of the living. We who must guard our own times and entrust their care to others have little choice but to make value judgments about the past as we apply it to the present. This kind of judgment has its place. At the same time, its place must be reserved at the end of the order of historical research. Value judgments come last, not first.

Methodological Model

Putting these presuppositions to work is the task of a methodological model. In the model to follow, historical research is conceived as comprising eight stages. Since these logically follow one after the other, they also can be called eight steps to a historical study. In brief outline these are:

    1) Set a focus on the object of study and delineate
       carefully the general scope of the research.

2) Collect the sources relevant to the study.
3) Select among the documents.
4) Organize the material and the data gathered.
5) Analyze the data.
6) Interpret the data.
7) Set forth reasonable judgments about the material.
8) Report the study in a clear and meaningful fashion.

This first step, to **set a focus and delineate the scope** is inherent to any research study. In some methods the nature of the method itself aids this process. In historical research the step is particularly critical because such research can be tremendously wide or distressingly narrow in focus. Careful attention to this step can save a lot of wasted effort and heartache later. In fact, by acquiring a sharp focus from the start the pursuit of steps two and three, in particular, becomes much easier. A simple but helpful guideline is: make the object of study large enough to be meaningful but small enough to be manageable.

Next **collect the sources relevant to the study.** A study of the fall of Jerusalem in A.D. 70 might accumulate to itself many sources touching at least partly on the topic. Thus even in collecting materials selection enters in. Studies are rarely exhaustive in nature. Gathering sufficient material is generally a better goal than trying to find all the possible sources. The guide has to be the purpose and scope of the study. If a study can only be served by utilizing every possible source, then either the study design needs adjustment or the researcher is faced with a long period of collecting sources.

How are sources collected? The answer depends on the exact nature of the study. In some cases archaeological artifacts might be collected alongside ancient manuscripts. But usually historical research means finding appropriate written **primary** and **secondary** sources; occasionally **oral** sources may be used as well. Historians make generous use of **libraries.** Wherever written documents pertinent to the study might be found, that is where they should be searched for and collected. Thus, a study of the nineteenth century theologian Albrecht Ritschl could lead a student to the public library, but a theological library, such as that found at a seminary, would be a more appropriate choice. When the student finds that several books and articles concerned with Ritschl exist in the library, the collection process may stop. However, in many instances it is profitable, even necessary, to use such aids as an **inter-library loan** to acquire materials not available in a given geographical area. **Book searches** through book dealers may produce a key document. At the professional level of historical research, the effort to collect sources may lead the historian to other parts of the country, or to other countries. Not only public collections of materials may be pursued, but also **private** archives or unpublished materials (like letters and diaries). Interviews might yield valuable information. Collecting sources, then, can challenge the creative imagination of the researcher.

Once the relevant materials have been collected a process of selection among the documents must take place. Three general sub-steps can be enumerated in this process:

1) Divide the materials according to their nature. This is a task involving distinct steps:
    (1) Separate any nonwritten materials from written sources.
    (2) Distinguish between primary and secondary sources.
    (3) Place like materials with like.
2) Prioritize the materials. This also entails more than one operation:
    (1) Prioritize according to the most relevant materials for the study.
    (2) Prioritize according to the credibility of the material.
3) Treat inauthentic material separately. This means:
    (1) Select out from the materials gathered any that are clearly inauthentic or suspicious.
    (2) Decide whether the study should exclude inauthentic materials from consideration.
    (3) If inauthentic materials are considered, they should be set aside for special appraisal.

Selection, like any other step in a research study, means making decisions. Some of these are easier than others. It is generally not too difficult to distinguish a primary source from a secondary one. A primary source is one derived from a firsthand witness; a secondary source is one or more steps removed. Thus a book written by a theologian is a primary source for the study of that individual's theology; a book written about that theologian's thought is a secondary source. But the theologian's own book may be a secondary source if, for example, her or his work is a study of an earlier thinker who is the focus of the researcher's own study.

Other decisions are more difficult. How should materials be set in an order according to priority? Success in doing this reflects on how firm a grasp the researcher has on what he or she wants to do. If the historian is clearly focused, then the most relevant materials are easier to identify. Success in prioritizing according to credibility is usually a more difficult task, especially for the inexperienced. Many factors enter into determining the relative credibility of a source. Some witnesses have proven themselves to be more dependable than others. But even undependable sources might contain some credible data, while very dependable sources can hardly be called inerrant. So, both the sources as a whole and their particulars have to be judged. Four basic questions must be put to them:

1) Does the witness possess the ability to be credible? In other words:
   (1) Was the witness close enough in time and place to know firsthand what went on?
   (2) Was the perspective and attention of the witness such that the source is not only relatively unbiased as to fact but also relatively complete?
2) Does the witness possess the interest to be credible? In essence this means:
   (1) The witness had no special interest in falsifying the report or omitting critical data. Or,
   (2) The interest of the witness is recognizable and can be adjusted for by the research so that the facts still can be obtained.
3) Does the witness accurately report? This means, among other matters:
   (1) The details hold up under examination.
   (2) Good internal reasons exist to accept the witness's report. Such reasons might include:
      a) The testimony is such that the witness has nothing to gain from it and, indeed, might stand to lose from it.
      b) The testimony is about matters commonly known.
      c) The testimony is probable, that is, more likely to be true than not on the face of it.
4) Does the witness enjoy the independent corroboration of other witnesses? Historians are more comfortable about the credibility of any witness when it is substantiated by others.

The most difficult decisions are sometimes those about the authenticity of a document. Many factors enter into making such a decision, including the kind of **material** used (is it of a kind unknown for the time in which the document purports to have originated?), the **date** (does it know of events it should not?), the **author** (any telltale identifying marks confirming or denying a suspected writer?), and the **style** (is the manner of composition what might be expected?). Just because a piece is found in a place where authentic materials abound, the assumption that it is authentic must not be made casually. Suspect documents should always be tested. Then, if identified as inauthentic, they should be set aside while the decision is made whether to use them in the study or not. Often an inauthentic document will serve a particular research need. If it does, then it should be used; if it is superfluous or misleading, then exclude it.

Step four involves **organizing the material and gathering**

203

data for analysis. Just as step three (selection) is already initiated in step two (collection), so organization has begun with selection. But now the organization must become more exact. From this organized material must come data. In a sense, these are two steps, and can be conceived of as such. But on the other hand, because data as it is gathered suggests the organization of the material, and vice-versa, the two are so practically intertwined as to merit consideration as one stage with two aspects.

Organization can follow one or more of various lines. These include the following guidelines:

1) Chronologically: the material is organized sequentially according to time period.

2) Special interest: the material is organized to reflect the special focus of the research.

3) Emphasis: the material is displayed so as to call attention to an emphasis inherent in what is being researched.

4) Availability of material: the organization proceeds according to what the study has to work with, which may be scanty in some areas.

5) Suitability of material: the organization may distinguish carefully between credible material and doubtful material.

The organization and arrangement of material will naturally be a reflection both of the study design and of the data at hand. It is very ordinary in historical research to organize material chronologically. Such an arrangement is simply common sense in many instances. However, a particular study may have a special interest. Perhaps a chronological arrangement would not bring out adequately what the study intends to focus upon. Then an arrangement to accomplish this focus should be used. By it some new insight may be attained. Or perhaps an emphasis is inherent in the material and the nature or character of the data might be disguised by any treatment which does not clearly display this natural focus of the material. In such an instance the organization of the material should follow the character of the data, allowing the emphasis to emerge unhindered. In many instances research is made difficult by a lack of material or a mix of very good data with barely acceptable data. In these instances it is often to the benefit of the study to take this situation into systematic account by the organization of the material, both in its treatment and in its presentation. Often, though, material can be organized utilizing more than one of the guidelines. However, when more than one principle guides organization the possibilities for confusion are quickly multiplied.

Even as the material is being organized, data is being gathered. The term "data" here is used in a broad sense, meaning information to be analyzed. The kind of data gathered may vary from study to study. Five kinds of data that might

be gathered are:
1) Stated facts relevant to the study as a whole, or to individual parts of it.
2) Implications of the stated facts.
3) Questions raised by the facts and by their implications.
4) Incorrect assumptions, statements, and implications.
5) Speculations by the witness.

It is obvious that the data has gradations of value, though the precise ordering of most valuable to least valuable may vary according to the study. Generally, facts are what a historian is after, first and foremost. A "fact" in historical research is commonly not the same "objective" fact of the natural sciences, but a credible particular of historical testimony. Facts often suggest more than what they merely state. These implications, especially the more obvious ones, should not be overlooked. Neither should questions raised by the facts, especially when raised by the witness itself. All of these pieces of data are relatively positive in character. But negative data, incorrect information in the witness, should also be considered. Often incorrect assumptions, "facts," and implications can lead to the discovery of correct ones. Finally, the speculations ventured by the witness, in addition to being interesting, may also shed important light leading again to true facts.

Step five, **the analysis of the data,** follows hard on the heels of its gathering and organization. Some analysis has tacitly begun much earlier, in collection, selection, and organization. But once the data has been gathered and arranged for treatment, the real bulk of the labor of analysis begins. Among the many facets of such analysis, at least fifteen basic principles should be stated:
1) The **language** of the witness should be understood by the historian.
2) Primary sources should be distinguished from secondary sources and the **characteristics** of unpublished sources should be taken into account.
3) A **literary analysis** of the documents should be undertaken.
4) The **authenticity** of every document should be assured, or the inauthentic nature of it recognized and accounted for.
5) The **author** of the document should be identified, whether by name or by the characteristics evidenced in the testimony.
6) The **audience** intended by the witness should be known.
7) The **date** of the witness should be identified.
8) The **viewpoint** of the witness should be recog-

nized, and also that of the surrounding culture, etc., if relevant.

9) The **effect of groups or tradition** on the witness should be known.

10) The **structure** of the testimony should be at least outlined, and the **direction** of it noted.

11) The **facts** should be ascertained and **tested** for credibility as many times as needed.

12) The **relationships among sources** should be established.

13) The **relationships among facts** should be established, with the implications and questions these relationships raise.

14) An **interiorized comprehension** of the witness should be achieved. In other words, the witness must be understood first as a contemporary of the witness would understand.

15) **References** and **allusions** made by the witness must be identified and traced.

A good deal could be said about each of these principles. A complete historical study will not neglect any of them. Yet frequently the constraints of time, materials, and ability make it necessary to give little if any attention to some of these. Which, then, are generally beyond sacrifice? Remembering that the actual purpose and needs of the study must always give the final word on such matters, there are three principles that deserve special place. These three ought never to be passed by or given anything less than exacting attention:

1) Ascertain and test the facts.
2) Identify the viewpoint of the witness.
3) Achieve a perspective that permits seeing the witness as a contemporary of the witness would.

These three stand out because they are so central to the heart of the task of historical research. Historians want facts, and they want them in the framework of the past. Time is a tremendous obstacle to bridge. The imaginative use of perspective to try to understand a witness as the audience addressed by the witness would: that is bridging the gap of time and space, of language and ideas.

In identifying three preeminent principles, no intention exists to lessen the importance the other principles have. Historical research, like any research, is as good as the effort put into it. The more complete the analysis, the likelier the study will produce accurate and useful results. Analysis is not everything in research (contrary to what some may say or think), but it certainly is basic and central.

Step six, **the interpretation of the data,** is a creative one. But the creativity involved must be harnassed by a faithfulness to the data. Four broad guidelines for interpretation are:

1) The interpretation should be suggested by the material itself, not by what the interpreter thinks it should suggest.
2) The interpretation should be liberally supported by evidence.
3) The interpretation should aim at going beyond the obvious (self — evident) meaning **without neglecting the obvious**.
4) The interpretation should indicate, where possible, the cause-effect relationship at work, the motives behind events, etc.

Interpretation is more exegetical than eisegetical; it reads out from the evidence, rather than reads into the evidence. The historian must be prepared to have cherished notions rudely shattered by hard evidence. Otherwise, the interpretation may bear so little resemblance to the facts that it will have no credibility, and the historian will appear (rightly) foolish. If an interpretation is suggested by the data, it also should have as its accompaniment a liberal entourage of substantiating facts. In other words, an interpretation does more than just **say** it is warranted, it **shows** its merit. Of course, it is possible to give more evidence than is necessary, but it is better to err on the side of liberality in supporting an interpretation than it is to err on the side of stinginess.

Interpretations which only state the obvious often belabor it, too. The obvious ought not to be overlooked, nor dwelt upon to the point of tedium. Interpretations that are able to infer beyond the obvious are valuable. They promote insight and spark debate. As long as they also are reasonable, and supported by evidence, they are beneficial partners in historical dialog. But interpretations that merely aim at promoting a novel view, that stretch the evidence past the limits of probability, only accomplish muddying the very waters historians are trying to see clearly through. Interpretations that go meaningfully beyond the obvious disclose hidden cause-effect relationships, unearth shrouded motives, and illuminate dark corners. Of course this requires imagination, for it is detective work of the first magnitude. But it is imagination guided by realities, disciplined by probabilities, and stated as informed opinion rather than as assured fact.

Step seven, **setting forth reasonable judgments**, is a complementary step to that above. In fact, it is not uncommon to find the terms "interpretation" and "judgment" used synonymously. Here, though, they refer to different foci. Judgments also should follow guidelines, and the four that follow can be set usefully alongside those given for interpretation:
1) Judgments should be attached to interpretations, complementing them and completing their utility.
2) But judgments should preserve their unique focus: evaluation and application.
3) Judgments should not overreach themselves.

4) Judgments should be personal, but also
   professional. This means they should be honest
   and also purposeful.

Historical judgments belong alongside interpretations. Where an interpretation aims at establishing the meaning of a witness, historical judgment aims at evaluating this meaning for today and applying it as meaning for today. This is unavoidably a creative process of interpretation itself, but an interpretation aimed at the historian's audience, not one meant to uncover the witness's meaning for a past audience. So the difference in focus needs to be maintained in the interest of clarity. Good historical judgments make use of sound interpretations, fully maximizing their utility for a modern audience.

But if it is easy to overstate an interpretation, it is much easier to overstate a judgment. This is because historical judgments are a step back across time from the past to the present. It is all too easy to misuse the past to serve the present, or to try to bring the past and its meanings whole and uncritically into the present. Naturally, it is at the point of judgment where the historian has the greatest latitude in expressing personal opinion. There is a temptation to go beyond what is appropriate. While the historian must be honest in his or her judgment, that judgment should carry with it some definite purpose. Why make this judgment? That question should be asked before any judgment is made, and the statement of the judgment should answer clearly that question for the audience. A good historian is most professional while being uncompromisingly personal, because no abuse of the historian's vocation is indulged at the very point where the risk of such is greatest.

Step eight, **reporting the study,** is the final, but not the least consequential step. Historical research has the onus of an unfortunate reputation for being **boring.** Yet most people like doing historical research, and all people engage in it at some point, so why does this reputation persist? It is because too many reports of historical research are uninteresting though their topic is fascinating.

Chapter six (in Part One) should be reviewed carefully. In addition, the ideas about organization mentioned earlier in this chapter are worth reviewing before setting down a historical study in a report. Careful attention to structure and style are important keys to making a study readable. But even more critical are enthusiasm and a genuine concern to communicate. A historian who cares about the research that has been done, who is not afraid to display a little passion, that historian can do much to make an audience want to read his or her studies. But, the burden of exacting attention from a public constantly harassed by published material is upon the writer, not upon the reader.

A good historical report does not depart from history in

order to become interesting reading, but instead makes history come alive by intelligent and creative presentation. It is perhaps harder to do than it is to enjoin, but the labor of historical research is repaid fully only when a report is issued from it that successfully invites readers to become partners in the historical dialog.

Conclusion

The methodological model put forward in this chapter is broad and flexible, but then so is historical research. The model affords an outline of concerns such research can address, but it still remains the task of any given research study to flesh out the outline and place its distinctive emphases in plain view. While it is true of all of the models of Part Two that they should be used in connection with more extensive treatments of the same methods, this is particularly true of historical research. What barely has been touched by this model may elsewhere be the subject of a major discussion. The more a student can discover about historical research, its problems and its tools, the better able the novice historian will be to use this model and ply the historian's trade. At the same time, while learning more from other books, there is no better teacher than experience. Try the model, and learn firsthand the excitement of historical research.

Suggested Exercises

The discussion of historical research in this chapter has been very broad. Probably the most profitable way, then, of acquiring some level of competency in historical research is to begin with some limited and quite definite projects that focus on one or two aspects of historical research. Later, more comprehensive efforts can be attempted. Each of the following exercises focuses on one part of historical research.

Exercise 1. Use one of the topics from the list provided in the third exercise for library research (p. 79), and build upon what you have already accumulated. Examine how your library research has accomplished, at least in part, the first three steps in historical research. Compare and contrast the aims of library research with those of these three steps in historical research. Are they precisely the same? If they differ, how do they differ? Can library research serve as the first part of historical research?

Exercise 2. Still using the materials gathered for Exercise 1, focus on the principle of organization. Which of the five guidelines suggested for organization best fits your material? Why? How might your study vary in its findings and/or presentation by the selection of this guideline instead of another?

Now, attempt the organization of your material according to chronology. Place all of the evidence in a sequential order. Does this arrangement work well for your study? Why, or why not?

Next, organize the same material and data according to emphasis. This means making decisions as to what is most important among the things you have collected. How can these be arranged so that the right emphasis is clearly visible?

Exercise 3. Once more build on what you have gained in the first two exercises. This time focus on the data. Divide it into five categories, each one answering to the kinds of data that might be gathered (i.e., stated facts; implications; questions raised; incorrect assumptions, statements and implications; and speculations). Does your study provide data fitting each category? If not, why not? Has something been overlooked?

After dividing the data into kinds, assign value both to the different categories and also to the individual pieces of data. What categories of data are most important to your study, and why? What pieces of data, and why? Can the matter be handled in such a black-and-white manner, or does your data elude such an easy valuation?

14

Content Analysis

The Promise of Content Analysis

Many researchable problems flounder on the shoal of an inappropriate research design. This is as true in theological research as it is anywhere else. Since so much of theological research has been traditionally qualitative in nature, with its corresponding emphasis and dependence on expert opinion, the problem of design always has been acute. Scholars employing the same method have done so at times in such a fashion that an outside observer scarcely can believe that the same method has been invoked. Quantitative alternatives, while also very versatile in application, tend to be more formal in design, giving themselves over easily to replicability. Theological research should turn more frequently than it has to the use of quantitative research strategies, both because of their utility in replicating critical studies, and for their relative exactness. The problem, of course, is finding quantitative designs suitable to the qualitative kinds of problems so common to theological research. One appropriate alternative is found in content analysis, an approach to research that may well be the deep water channel by which many difficult problems can be steered safely to shore.

Content analysis is a quantitative methodology. It provides a means to treat materials of communication so that the tasks of description, and sometimes inference, can be expressed by precise numbers as well as words. Where **qualitative** research relies on qualified, expert opinion to pass judgment on matters under study, **quantitative** research relies on quantities expressed numerically and amenable to statistical analysis (cf. Chapters 17-19). Thus, qualitative research is relatively subjective in nature, with an inherent difficulty in providing results that can be generalized. Quantitative research, on the other hand, is relatively objective and lends itself to generalizable results with greater facility.

It is doubtful any theological researcher would believe that quantitative research is so clearly superior to qualitative means that it should replace those traditional approaches. But why is it so hard for many theological researchers to grant that, in many instances, quantitative treatment is not only an acceptable alternative but actually a preferable one? The answers to this query are not hard to find. In the first place, the question itself rarely has been asked if quantitative research should be used for a particular study. Two factors militate against asking that question: strong training in traditional, qualitative strategies plus little, if any, training in quantitative strategies. If more theological researchers understood the ideas behind quantitative research, and were trained to employ such methods, the increase in applying such strategies would be dramatic.

Its Adaptability

Content analysis is suitable particularly to studying the diverse forms of human communication. It is a sound method for investigating biblical and theological writings. In fact, it is so adaptable that it can serve as a tool to date disputed materials (see Part Three), or to detect an author's style, or analyze a speech. This adaptability comes from broad assumptions and flexible techniques. To make content analysis succeed, the scholar must creatively employ quantitative tools based on qualitative decisions. But what is produced by the resulting study is expressed quantitatively.

The Definition of Content Analysis

Content analysis is any technique for the description of a text which is objective, systematic, and **quantitative,** and which can permit valid and reliable inferences from the analysis of the data. Now this is a rather general definition, but it is a correct one because content analysis can embrace several techniques, all of which retain the critical elements of objectivity, systematic and quantitative treatment, validity, and reliability. On one hand, the key term is "description." While inference is aimed at, in essence content analysis is an approach to description. It first permits seeing what is there, before making any inferences about it. On another hand, the key term is "quantitative," because content analysis uses numbers in the study of texts. Since theological research has frequent occasions to work with texts, content analysis is an attractive quantitative tool.

Content analysis is **objective** because it specifies precisely the criteria and procedures it utilizes in describing content, while also establishing a process by which it may be replicated by others. It tries to avoid uncertainties that cause the scholar to rely heavily on personal judgment rather than clear characteristics within the data. Its goal is to provide a research design with constituent parts so clear that those who follow the researcher can study the same content the same way and gain the same results.

Content analysis is **systematic** because it follows an unbiased plan formulated prior to analysis of the content. The material under study is treated methodically, in an orderly manner, according to this plan. The system employed yields **quantitative** results because it is designed to do so. The content is expressed numerically because within the language of mathematics and statistics there is substantial agreement as to whether an analytical procedure is appropriate and correct. This provides an added advantage in making the study objective and systematic.

Assumptions

It is common in content analysis to identify three fundamental assumptions:
1) Quantitative description of content is both possible and meaningful.
2) The study of manifest content is meaningful.
3) Inferences can be drawn validly from the study of content.

The first assumption has its stress on the idea of meaningfulness. It is possible to describe content quantitatively, but is it meaningful to do so? Implied by this assumption is another assumption: producers of content are relatively more interested in frequent units than in infrequent ones. In more familiar terms, an author shows emphasis by quantity of attention, indicated usually by the frequency of occurrence of various content characteristics. So Paul, in writing to the Philippians, says, "Rejoice in the Lord always; again I will say, Rejoice." The repetition of the term "rejoice" is an important (and measurable) factor in the Apostle's communication. In content analysis the manifest and objective characteristics of content are focused upon.

So the second assumption is that manifest content can be studied meaningfully. But what is manifest content? **Manifest content** is that which is readily perceived or easily recognized. It is, quite simply, what is **there.** It is the direct communication of the content, its obvious form and substance. It differs from **latent content,** which is content that is present but not immediately obvious. Roughly, the distinction between manifest and latent content is that between reading what is on the lines and reading that which is between the lines. While some scholars have applied content analysis to latent content, in this chapter only manifest content is considered. It is assumed that this content is meaningful (else why would it have been communicated and preserved?), and can be meaningfully studied (otherwise how could its meaning be surely attained?).

The third assumption states that inferences can be validly made from what is essentially a descriptive research approach. Content analysts reason that a relationship exists between a communicator's intent and the content actually expressed. A study of the content should then permit inferences about the communicator's intent. What is valid on one side should hold relatively true on the other side. This is somewhat the assumption that a communicator "says what he means and means what he says." But there is another relationship about which content analysts are concerned. Content creates an effect. Scholars often are very interested in making inferences from content about these effects. By studying this relationship valuable insights can be gained into the communication process, and may reveal interesting things about the communicator and his audience.

Methodology

Content analysis is very practical. Even its assumptions are cautious and without controversy, characterized by a very practical bent. The methodology of content analysis is so practical that it can be applied to a wide variety of materials in a wide range of styles without losing its distinctive features. It may not always be complex and intricate in its beauty, but it generally gets the job done.

The steps used in content analysis can be rearranged according to the specific need or interest of the researcher. Content analysis serves two ends: to secure the researcher's answers to specific questions, and to do so in an objective, systematic, and precise manner. The stages incorporated by a content analysis study include elements that we have repeatedly seen are basic to research: an initial question or problem; an hypothesis in response; the design of an appropriate research approach; and coding and analysis of data. The specifics often can be juggled.

In the case of content analysis it is probably better to conceive of stages rather than steps, since most people can more readily grant that stages may be mixed than steps. The basic stages, then, are:

1) Select an initial question or problem.
2) Formulate hypotheses.
3) Sample.
4) Categorize the data.
5) Unitize the data.
6) Code the data.
7) Analyze the data.

Selecting an initial question or problem has been discussed before. What must be particularly mentioned about selecting for a content analysis is what is appropriate for such study. It is communication content (in literary texts, in oral communications, on film) that content analysis was designed to study and for which it is particularly suited. Naturally, since so much of what a theological scholar desires to study is in the form of some kind of communication, this makes content analysis very appropriate for most theological studies. It can be applied with profit to questions of introduction about the biblical books and to specific questions or problems of the biblical content. It can be used to study the style or themes or development of a religious thinker. In one of the earliest uses of content analysis it was applied to the study of two sets of hymns to test them for their religious ideas in order to determine their suitability for worship services.

Formulating hypotheses, the second step, follows as a natural response to what has been selected as the object of a study. What hypothesis formulation does is focus the scope of the study and provide something tangible which can be tested. Formulating hypotheses in content analysis is the same as in other kinds of research. The general hypotheses spark the development of the general research program, while the specific hypotheses refine this program into a set of working directives.

Often it is necessary to reformulate the hypotheses as the study progresses. This occurs as the analyst becomes able to specify in terms of the study how, for example, the incidence of units in one category is expected to differ from the incidence in another category. In other words, reformulation is able to make specific hypotheses more precise and concrete, and hence more practical for testing. A scholar sets hypotheses to guide the investigation; these are adjusted to reflect the actual course the study takes.

Hypotheses, it must be remembered, are only as good as the research questions behind them. Good questions, meaningful questions, can lead to productive and beneficial research. Bad questions lead nowhere. In any quantitative research it is easy to forget that it is the question that matters, not the numbers. The numbers only have their relevance in connection with the questions. Superficial questions may yield tons of numbers, but superficial answers. The nature and number of research hypotheses should answer to the research questions. These questions in turn, should reflect the researcher's interest or need.

Sampling is a concept long utilized by various methodologies to make large volumes of data more accessible and manageable without also sacrificing objectivity, validity, and reliability. This third step is as critical as any other since incorrect sampling can deceive a researcher into believing that the data gathered is representative of all the material in the universe from which the sample is taken. If it is not representative, then the researcher who generalizes about what has been found is in deep trouble, as the first correct sample and study that next comes along will bluntly point out.

Sampling is a practical necessity when the researcher's problem embraces so much material as to make dealing with all of it an impossible or infeasible task. When inundated by content, the scholar has to make some decisions. What is relevant? What can be discarded, or excluded from this particular study? Once these questions are answered it may still be that a vast volume of material remains. Then the researcher must decide to sample; the only remaining question is how. A properly selected sample is capable of accurately describing large quantitites.

But what constitutes a properly selected sample? Two ideas are critical:

1) Samples must be manageable.

215

2) Samples must be meaningful.

Manageability refers to size. A manageable sample is one large enough to have meaning but small enough to permit treatment in the time and under the constraints placed on the researcher. It is impossible to set down a law about size because each study has its own requirements and the universe (or total possible number of items from which a sample may be drawn) under consideration may vary in size itself (even though most are commonly regarded as unlimited in number). **Meaningfulness** refers to representativeness. A meaningful sample represents the universe from which it is drawn. It renders an accurate picture of the whole. When the ideas of manageability and meaningfulness are put together a general rule is produced: samples should be only large enough to ensure representativeness.

How can this general rule be honored? The following steps are an assist:

1) Specify the dimensions of the universe from which the sample is to be taken.

2) Use a sampling procedure which guarantees the known probability that any unit might be selected for the sample.

To depict the universe is not as impossible as it might first appear. In essence, what this entails is identifying one or more characteristics decisive for determining whether or not any given item belongs to that universe. Thus, as a very simple example, the universe of the Bible includes any item with the decisive characteristic of canonical status. Another characteristic might reflect some quality, such as the assigned range of dates of composition, a characteristic that holds true for all biblical literature. But the best characteristics for use in delineating a universe are those true only for items in that universe, and not characteristics shared by items outside the universe (as, for example, range of date, which applies to many non-canonical books composed during the time biblical books came into existence).

More than one sampling procedure can satisfy the second consideration. The most preferred process is called **random sampling.** It is designed to assure that every item in the universe has an equal chance of being selected for the sample. Sometimes this process is modified in a **stratified random sampling.** Here the goal is drawing a random sample from different parts of the universe. Thus the universe might be classified according to several criteria (length, place of origin, time of origin, etc.). Each criteria produces a strata and from each strata a random sample is drawn.

Commonly, however, the analyst desires to incorporate into the sample particular features pertinent to the study. It may be that a stratified random sample cannot adequately accomplish this task. Perhaps the material can be stratified but not drawn from randomly. Then the sampling process is simply a strati-

fied sampling. Can this produce a representative sample? Perhaps, but such is not guaranteed by the process. The result is that the ability to generalize from the sample to the universe is called into question.

Yet many times the practical demands of a study make it imperative to use a sample where representativeness cannot be ensured. A **purposive stratified sample** serves the particular demands of a study by offering a best-guess selection of materials. This is a clearly qualitative decision and while generalizing from such samples occurs, it must at best be cautious and limited. Any study utilizing a random sample will likely eliminate extremes at either end of the universe. If these extremes are a desired focus of the study, then a random sample is inappropriate (and perhaps any sampling may be inadvisable). Thus, it is by no means a hard and fast fact that random sampling should be used in content analysis. But the sampling should always serve the study's purpose.

Content analysis sampling often is complicated by the difficulty, sometimes even the impossibility, of securing the desired materials. In such cases, for the study to proceed the analyst must use what is available. Samples drawn under such conditions need not be viewed as undermining the research but they must be seen as qualifying it. Scholars can gain profitable results even from samples where the materials are less than ideal. But they must be honest about the quality of their materials and samples, and they must adjust their expectations and interpretations in accordance with the limitations so imposed. The critical factor in choosing a sampling procedure is its appropriateness to the study at hand, not its inherent strength as a sampling tool. Theory is shaped by the demands of practice.

Categorization, the fourth stage, also can be called **classification**. It is a step in measurement; in fact, it is the simplest step. It means assigning individual things (subjects) to classes or categories on the basis of some specific attribute or trait. Frequently called the most crucial aspect of content analysis, it definitely is located at the heart of such analysis. The construction of categories, and the subsequent classification of material, is the step where specific hypotheses are tied to actual data. It thus begins a rigorous testing of the hypotheses while preparing for the possible inferences which will follow.

The kinds of categories and the schemes for classifying material are as varied as the number of content analysis studies. They depend in part upon the researcher's conceptions and hypotheses, and in part upon the data available. What generally limits the production of relevant categories is the imagination of the scholar. A creative researcher can wrestle with a significant problem so as to find appropriate categories that will fit it. But the categories must be appropriate. Category construction and classification are not arbitrary or capricious, though they are flexible. Instead, they must proceed

217

both logically and relevantly.

The following considerations are important for categorization:

1) Categories should reflect the purpose of the study.
2) They should be exhaustive.
3) They should be independent.
4) They should be mutually exclusive.
5) They should be explicit.
6) They should be functional.
7) They should be manageable.

Categorization is where, as the saying goes, "the rubber meets the road." Categories having no relation to the research question are just superfluous and hinder the study. Every category should mean something to the scholar and fit naturally within the framework of the study.

The categories must also be **exhaustive**. This simply means that every item under study can be placed somewhere. If an item is left unaccounted for, think what havoc that creates for the study! It makes sense, then, to choose categories wisely and to have in mind beforehand the nature of the data being classified.

For categories to be **independent** they must be unable to influence the classification of other data. Sometimes this consideration is not practical, as in situations where only two categories exist and not to be in one means logically to be in the other. Obviously, where many categories are in use each should be clearly distinct from the others.

Closely associated with this thought is the concept that categories should be **mutually exclusive**. This means that no item can belong to more than one category. Of course, it is possible to think of specific situations where a study might violate this precept. But the general idea in creating a strong content analysis design is to use these ideas whenever and wherever possible and, most important, appropriate.

Categories must always be **explicit**, as explicit as they can possibly be made. This is not a luxury, but a necessity if the study is to be faithfully replicated. Explicit categories demand explicit rules for why something belongs here and not somewhere else. The statement of such rules constitutes what is called the **operational definition** of a category. Without these definitions other analysts could not classify the content the same way.

That categories need to be **functional** should pass without comment. But creating functional categories is not always that easy. To be functional a category should work, that is, really serve the purpose for which it was made. All of the other considerations about categories are aimed, ultimately, at this end. Well-constructed categories facilitate classification.

Finally, categories, like samples, should, be **manageable**. This idea applies as well to the whole system of categories.

Each individual category should do only its job and that job should not be too broadly conceived. Likewise, the entire system should do the job it is designed to do without entailing the creation of so many categories that the researcher needs an index to remember them all. Large numbers of categories does not necessarily mean greater analytical power or increased sophistication. In fact, it may mean only mass confusion.

Certain kinds of categories are natural and quite common. Since simple operational definitions for categories make categories easier to follow and understand, it is to the researcher's advantage to use natural or common features in creating categories. Categories formulated, for example, on the basis of a particular vocabulary item are operationally easier to define than those formulated on a theme. Yet both vocabulary and themes are natural and common features of content. Other such features are subject matter and statement form. They are essential parts of the manifest content and generally easy to identify.

So far the focus has been upon category construction. But, as was first noted, categorization entails not only creating categories but also classifying the material. While the terms "categorization" and "classification" can be interchanged, they have been separated in this discussion. Here the former refers to the specific area (class or category) to which an item can be assigned. The latter term refers to the actual process of assigning items. In theory it might be said that categories precede classification. In practice the two operate more dynamically, with items suggesting their own place, and places helping to identify items. Categorization and classification are two aspects of one movement.

In classification the ideas guiding category construction impose themselves on the placement of items. Thus, for instance, an item placed in one category is usually not to be classed in another place as well. An item defined one way should not be defined in several other ways, too. Clarity is the goal, and confusion the obstacle to be avoided. The guiding principle in classification is simple: identify an item by a specific trait and match that trait to the appropriate category.

Unitization, the fifth stage, is a complementary process to categorization. Practically, where there is categorization there is also unitization. In fact, unitization is a kind of categorization in that it is the classification of material according to specific identifiable units. It is distinguished from categorization as discussed above in that unitization entails the division of the content into manageable portions from which items are drawn for classification. By its nature unitization often takes place before categorization, although the order for many of these steps is relatively interchangeable.

Most content analysis studies express their findings in terms of the relative frequency of occurrence of some unit. This means that units are determined, then content classified, then the frequency of recurring items calculated. A common plan used in content analysis that displays the practical intertwining of categorization, unitization, and classification is as follows:

1) The researcher establishes categories and defines them.
2) Then the researcher divides the material into manageable portions in order to make classifying easier.
3) Finally, the researcher classifies the material found in the units.

Communication content, particularly that which is written, lends itself to unitization. Written documents have many natural features that make the task relatively simple. Units might be sentences, or even words. They can be paragraphs, or chapters. What determines what they should be for a given study is the scholar's material. As this material is examined with unitization in mind, four basic guidelines can help produce a wise decision:

1) The unit should be large enough to be easily identifiable.
2) The unit should also be large enough to contain meaning.
3) But the unit should not be so large that it contains too many meanings or yields too few units for analysis; conversely, it should not be so small it produces too many units to be manageable.
4) The total number of units should fall within the range and limitations specified above and also be well suited to sampling (if sampling is to be used).

Unitization may commonly yield more than one kind of unit. The most essential of these is the **basic coding unit** (or **recording unit**), the smallest division of the content in which the appearance of an item is counted. Another way of expressing this is, the basic coding unit is the unit at the focus of analysis, the one to which the scholar wishes to give a score. Depending on the nature of the research this smallest unit may be a word or an entire document; the size is relative to the study. But within the study, that unit, whatever it is, is the smallest to receive a coding score. If a document will do as well as a word in a study, then the document is preferred since it is easier to work with, and because large units generally provide as accurate a picture of the content as smaller ones in such situations.

Sometimes studies utilize space-and-time measures. Thus, instead of using subject items the content is divided along physical dimensions: when was the item created? How much space (or attention) does it receive? A subject unit counts kinds of words or ideas while a physical unit measures amounts of words or time devoted to a subject. This kind of unitization may be most appropriate where nonverbal materials are involved.

Sometimes to accurately score a basic unit its context must be considered. The **context unit**, in contrast to the basic unit, is the largest division of material a researcher might consider in coming to a score for a basic unit. Thus a basic unit might be a word, its context unit the paragraph. But context units are less frequently employed than other kinds of units and require care in their utilization. While they suggest the scholar's awareness of the effect of context, they also may unnecessarily complicate the study or even mislead the analysis.

The following brief list indicates the different kinds of units content analysts might use:

1) Basic coding unit/recording unit: the smallest division of content to receive a score.

2) The context unit: the largest unit having direct impact on the scoring of a basic unit.

3) The physical unit: a non-subject way of dividing material according to such physical means as time, length, size, or volume.

4) The syntactical unit: division of content according to words.

5) The referential unit: division of content according to some particular point of reference such as specific objects, events, persons, or places.

6) The thematic unit: division of content according to the correspondence of content to a particular structural definition.

Two designations can refer to the same unit. A syntactical unit, for example, might be the basic unit for a study. Some studies may treat the content under analysis using one unit form then return to it using a different unit form to yield different results. Like so many features of content analysis, unitization is versatile and can be adapted to the specific demands of virtually any study of communication content.

Coding is scoring content. As items of content are classified from the units, they are assigned a score which later will be analyzed along with the other scores gathered. It is normal, though not essential, to code using the **nominal level of measurement.** This is the simplest level of measurement and refers to dividing content according to categories distinguished from each other by their names. The data gathered from the content is identified and assigned to a category that corresponds to it. As a simple illustration, imagine dividing the books of the New Testament into nominal categories. The categories might be: Gospel, Epistle, Apocalypse, etc. Each book is identified as to whether it is a Gospel or Epistle, etc. The measurement, then, applied to each book is signified by the name. It separates the content into classes in a very basic fashion, with no statement made about such matters as how the classes are related to one another. (For more about nominal level measurements, see the section on Chi Square in chapter

16.)
Coding itself entails three basic components. These are:
1) It renders content into scores, thus creating numbers for statistical analysis.
2) It must take into account both the units being observed and those being analyzed.
3) It must make its record counting base clear.

The first goal of coding is to produce numbers susceptible to statistical analysis. When the nominal level of measurement is used, scholars talk about identifying nominal data. All this means is that the information being coded is named. Whenever a name A occurs identifying an item (as in A = Gospel), that item is placed in the category bearing the same name. Thus the data can be expressed in terms of how often things occur in each category. There are four Gospels (Matthew, Mark, Luke, John); each time one is found, it is given its identifying name and placed in the appropriate category. Its identifying name is a label to help the researcher score it so that the numbers produced may be analyzed later. Each category will have a score reflecting the number of items assigned to it (so for the nominal category of Gospel there will be a score of 4, since there are four items in it).

A second goal of coding is to distinguish between different things. On the one hand, the scholar has materials which are being observed and which contain units. On the other hand, there are the units themselves which need to be analyzed. The researcher has a broad and a narrow concern. The materials as a whole cannot be dismissed because it is likely that they will be needed in making full sense out of the results taken from the basic units. The basic units cannot be ignored because, after all, they are the proper focus of the analysis.

The third goal goes beyond the second. The record counting base is a way of relating the narrow and the broad concerns of the researcher. This base refers to a comparison critical to the scores if they are to make sense. For example, the ratio of lexical items (basic units) compared to the whole vocabulary of a document (the material as a whole) might be the record counting base of a study. The idea behind this base is to provide a framework within which scores have meaning.

Coding is a very practical operation. It requires making decisions about items, but this should not be too difficult if the work preparatory to coding has been done with care. Coding should be logical, not arbitrary. Care should be given to coding all of the data relevant to the study but also only the data relevant to the study. Clear coding helps later researchers follow the process, understand it, and replicate it.

Analysis, the last stage, is the goal of the others. A variety of ways of analyzing the data are available. The term "analysis" here refers not to that analysis which has already taken place in classifying the data, but to the statistical measures which can be applied to the material that has been coded. Among the statistical techniques particularly useful to content analysis are Chi Square, correlation measures, and even simple frequency counts (all of which are discussed in chapters 15-17).

Special Note

Both because quantitative research strategies are unfamiliar ground to theological researchers, and because content analysis can be so helpful in a wide variety of studies, Part Three of this text has been provided. There can be found a mixed research design that has at its heart a theological problem addressed by a content analysis and appropriate statistical aids. Content analysis is not easy to specify in an exact set of rules and steps. Learning it is mostly a matter of practicing it until the process makes full sense. But the sample study in Part Three may aid this chapter in paving the path of early practice.

Validity

Two important considerations, which are not themselves identifiable as separate stages in content analysis, are validity and reliability. Both concepts have been discussed before. Validity, it will be recalled, addresses the question, Does the measurement tool measure what it is supposed to? Is the researcher able to see what is really there? This is a practical concern for every study because validity reflects on the usefulness of a measure for the researcher. It is quite possible for a measure to be valid for one study but not for another. Once more the basic truth that the researcher's own special purpose reigns supreme is evident. It is most important for a scholar to know what he or she is trying to accomplish, what the purpose of the study is. Measures consistent with that purpose, and the resultant design from that purpose, will be more likely to be valid.

Five different ways of testing for validity can be mentioned:

1) Face validity: a measuring instrument so obviously does what it is intended to do that, "on the face of it," it is valid.

2) Agreement: a measuring instrument is commonly agreed by many researchers to be valid for such a use in such a situation.

3) Comparison: a measuring instrument is compared against another that is known to be valid.

4) Correlation of results: a measuring instrument is judged by its ability to produce valid results as gauged by comparing the results to others known to be valid. (This is similar to #3 which compares instruments, not results.)

5) Prediction: a measuring instrument is used as a predictor to see its success in terms of valid-

ity.

Where latent content is analyzed the validity is lowered. This is because direct data, as in manifest content, is lacking. But the magnitude of validity is of relatively less concern than whether there is any validity at all. For a study's results to be trusted the question of validity must be satisfactorily answered.

Reliability

Objective research is so only when the requirement of reliability is met. Measuring instruments and procedures should be reliable. This means repeated measures should yield similar results when the same instrument and data is involved. Reliability, then, is the concept of constancy. Validity implies reliability, and is relatively more critical. But reliability should not be neglected, nor simply assumed, though a level of validity has been established.

Reliability is increased by precision in categories and units. Ideally, any number of coders should be able to treat the same content the same way because the directions, labels, and content are so clear that differences of scoring are eliminated. In practice the ideal is rarely realized. Often studies seek to alleviate this situation by using many coders and testing for inter-coder reliability to help ensure that the categories, units, etc., are reliable. This is not always feasible, of course, and reliability is frequently a persistent problem. However, it should not be unduly exaggerated. Sufficient care by the researcher should produce enough reliability to make the study objective.

Conclusion

Content analysis shares many of the features basic to quantitative strategies. Yet it is also amenable to the kinds of problems common in theological research. It thus commends itself as a methodology for the theological researcher who desires the more objective and precise ability of a quantitative approach. While it introduces the researcher to a new way of looking at, and doing research, the effort put into mastering it is more than repaid by the results.

Suggested Exercises

If the concepts of content analysis are unclear, take the time to review the chapter before attempting any of the exercises. It may be advisable, too, to consult Part Three of this text. There an actual content analysis is shown, from conception through data analysis. If you are confident that you have a basic starting point, then try one or two of the exercises. Afterwards, read through Part Three. Then return and review your work. Finally, do exercise three.

Exercise 1. The focus of this exercise is the concept of sampling. Take your Bible and turn to the Old Testament. You wish to study the theme, "the fear of God." To accomplish this in a reasonable amount of time means making a decision of how much material to examine, and what that material will be. Thus, you must create a sample.

For your sampling procedure, use a stratified sample. Set your categories for selection as: length of the document, date, and kind of literature. This is a purposeful sample because you are interested in the theme as treated across a span of time in different genres. To make the later work easier, you decide to keep each document about the same size.

Now, establish the size range you will accept (in terms of words per book, or pages of space the book takes in an English version of the Bible). Determine which Old Testament books meet that qualification. Then sample among them according to date and genre. This will mean establishing select periods from which you want to draw literature and, as well, different literary kinds (e.g., wisdom literature, prophetic literature, etc.).

How many documents do you finally have in your sample? What are they? Are you satisfied that your sample is both manageable and meaningful in size?

If you have time, perhaps you could follow the same procedure but change the size range. What effect does such a change make on the sample?

Exercise 2. This exercise focuses upon categorization. The object of your study is a treatment of four doctrines as considered by select contemporary theologians. You select the doctrines and establish a sample of theologians and/or theological writings.

Now, check your categories against the criteria set forth in the chapter. Remember, the doctrines you have selected are the categories.

If you wish to take the exercise a step further, try classifying material from your sample documents into each category. This will also mean coding, since you will be assigning a score to each item as you classify it and place it in its appropriate category.

Can you see how, in practice, categorization, classification, and coding so closely tied together?

Exercise 3. This exercise focuses on classification and coding. The object of your study is an analysis of hymns found in a hymn-book your church is considering purchasing. The question has been raised whether the hymns included in this book are reflective of your church's theological tradition. Your task is to answer this question.

Select a hymnbook. Obviously, to analyze each hymn or hymn verse would involve a tremendous amount of time. You decide to try two ways of approach. In the first, you use a random sample to select hymns to analyze. The numbers come up as follows: 3, 5, 18, 33, 156, 157, 169, 200, 210, 354, 402. You establish categories suggested to you by the hymns themselves(perhaps by using the designation for the theme of that hymn as given in the hymnal). Each hymn is then classified. You use each hymn as the unit being coded, and assign a score matching hymn to the name of the category to which it belongs (nominal measurement). How many categories do you have? What are their names? How many hymns belong to each? Are you satisfied that this design does the task of answering the question? If not, why not?

Since you wisely saw that the first approach was inadequate to the aim of your intended study, you try a different tact. This time, you set your categories first. Each category names an important theological point especially valued by your church. Now you must determine an accurate way to sample the hymns. Shall you again use random sampling, though perhaps with a larger number of items? Or perhaps a stratified sample would be more appropriate. Once you have settled your sampling procedure, create a sample. Now classify the units (still individual hymns). Assign each one to the category, or categories, to which its contents belong. Use nominal measurement and check to be sure your coding is done accurately.

When you have completed this exercise, save it for use later when statistical analysis has been learned. Then, return to this example and reflect on what statistical tools you might use to best answer your question. Try one or two statistics and see what results you gain.

15

Simple Descriptive Statistics

Descriptive Statistics Defined

Researchers in many fields commonly make use of statistics. The word "statistics" itself can carry more than one connotation. But in research the essential meaning of the term is the collection of specific theories and methodologies that are available for analyzing information which has been collected in numerical form. Established strategies can be brought to bear on this numerical information to yield other numbers, which either summarize the information or make it possible to venture generalized statements about the information presently at hand. The former of these two ends, summarizing large groups of numbers, is the work of descriptive statistics.

Descriptive statistics are, simply, numbers that describe larger sets of numbers. They may do this by a statistic that summarizes the entire collection of data or by statistics that characterize the data. In either instance, descriptive statistics render large groups of numbers into a more manageable form for the researcher. They make it possible for the researcher to make accurate statements about the data at hand without constantly having to discuss each particular item of information. Such statistics are the simplest to use and the easiest to understand. They make a ready tool for many kinds of theological research.

Value, Applicability, Limitations

Description is a basic facet of research. Description points out what has been observed and thereby paves the way for eventual attempts at explanation. Typically, in theological research description is verbal. For example, in studying the Gospel of John a researcher might describe the writer's emphases by calling attention to such terms as "light," "spirit," and "door." He or she may say that these terms are used often by the author; that is a descriptive statement. If the scholar goes on to suggest that such recurrent terms are important because they occur so frequently, he or she is making an inference about them based on the idea that nouns or concepts favored by an author are significant. Thus, an observation is described and the description stands as a foreword to an important inference.

Often this kind of verbal description is accompanied by a numerical aid. The scholar may state that "light" ($\varphi\tilde{\omega}\varsigma$) occurs 22 times in the Gospel, "spirit" ($\pi\nu\epsilon\tilde{\upsilon}\mu\alpha$) 17 times, and "door" ($\vartheta\acute{\upsilon}\rho\alpha$, $\vartheta\upsilon\rho\omega\rho\acute{o}\varsigma$) 7 times. These numbers are statistics. They express the frequency with which each term occurs. Of course, the reseacher could choose to list each occurrence for each term. But why should she or he? Generally, the study is better served by merely reporting the total number of occurrences. This number summarizes a body of numbers (i.e., each occurrence considered as an individual member of a large group).

The obvious values in utilizing numbers include sharpness and clarity in description, economy, and a certain persuasive force. Consider the following two sentences:

The Gospel of John uses the term "spirit" many times.

The Gospel of John uses the term "spirit" 17 times.

The only change is the substitution of a numeric descriptor ("17") for a verbal descriptor ("many"). Yet the second sentence is preferable because it answers the question raised by the first sentence ("How many?") before it can be asked. The number makes the observation a more clearly focused one. It also is economical in that it says with one number what otherwise could be said only as exactly by the actual listing of all occurrences. It carries, too, more force to the reader than the ambiguous word "many."

These values become even more apparent when relatively sophisticated descriptive statistics are brought into play in order to render large, and often obscure, bodies of data into short and understandable statements. In one or two such numbers a description might be made precisely and clearly that otherwise would require a massive proliferation of words. Yet these values only can be appreciated by those who have acquired a competency to understand and use descriptive statistics. Then, statistics can be blended into verbal description to sharpen the research and facilitate comprehension.

The applicability of numbers to theological scholarship probably is clearer in some areas than in others. It may be apparent that reporting frequencies of terms is helpful in a biblical word study. But what about research into, for example, the dating of a biblical document (see Part Three)? The surprising truth is that numbers are far more applicable to theological work than most people imagine. But to utilize them, and to gain maximum benefit in so doing, requires creativity, competence in statistical theory, and a practice of different statistical methods. While a few brief chapters cannot suffice in themselves to provide all of these things, they can introduce enough ideas and aids to demonstrate the genuine possibility and desirability of including statistical work in theological scholarship.

However, a disclaimer is in order, too. Statistics, as helpful as they can be, cannot be pushed beyond their own limitations. Descriptive statistics may prepare the way to making inferences, but that task is better left to **inferential statistics** (see chapter 17). Nor are statistics always the most appropriate means available to the scholar. Someone has said, "figures don't lie, but liars figure." In other words, statistics can be misused as well as used properly. All theories and methods have inherent limitations and a range of uses that are most appropriate to them. To ignore these limitations is to risk misunderstanding at best and, at worst, to become one of the "liars" who "figure."

Frequency Distributions

A very simple descriptive statistic is the frequency distribution. By it a set of scores (numbers) are arranged in an orderly fashion, either in an ascending or descending order, the better to see how many times each score occurs, what the most frequently occurring score is, and whether any identifiable pattern in scores exists. Teachers commonly resort to this practice in handling scores obtained from tests. Thus, for instance, a test in an Old Testament course might yield the following scores as the teacher grades each paper: 65, 58, 72, 80, 97, 84, 85, 80, 97, 80, 90, 72, 80, 86, 83, 80, 97, 90, 80, 95. In such a list these twenty scores are not very manageable. So the teacher makes a different list:

Score	Frequency
97	3
95	1
90	2
86	1
85	1
84	1
83	1
80	6
72	2
65	1
58	1

Now the scores are arranged from highest to lowest, and it is easy to see how many times each score occurs. It soon is evident that a score of 80 is the most frequently occurring. From this list the teacher might go one step further and create a group frequency distribution:

Scores	Frequency
90-97	6
80-89	10
70-79	2
60-69	1
50-59	1

From this list might be created the actual grades, e.g., 90-97

229

are "A", 80-89 are "B", 70-79 are "C", and below 70 are "D".
But the use of frequency distributions need not wait until a teaching job is landed. They can be used in scholarly research. Suppose the statement is made that the doctrine of revelation was studied more in the 1950's than in any other decade of this century. If the assumption can be made that this doctrine is studied because it is of interest, and what is of interest at a given time is discussed in print, then the statement can be tested by looking at the literature about this topic, and by using a simple frequency distribution as an aid to describing the actual situation observed in the literature. In this instance, the year of publication of a book or article becomes the score. Each time a year occurs it is noted. If the year 1955 occurs in the citations of fifty pieces of literature, then the "score" 1955 would have the number "50" as its frequency. The twentieth century would be a list of scores from 1901 to the present, with each year followed by a number designating its frequency of occurrence in the literature. Thus, a given five-year period from that list might look like this:

Score	Frequency
1953	37
1954	40
1955	58
1956	50
1957	44

But, since the number of available years is considerable, the scholar probably would want to use a grouped frequency distribution, especially since the statement being tested referred to a decade (the 1950's), and not a year. In fact, had he or she desired, the study could have as easily begun with decades as the scores rather than individual years. At any rate, the new table might look like this:

Scores	Frequency
1910's	79
1920's	88
1930's	110
1940's	230
1950's	430
1960's	150
1970's	90
1980's (incomplete)	35

Assuming that the researcher had adequate access to the literature so that the observed frequencies are reliable indicators of the actual situation, the statement about interest in the doctrine of revelation peaking in the 1950's is borne out. Moreover, a pattern also has surfaced. Interest grew until that decade, exploded during it, and then sharply declined after it.

The frequency distribution, therefore, garnered more information than was originally sought. (Please remember, though, that this example, like the others in this chapter, is an imagined study.)

Of course, such studies are limited in range and value. The researcher must be as wary as always, trying his or her best to consider rival hypotheses for the data, and owning up to deficiencies. For example, the data above may not reflect accurately the real situation if a factor such as delay in publication from the time of composition is considered, too. Suppose that 109 of the 430 occurrences in the 1950's were in the year 1950. Perhaps these reflect the interest of the late 1940's, when they were written, rather than the early 1950's. Adjusting all of the decades by this consideration might reveal that the true 1940's score should be 339, and the 1950's score only 321! Or suppose that the number of journals and books published in the 1950's was substantially greater than before that time. Then the data is greatly prejudiced. A more accurate indicator in this situation would be the relative frequency of the topic to all of the literature published by theologians in that decade. Then the relative frequencies could be subjected to a frequency distribution. Finally, the whole notion of using decades as an indicator seems rather arbitrary. Was there really such a marked difference between 1949 and 1950, or between 1959 and 1960? Calculating by decades may lead to a static and misleading picture of the actual situation. Again the maxim comes into play: "figures don't lie, but liars figure." Be sure the method is appropriate to the study's aims and the available data.

Measures of Central Tendency

Frequency distributions can be supplemented by three other simple statistics: the mode, the median, and the mean. These three are **measures of central tendency**. They help identify the most typical or representative score in a set of scores. Each of these measures provides a numerical index, a point of reference with regard to the group of scores. But each measures a different reference point.

The **mode** is nothing other than the most frequently occurring score. It is the simplest measure of central tendency. No special calculation is needed to determine the mode. All that is necessary is counting the scores and reporting the one which occurs most often. The value of the mode, therefore, is severely limited. But it is not useless. For example, in a survey of frequently occurring terms in the New Testament it is certainly of some interest and benefit to know what term may occur the most. At the same time, a study which merely aims at discovering the mode and reporting it is unnecessarily self-restricted.

The **median** is a statistic that functions much like the median stripe on a highway. It divides the scores in half.

231

The median is the number found at midpoint in the frequency distribution. If there are an odd number of scores in the distribution, the median will be that number in the distribution above and below which are an equal number of scores. If there are an even number of scores in the distribution, the median will be a number halfway between the two middle scores. Like the mode, the median is a limited measure. It often can be helpful to know the midpoint in the scores under study, but because the median is insensitive to the effects of extreme scores (which cannot raise or lower the median), its value often is mitigated.

The **mean** is both the most popular and the most useful measure of central tendency. Properly called the **arithmetic mean**, it is the arithmetic average of a distribution of scores using at least an interval level of measurement (i.e., the distance between scores is in known intervals, as in the temperature scales). It is calculated by adding all of the scores together and dividing the resulting sum by the number of scores. The mean is sensitive to extreme scores which means that very high or very low scores will pull the mean toward themselves. This is easily illustrated. Consider the following ten scores: 10, 12, 13, 14, 43, 17, 12, 10, 18, 16. The sum of these scores is 165. This sum divided by the number of scores (10) yields a mean of 16.5. The 43 has pulled the mean toward itself, making it higher than it would be had the 43 been a score in the same range as the others (between 10 and 20). Thus, if the 43 had been 17, the mean would have been 13.9. Despite this sensitivity to extreme scores, the mean usually is the preferred measure of central tendency because it is based on all the scores and takes the quantity of scores into account in its calculation.

The pertinent question again is how these simple statistics can be usefully incorporated into theological scholarship. In any given study it is likely that only one of the three measures will be appropriate or helpful enough to use or report. For instance, in considering Paul's use of the terms "faith," "law," "righteousness," "spirit," and "hope" in Romans, the most likely measure to be employed will be the mode. Many people would be interested to know which term occurs the most. But the median and the mean probably have little meaning in this situation.

Or consider a study interested in comparing similarly sized literary documents. Perhaps the scholar has in mind the acceptable range of words each document can have, wants to use eight documents, and desires to have these documents be as close to one another in size as possible. He or she sets the range at 1000 to 2000 words, and finds 15 documents within this range. A frequency distribution is established using the number of words in each document as its score. The resulting order is: 1014, 1026, 1035, 1247, 1248, 1300, 1488, 1497, 1503, 1512, 1516, 1525, 1533, 1690, 1901. The mode obviously is irrelevant since every score appears only once. However, either the median or mean could be used to help select eight documents. The median score is 1497. Selecting the three documents before and four after produces a difference of only 269 words between the smallest and largest documents; selecting the four before and three after produces a difference of 277 words. Calculating the mean (the sum of all the documents, 21,135 ÷ the number of documents, 15 = 1409), leads to a selection of eight documents where the difference between the smallest and the largest is 377 words (largest: 1512; smallest, 1135). In this case, the median is a more helpful statistic to the researcher in setting up the study.

Now consider a study where the problem is discovering the relative frequency of various Greek terms in Matthew's Gospel and Mark's Gospel. It easily is seen that simply noting the number of occurrences is misleading because of the size differences between the two books. Instead, each term must be measured against the total number of words in each book. That means the scholar must calculate the number of words in each book. Unfortunately, she or he is unable to locate a reference aid listing such information, and must make the calculation by hand. He or she selects the edition of the Greek New Testament intended for use, and ponders. The researcher can, of course, count all the words. Naturally, though, he or she shrinks from such a tedious and time-consuming task. There must be an easier way!

There is. The scholar can use statistics. Taking the New Testament in hand, the researcher begins counting the number of Greek words in each of the first 25 lines in Matthew. The same is done for the last 25 lines. Now there are fifty scores, one for each line. These are added, then the sum is divided by fifty. Suppose that the mean is 7.5. The researcher then counts the number of lines in Matthew, and multiplies by 7.5 for the approximate total of words in the Gospel. The process is repeated for Mark. The work still has been relatively long, and even boring, but not nearly as long and boring as it might have been. In this situation, calculating the mean was an invaluable aid. But the mode and the median were not of enough value to use or report.

Obviously, not every study needs, or can benefit from measures of central tendency. Yet some can, and knowing which measure to use may prove an invaluable help. As the examples above show, this aid may appear early on, in the setting of the study's structure. The statistic often does not at all represent the end, or goal, of the study, but only a minor means to help arrive at the desired destination. Thus, several different statistical tools might be incorporated into a study to help it on its way. Maybe a frequency distribution and a calculation of the mean might both prove helpful at different steps in a study. Creativity and competence combine in the good researcher to make these aids work in achieving his or her goals.

Measures of Variability

The measures of central tendency provide a single numerical index to help describe, or represent, a large group of scores. Such a function is a limited one, and more information may be desired from the scores. Since most groups of scores vary within themselves, a **measure of variability** (or dispersion) among the set of scores can be very valuable. It already has been observed how the mean is pulled by extreme scores, occasionally to such a degree that it becomes a quite misleading index. By using a measure of variability the entire set of scores can be better understood. Three common measures of variability are range, variance, and standard deviations.

The **range**, the simplest measure of variability, is the difference between the lowest and highest scores in a group. In the example of the 15 documents (above), the researcher had occasion to use the range as a part of the determination of which eight documents to use in the study. The range can be reported as either a single number representing the difference, or the two extremes. Thus, in this distribution: 1, 5, 7, 11, the range can be reported as either 10 or 1-11. The reliability of the range as a measure of variability is not great because it rests on only two of all the scores. It cannot reflect anything about the variability of the scores in between the extremes.

The **variance** is a much more sophisticated, and important, statistic than the range. The mean is used as a reference point in measuring the extent to which scores of interval level data vary. All the other scores then can be subtracted from this reference point, or subtract this point from themselves. This procedure would show how much scores vary (or deviate) from the mean, but the total of all such variations would have to add up to zero, with all the positive deviations equal to the sum of all the negative deviations. This is seen easily enough by using the numbers of the distribution just cited: 1, 5, 7, 11. The sum is 24; the mean is 6 (24 : 4 = 6). The deviation of each score from the mean is, respectively: -5, -1, +1, +5. The negative sum is -6, the positive sum is +6. Added together, the sum is zero.

Because the sum of these deviation scores must be zero, it is insufficient as a procedure to determine variance. The procedure has no meaning because it cannot be interpreted. For practical and statistical reasons it is necessary to square the deviation scores to obtain a value different from zero; this value can be meaningfully interpreted. The squared deviations from the mean are added together and divided by the total number of scores to produce the variance. Where less than thirty scores are involved an adjustment for greater accuracy is used. In such cases, the sum of the squared deviation scores is divided by the total number of scores **minus one**. The formula for computing variance, then, can be either:

$$\text{Variance} = \frac{\text{Sum of the squared deviation scores}}{\text{Number of scores minus one}}$$

which is correct where less than 30 scores are involved, or:

$$\text{Variance} = \frac{\text{Sum of the squared deviation scores}}{\text{Number of scores}}$$

Variance is simply a measure of the extent to which scores differ from the mean score. It provides a measure of the average distance of the scores from the mean, but in different units of measurement. The variance is essentially an average squared deviation from the mean. If the deviation, for example, were measurable in feet, the variance would be expressed in square feet. Naturally, this makes variance rather unsatisfactory as a descriptive tool. Consider once more the distribution: 1, 5, 7, 11. The variance can be calculated by summing the squared deviation scores and dividing the total number of scores minus one, as follows:

Mean = 6

$6 - 1 = 5 \qquad 5 \times 5 = 25$
$6 - 5 = 1 \qquad 1 \times 1 = 1$
$7 - 6 = 1 \qquad 1 \times 1 = 1$
$11 - 6 = 5 \qquad 5 \times 5 = 25$

$25 + 1 + 1 + 25 = 52$

52 = the sum of the squared deviation scores.

Total scores = 4; 4 - 1 = 3; 52 ÷ 3 = 17.3.

The variance is 17.3. But again, this measurement is in different units than is the mean. To translate the variance into the same unit as the mean is to calculate the **standard deviation** (often symbolized by SD). The square root of the variance is the standard deviation. In the example above the standard deviation is 4.16. This can be used as a unit of measurement. A standard deviation of 4.16 would mean, for the above example, that a score of 10 is approximately one standard deviation above the mean (which is 6).

Because the standard deviation is given in the same unit of measurement as the mean it generally is much more useful, and readily understandable than the variance. It is only natural that the two statistics should be used together, although frequently it is necessary to report only one or the other. Standard deviations often are a handy unit of measurement in comparing a given score against the mean, as in the example above.

Very often scores in a group are distributed normally, that is, the scores tend to cluster about the mean, with a symmetric pattern of distribution. In such normal distributions the range between one standard deviation above the mean and one standard deviation below the mean contains 68.26% of all the scores. The probability, then, of any score above or below one standard deviation sharply decreases, and all the more as

235

the distance from the mean increases. This means that in a normal distribution the standard deviation as a unit of measurement can be quite significant. A score two or three standard deviations above or below the mean is much rarer than those within one standard deviation.

However, not all distributions are normal. How the standard deviation is interpreted depends upon the distribution. In normal distributions what holds true for scores above the mean, in terms of the probability of obtaining them, holds true, too, for scores below the mean. Scores two standard deviations above the mean are as probable as those two standard deviations below the mean. But this is not necessarily true in non-normal, or **skewed distributions.** It is essential that the shape of the distribution be kept in view in working with standard deviations.

But how can range, variance, and standard deviations be incorporated into theological research? Again, creativity and competence alone can provide the answer. However, let us imagine a specific research situation and problem. Suppose someone is interested in discovering if the various New Testament books give varying amounts of attention to a theological problem like the relation of faith and works. Not being content with vague impressions, the researcher resolves to use statistical aids to answer the question. The 27 books are analyzed in terms of the relative frequency with which the topic occurs. This produces 27 numbers, each representing the proportion of space, or attention, given by the books. The scholar arranges the scores in a distribution of descending order. He or she notes immediately the range. Since the lowest score found was .0100, and the highest was .0410. the range, or difference, is .0310. A calculation of the mean produces the number .0200. Each score then can be compared to the mean, and the deviation of each from the mean squared. Then all the squared deviations may be added and divided by the total of scores minus one (26). Suppose the sum of the squared deviation scores is .0014612. This divided by 26 gives a variance of .0000562, a not very helpful number in itself. But, by simply calculating the square root of the variance, the standard deviation (.0075) can be determined. Suppose, too, that the scholar had found the scores to be distributed normally. His or her labor now is ready to yield some very helpful information.

First, the researcher knows that no book gives less than 1% (cf. lowest score) of its attention, nor more than 4% (cf. highest score) of its attention to the topic (range). Second, the extent to which scores differ from the mean is known (variance, expressed in a different unit than the mean). Third, a unit of measurement comparable to the mean has been established that makes it possible to get an accurate idea of the relative position of the scores within the distribution (the standard deviation). A score of .0125 is one standard deviation below the mean (calculated by subtracting the standard deviation from the mean; .0200 - .0075 = .0125). A score of .0275 is one standard deviation above the mean. If the distribution of scores is normal, then some 68%, or 18 books of the New Testament, are within one standard deviation of the mean. By examining each score in this fashion, the scholar can see that book's relative position in the distribution, and begin to form ideas about the significance of that position. The statistical work has made possible for the researcher a very exact picture of the actual situation which he or she is studying.

Measures of variability, like those of central tendency, have limitations. Yet they are, within these limitations, precise and clear tools of description. Descriptive statistics, like frequency distributions, may reveal broad patterns. Or they might, as in measures of central tendency, show averages characteristic of a group of things. They even may disclose, as in measures of variability, how scores differ from each other and from their average. But they only can do these things if they are used.

Suggested Exercises

Exercise 1. The aim of this exercise is training in calculating frequencies and creating a frequency distribution.

Use a concordance and select ten to twenty terms (such as "law," "grace," "faith," and "love"). Count the number of occurrences of each of these terms in the Bible. Create a list of the terms from most frequently occurring to least frequently occurring. Also, using the scores, create a grouped frequency distribution to specify which terms occur in the most frequent group, etc.

Exercise 2. The aim of this exercise is the practice of calculating measures of central tendency.

Suppose a researcher wants to study various ideas occurring in the New Testament. He or she creates a list of twenty-five such ideas. Using predetermined indicators he or she works through the New Testament counting eachoccurrence of an idea as he encounters it. He then arranges the frequencies in order, as follows: 54, 29, 28, 28, 22, 19, 18, 17, 16, 15, 14, 11, 11, 11, 11, 10, 10, 10, 9, 6, 5, 5, 3, 3, 2.

From this list he or she figures first the mode, then the median, and finally the mean. What are the results?

As best as you can, discuss the strength and weakness of each of these measures as they apply to this scholar's specific study. Which of the three measures appears best suited to the study? What kind of unspecified factors in the study might best indicate to you what measure of central tendency the researcher should focus upon?

Exercise 3. The aim of this exercise is practice in measures of variability. Using the list provided in Exercise 2, calculate the range, variance, and standard deviation.

Using the standard deviation as a unit of measurement, specify which scores are within one standard deviation of the mean, either above or below it. Then do the same for those scores two standard deviations from the mean, etc. If you were to graph what you have discovered, what kind of shape would it have? Do you think the scores are distributed normally?

Answers: Ex. 2. Mode, 11; Median, 11; Mean: 14.68
Ex. 3. Range, 52; Variance, 122.99; SD, 11.09

238

16

Measures of Association

The Nature of Correlation

The descriptive statistics examined in the last chapter all concerned single variables. A **variable** is a thing or an event that either can be measured or manipulated. In an example in the last chapter an investigator was interested in whether the doctrine of revelation was studied more in one decade than in others. The research attempted to measure a specific thing, namely, the doctrine of revelation, in terms of the attention it received in literature. The statistical procedures of the last chapter describe the distribution of a single variable. Measures of central tendency and measures of variability are descriptors of a distribution of scores on one variable.

But frequently a researcher desires to study two or more variables and examine the relationships among them. For example, **correlations** are common measures of relationship. The **correlation coefficient** is the statistical descriptor of the relationship between the variables. By using a measure of relationship a researcher can both discern the nature of any relationship between variables, and the extent of that relationship possible. If no relationship exists between the variables it is a zero correlation. If one variable varies similarly to another, a positive correlation is said to exist. If one variable varies inversely to another (i.e., high scores on one variable go with low scores on the other variable), then a negative correlation is said to exist. These relationships are said to have **direction**, and the direction is named by the way in which the variables vary with one another (positive/negative), and shown in writing by a symbol (positive = +; negative = -) which appears before the correlation coefficient.

In addition to direction, these relationships also have **magnitude**. The magnitude of the relationship is its strength. A correlation may be positive and either relatively weak or relatively strong. In other words, the relationship between the variables may be such that as one varies the other varies similarly, and very strongly or only mildly. The magnitude is expressed by the value (number) of the correlation coefficient. So a perfect positive correlation, one where the strongest possible positive relationship exists is indicated by the correlation coefficient +1.00 (where + shows positive direction and 1.00 shows magnitude). A perfect negative correlation, where the strongest possible negative relationship exists, is shown by the correlation coefficient -1.00. A zero correlation is written 0.00 (with no direction sign, of course). The closer the coefficient is to either +1.00 or -1.00, the stronger the relationship. The nearer to 0.00, the weaker the relationship.

There are definite advantages to a correlational study. It can lead to an awareness of whether and how two or more variables are related. In so doing it is able to reduce large sets of data into a simple statistical statement. In one index, the correlation coefficient, the scholar is able to state both the nature and the extent of any existing relationship. Moreover, in some instances prediction is made possible. If two variables are known to be correlated, and a score for one variable is known, then a score for the other variable can be predicted. The greater the magnitude of the correlation, the greater the accuracy of the prediction will be. Prediction must not be confused with causality, however, because a correlation study does not make it possible to state that one variable causes another, no matter how strongly related they may be. Still, the value of correlations for prediction should not be minimized (for more on this idea, see Part Three).

Pearson Product-Moment Correlations

Probably the two most common correlation techniques are the **Pearson product-moment correlation** (commonly called the Pearson **r**), and **Spearman's rho** (discussed more fully below). The former is a **parametric** statistical test, which assumes that the samples of scores being studied are distributed normally, and that the variances within the groups being compared are the same (called "homogeneity of variance"). The Spearman's rho is a **nonparametric** statistical test, which does not make the assumptions of a parametric procedure (and hence ocassionally is called a **distribution-free** procedure). Simple in design, easy to apply, and readily comprehensible, the Pearson **r** is likely the most used of all correlation procedures.

The Pearson product-moment correlation coefficient (**r**) is an index of the relationship between two variables which expresses both direction and magnitude. The problem which the correlation coefficient addresses is how to state accurately the degree of relationship discovered to exist between variables that are themselves quite frequently measured by differing units (for example, height and weight). How can the measured relationship be expressed when the variables being measured are most likely in different units of measurement? To make the scores of the variables comparable, some way of converting them into comparable measuring units must be found. Karl Pearson found such a way. The Pearson coefficient (**r**) is a pure number, independent of the units of measurement, and useful whenever it is desired to compare sets of data. With a single number it is able to provide an index of the relationship between the variables, independent of the measuring units used for each variable. A more formal manner of putting this is to say that the correlation coefficient can be expressed as the average cross product of the variables in a standard score form.

Because it is far too time consuming to compute correlations by hand (unless the data set is less than 20), scholars use one or another of the various statistical programs available, such as the **Statistical Package for the Social Sciences** (abbreviated SPSS; available through the McGraw-Hill book company). These programs provide directions concerning the correct procedure for placing the accumulated data into a computer. The computer then does the mathematical work and provides information, which the researcher must interpret. But, before any data can be given to the computer it must be collected. Prior to any computer analysis is a background of careful research design, patient identification and collection of data, and proper preparation of that data so that the computer can recognize it and interpret it.

To conduct a Pearson product-moment correlation, two or more variables must be studied. These variables must be subject to a level of measurement which is **interval** in nature. In other words, each variable can be set in order and assigned a number, and equal differences between numbers reflect equal differences in the amounts of the variable measured. A temperature scale reflects an interval level of measurement, as does calendar time. In interval levels of measurement the data categories for the variables are mutually exclusive, follow a logical order, and are arranged on the scale in accordance with the amount of the characteristic they actually possess.

To make this easier to visualize, let us consider a specific theological research problem. Suppose a scholar is interested in measuring the supposed relationship between two important New Testament concepts, repentance and the kingdom of God. These concepts are the variables he or she wishes to compare. The researcher constructs a list of vocabulary items that are associated with each of these variables. He or she selects the Synoptic Gospels as the material base from which to draw data, and elects to divide that material into manageable chunks by considering chapters as separate textual units.

Now the scholar could simply determine how frequently each vocabulary item appears in each textual unit. But that would be misleading in the long run because the chapters are of varying lengths. Instead, he or she opts to compute relative frequencies (taking the actual count of the item in a chapter and dividing by the total number of words). Because he or she already has found the average number of words per line in the Bible being used, the task of computing words per chapter is relatively easy (i.e., number of lines per chapter times the average number of words per line). The calculations produce a series of proportions for each lexical item per textual unit. Because the use of relative frequencies permits the establishment of an interval level of measurement the scholar now is able to use the Pearson **r** to analyze the data.

Eventually the researcher arrives at two sets of scores. One is the total proportion of material concerning repentance in each of the 68 textual units (remember that each textual unit is a chapter, and there are a total of 68 chapters in the Synoptics). The other is the total proportion of material concerning the kingdom in each of the textual units. But the researcher does not want just two lists; he or she desires an index of the relationship between the two lists taken in their entirety. After all, the goal is still a comparison of the two variables.

The scholar consults a program that provides directions for the proper placing of the information collected (i.e., the lists) into a computer. Sometime later the computer reports the results. Among other bits of information, it will divulge the awaited correlation coefficient: +.8020 (the computer may print the number without a sign when the correlation is positive). This tells the researcher that a positive relationship exists between the concepts of repentance and the kingdom of God in the Synoptics, and the magnitude of that relationship is .8020. Consulting a scale like the one below sheds further light:

.91–1.00 Very high correlation
.71– .90 High correlation
.51– .70 Moderate correlation
.31– .50 Low correlation
.01– .30 Little, if any correlation

The researcher now knows that the supposed relationship actually exists. When the concept of the kingdom of God appears it can be reasonably expected that the concept of repentance will too, because they are positively related to a high degree. Thus, the one concept can be used to predict the presence of the other. What previously had been a matter of expert opinion now is buttressed by statistical analysis. (Remember, this example and the others in the chapter are fictitious). The analysis, of course, does not make the situation "more real," but it probably does make it clearer, and that is a preeminent goal of descriptive statistics.

But correlations can move beyond description to inference. It is likely that the computer also has printed the significance of the coefficient. **Statistical significance** refers to the probability of a result occurring by chance alone. Commonly, the level of significance accepted by researchers is the .05 or .01 level, which means that a given result has five chances in a hundred (or one chance in a hundred) of coming up sheerly at random. The level of significance can be stated as $p < .05$, which means, "the probability is less than 5% that the result occurred by chance alone." Thus the computer printout may appear as:

Repentance

Kingdom of God   .8020
                   (68)
                 S = .001

242

Beneath the coefficient is listed the number of cases (68: the number of chapters, each of which has a proportion for both concepts, so that 68 also represents the number of paired observations). Beneath the number of cases is given the actual figure for significance. In this example, the level of significance is .001, which means that if the researcher has adopted either the .01 or .05 levels he or she has found a statistically significant result. This gives added confidence that a similar relationship would be found by future study.

Spearman's Rho

Spearman's rho is another correlation technique. It occasionally is called the **rank-order** correlation procedure because it uses data in the form of ranks. Unlike the Pearson **r**, Spearman's rho requires nothing more than an ordinal level of measurement. An **ordinal** level of measurement places a set of things or events in an order determined by rank. Numbers assigned to the things or events do not imply equal differences between what is being measured. Classic examples of such scales are those for the hardness of minerals, and military ranks. Moh's scale of ten minerals presents an order of hardness:

1) Talc	6) Orthoclase
2) Gypsum	7) Quartz
3) Calcite	8) Topaz
4) Fluorite	9) Corundum
5) Apatite	10) Diamond

Gypsum is not twice as hard as talc; the number 2 here does not mean twice the number 1. What the number 2 does mean is that the gypsum is harder than talc (1), but not as hard as calcite (3).

Spearman's rho also needs a large number of categories or ranks on each of the variables being studied. The statistic aims at determining whether two rankings of the same cases are similar. Thus Spearman's rho assumes, too, that there will not be a great number of cases with identical scores. The correlational coefficient produced by this statistical procedure is a summary measure. It is represented by the symbol r_s .

Spearman's rho can be a useful tool in theological research. Suppose a scholar wished to compare the assessments of two prominent church historians on the question of who has made the greatest impact on theological thought in this century. The historians each have ranked twelve theologians. Their comparative rankings look as follows:

Theologian	1st Historian's ranking	2nd Historian's ranking
1	2	3
2	5	4
3	3	5
4	1	1
5	9	9
6	10	11
7	11	10
8	7	6
9	6	7
10	8	8
11	4	2
12	12	12

As with the Pearson product-moment correlation, the researcher could now consult a program for instructions as to the loading of this data into a computer. But, having the computational formula close at hand, and realizing that the problem is not overly difficult, the scholar uses a pocket calculator instead. He or she first notes the difference between the rankings for each theologian:

$$2 - 3 = -1 \qquad 11 - 10 = 1$$
$$5 - 4 = 1 \qquad 7 - 6 = 1$$
$$3 - 5 = -2 \qquad 6 - 7 = -1$$
$$1 - 1 = 0 \qquad 8 - 8 = 0$$
$$9 - 9 = 0 \qquad 4 - 2 = 2$$
$$10 - 11 = -1 \qquad 12 - 12 = 0$$

The differences all are squared, then totaled together to produce a sum of 14. Now the scholar has all the information needed to use the formula for computing the correlation coefficient. The formula is:

$$r_s = 1 - \frac{6 \text{ times the sum of the squared differences}}{\text{Number of pairs of scores (N) times } N^2 - 1}$$

The numbers 1 and 6 are **constants**; they always appear in the formula. Placing the relevant numbers into the formula produces the following equations:

$$r_s = 1 - \frac{6 \times 14}{12 \times (144-1)} = 1 - \frac{84}{12 \times 143} = 1 - \frac{84}{1716} =$$

$$1 - .0489 = .9511$$

The Spearman's rho coefficient is .9511. The direction is positive. The researcher concludes that an extremely strong correlation exists between the two assessments; the historians are in substantial agreement.

Imagine, however, that the rankings of the second historian were the reverse of what is listed above (so that theologian one is ranked 12th instead of 3rd, and so forth). Now a recalculation of the sum of the squared differences produces the number 298. The formula boils down to 1 - (1788 ÷ 1716), or, 1 - 1.0420. The coefficient now is -.0420, a mildly negative correlation.

Naturally, not all research problems are so amenable to hand calculations. A computer is practically indispensable for more complex problems. Suppose, for example, a scholar was interested in discovering the strength of relationship between various measures related to a knowledge of church history. He or she is able to find 102 college students who have been ranked according to their actual test scores in a church history program using six different measures. The test measures are: an ability to recall historical figures, dates, events, ideas, publications, and vocations. The interest of the researcher, who may be faced with teaching courses in this field, is to find which of these things are most strongly associated with one another in recalling history.

All of the rankings are readied, the information placed into the computer with proper instructions, and shortly afterwards a series of correlation coefficients for the variable pairs appears. It might look like this (in part):

Recall persons	.1436	Recall persons	.0303
with	N (102)	with	N (102)
Recall events	SIG .075	Recall voc.	SIG .381
Recall persons	.1057	Recall persons	.2365
with	N (102)	with	N (102)
Recall publ.	SIG .145	Recall ideas	SIG .008
Recall persons	.2206	Recall events	.2637
with	N (102)	with	N (102)
Recall dates	SIG .013	Recall ideas	SIG .004

(Where N = number of subjects/scores;
SIG = level of significance)

Of course, the printout would have 15 variable pairs correlated with 15 corresponding coefficients. These all could be summarized in a single table. To do this so that the information is clearly accessible, and easily understandable, requires some definite forethought. Not everything given by the computer is necessary to reproduce in the table. What is necessary are all the correlation coefficients together with an indication of which correlations are statistically significant, and at what level. Also, each variable name should be given and a number should appear showing how mant subjects were involved. A matrix format table such as that on the next page commonly is used:

245

CORRELATION (RHO) MATRIX OF MEASURES USED
IN RANKING STUDENTS IN CHURCH HISTORY

		1	2	3	4	5	6
1	Recall persons	--	.1436	.0303	.1057	.2365*	.2206
2	Recall events		--	.1556	.0846	.2637*	.0850
3	Recall vocations			--	.1218	.0743	.0376
4	Recall publications				--	.2129	.1299
5	Recall ideas					--	.2491*
6	Recall dates						--

N = 102   *p<.01

At a glance the scholar is able to tell that of the several correlations only three are statistically significant. These are: recall of persons with recall of ideas; recall of events with recall of ideas; and, recall of dates with recall of ideas. In very practical terms, this suggests that a recall of ideas is linked much more strongly to persons, events, and dates, than to publications or vocations of historical figures. These associations may spark ideas as to how best to approach the teaching of the subject.

The "N" in the table refers to the number of students who were ranked; they were the subjects involved in the study. The "p" relates to the level of statistical significance. A glance back will show that the computer had listed a number for each correlation (SIG .004, for instance, means "significant at the .004 level"). The researcher merely notes which coefficients are significant at the level (.01 in this case) that he or she has selected for the study. Any number printed after the letters SIG which is less than .01 is significant for this study.

As with the Pearson product-moment correlation, the coefficient for a Spearman's rho indicates both direction and magnitude. Thus, the correlations in the table all are positive. The magnitude of the coefficient will fall in the range of -1.00 to +1.00. In the matrix above the greatest magnitude is .2637. It should be noted that while this is statistically significant, it may not be very practically significant. Large samples lend themselves rather readily to statistical significance. But .2367 is not a correlation of great magnitude in itself, only in relation to some of the others in the matrix.

Chi Square

Another useful measure of association is the nonparametric procedure known as the Chi Square. This statistic often is used for description and inference. The Chi Square, represented by the symbol χ^2 (the Greek letter "chi"), has the advantage of being able to treat data on a nominal level of measurement. A nominal level of measurement specifies no order (rankings), or continuous measurements (as in interval or ratio levels). Instead, variables are classified, with each one receiving a label.

Numbers can serve as labels, with each number reflecting nothing more than that the variable to which it is assigned is different from the variables possessing other numbers. What is preeminent in nominal measurements is the category to which a variable belongs.

The Chi Square is appropriate where the scholar is interested in the number of things, or events, or scores that fall into two or more categories. Chi Square compares actual observed frequency distributions with expected (theoretical) distributions. It asks, Is the actual number of things in a category significantly different from the number that could be expected for this category? In other words, does the actual data fit what is expected? Because it aims at answering such questions, the Chi Square often is referred to as a **goodness-of-fit** statistic.

It is also a test of statistical significance. It makes possible a determination of whether a systematic relationship exists between variables. Thus, it is used commonly as a test in crosstabulation procedures. A **crosstabulation** simply is a joint frequency distribution of cases according to the classificatory variables (nominal level for Chi Square tests). What this means practically may best be seen in a typical crosstabulation table:

THE USE OF TEXTBOOKS IN CLASSROOM PREPARATION
BY PHILOSOPHY AND THEOLOGY TEACHERS

	Teachers		
	Philosophy	Theology	
More than 10 books	75	40	115
Less than 10 books	25	160	185
	100	200	

Preparation (row label for the two "books" rows)

The researcher is interested in testing a hypothesis. He or she believes that philosophy teachers more frequently use a large number of texts in preparing for a course than do theology teachers. To find out if this hypothesis is correct, the scholar took a survey and acquired the above results. As the column and row totals indicate, 300 teachers were surveyed. In each block (called a **cell**) are the actual figures. Even casual inspection indicates that the researcher's hypothesis is correct. This becomes more apparent when the actual figures are given as proportions. Among philosophy teachers 75% used more than 10 books, while only 20% of theology teachers did so. But is this difference in percentage a statistically significant one?

Application of the Chi Square test can resolve this question. To do this test the researcher must figure the cell frequencies he or she could expect if, given the existing row and column totals (called **marginals**), no relationship is present between the variables. In simpler terms, the scholar must use the existing data from the column and row totals to determine the theoretical cell frequencies that would be obtained if no relationship between the variables was present. A formula to do this is available, and since the work is not too difficult, the researcher quickly makes the computations:

$$\text{Expected frequency per cell} = \frac{\text{column frequency x row frequency}}{\text{total number of valid cases}}$$

Since there are four cells, four computations using this formula are needed, as follows:

$$\text{Expected frequency} \ (f_e^i) = \frac{100 \ x \ 115}{300} = \frac{11500}{300} = 38.33$$

$$= \frac{100 \ x \ 185}{300} = \frac{18500}{300} = 61.66$$

$$= \frac{200 \ x \ 185}{300} = \frac{37000}{300} = 123.33$$

$$= \frac{200 \ x \ 115}{300} = \frac{23000}{300} = 76.66$$

These four expected (theoretical) cell frequencies next must be compared to the actual frequencies listed in the table. As the mathematical work for this second step also is relatively easy, the researcher does it by hand, according to the formula:

$$\chi^2 = \text{Sum of } \frac{(\text{observed frequency} - \text{expected frequency})^2}{\text{expected frequency}}$$

for all cells totalled.

In other words, Chi Square is equal to the sum of four different computations (in this example). A value must be derived for each cell and the total of those values gives the Chi Square statistic. For the sake of easy viewing, the scholar enters the data and calculations into a simple table:

Observed frequency (O)	Expected frequency (E)	O-E	$(O-E)^2$	$\frac{(O-E)^2}{E}$
75	38.33	36.67	1344.69	35.08
25	61.66	-36.67	1344.69	21.81
160	123.33	36.67	1344.69	10.90
40	76.66	-36.67	1344.69	17.54
300	300.00	0	---	85.33 = χ^2

The Chi Square is 85.33. But what does this statistic mean? To understand it, some other things need to be known. First, the greater the discrepancies between the actual and the expected frequencies, the larger Chi Square becomes. Second, a large Chi Square indicates that a systematic relationship does exist between the variables. But, third, to check this indication, and verify if a systematic relationship in fact does exist requires further work. It means discovering if the value of Chi Square is great enough to warrant rejection of the idea that the actual results (i.e., the observed frequencies) are attributable to chance. Once again the notion of statistical significance has entered in.

However, in assessing the significance of the Chi Square reference must be made to a table of Chi Square values. But to be able to use this table requires an understanding of degrees of freedom. **Degrees of freedom** is a concept reflecting the number of useful bits of information created by a sample for estimating a given universe parameter. Another way to look at it is to see degrees of freedom as the number of obtained frequencies that are "free to vary" when both the sum of the frequencies and the number of frequencies are fixed. In practice, determining the degrees of freedom is quite easy, especially once it is recognized that the totals for both rows and columns are **not** free to vary: they are fixed. In a 2 x 2 crosstabulation table like the one in the example, only one cell frequency is free to vary, since as soon as one obtained value has been entered in the table the others are determined. As a general rule, the number of degrees of freedom for a Chi Square with two variables will be equal to the number of rows minus one, times the number of columns minus one. Hence the formula:

Degrees of freedom (df) = (rows - 1) x (columns - 1)

The researcher now consults a table of critical values for Chi Square (such a table can be found in most basic statistics texts). It might look like this:

Degrees of freedom (df)	Level of significance accepted (p)	
	p = .05	p = .01
1	3.841	6.635
2	5.991	9.210
3	7.815	11.341
4	9.488	13.277
5	11.070	15.086
6	12.592	16.812

Assuming the researcher has adopted the .05 level of significance, the critical value he or she obtains is 3.481. If the Chi Square statistic is larger than this critical value, then statistical significance has been acheived. Thus, the idea that the observed frequencies should be attributed to chance can be rejected. The researcher now is more confident in saying that a relationship does exist between a teacher's department

249

(philosophy versus theology), and the use of books in course preparation. The scholar is correct in thinking that something more than chance is operating in the observed relationship.

Unfortunately, Chi Square by itself only states whether a relationship exists. In itself it cannot state how strongly two variables are related. But Chi Square can be adjusted by such statistics as **phi** (φ), or **lambda** (λ). Some computer programs determine automatically these statistics and report them. Or, they can be calculated by hand. The formula for these statistics can be obtained from most basic statistics texts.

Phi has a value of 0 when no relationship exists, and +1 when a perfect relationship exists between the variables. It is a helpful measure of the strength of a relationship. Lambda, on the other hand, measures an improvement in the ability to predict variable values. It aims at a proportional reduction in error to attain the highest possible confidence in the research results. Whether and how Chi Square is corrected depends, of course, on the scholar's needs. It is not uncommon to find Chi Square reported alone, since often the study is interested only in discovering if a relationship exists that is statistically significant.

For the purposes of the beginning researcher in theological study, it is probably best to master simply the computation of Chi Square along with an ability to determine if it is significant at the .05 or .01 levels. Let the computer handle Pearson product-moment correlations, complex Spearman's rho problems, and statistical adjustments of Chi Square. What the theological scholar does need is a grasp of the basic concepts. An ability to do the mathematics for simple problems is useful because it can save time. But when large or complex problems are being studied access to a computer is invaluable. With patience and a handle on the ideas behind these procedures it is possible to utilize an established computer program to accomplish truly sophisticated research.

Suggested Exercises

Exercise 1. The purpose of this exercise is to better acquaint you with basic concepts of a correlation.

Suppose a researcher has conducted a Pearson product-moment correlation using two important concepts in the book of Deuteronomy. The scholar reports the results by the number +.55.

What is the name by which this number is known? What is the direction of the relationship? What is its magnitude?

The Pearson r is a parametric test. What assumptions are made by such tests. To conduct this kind of correlation, what level of measurement is needed? If the researcher had set the level of significance at .01 and discovered a result significant at the .10 level, should the result be reported as statistically significant? Why, or why not?

Exercise 2. The purpose of this exercise is to work through an example of rank-order correlation.

Suppose that a researcher must select a curriculum for a church's education program. There are ten available from which to make a choice. Not being an expert in such matters, the researcher turns to the church educators for help. They are asked to rank the curricula for suitability for a total Christian education program. The two expert educators rank the curricula as follows:

Curriculum	1st Educator	2nd Educator
1	9	2
2	5	5
3	10	8
4	2	3
5	7	6
6	1	4
7	3	5
8	4	1
9	6	7
10	8	10

Calculate the correlation. What is its direction and magnitude? Are the two educators in substantial agreement in their assessment of the ten choices?

Does this finding provide assistance in selecting a curriculum? Why, or why not? Would the researcher have been wiser selecting some other method to help make a good decision?

Answers: Ex. 1. Name: correlation coefficient; Direction: positive; Magnitude: .55; Assumptions: normal distribution, homogeneity of variance; Level of measurement: interval; No, .10 is greater than .01. Ex. 2. Correlation coefficient: .5030; Direction: positive; Magnitude: .5030. The correlation is moderate and not, in itself, very helpful for this problem. The scholar might have asked the experts for objective measures by which to score the curricula. The curricula could then have been ranked by total scores.

17

Simple Inferential Statistics

Inferential Statistics Defined

Not all statistics are merely descriptive in character. Some of the statistics already examined have usefulness for inference as well. Often researchers desire more than to describe their data. They want instead to use the data they have obtained to generalize to a larger group. The use of data characteristics to make generalized remarks about sets of data that have not been measured is the province of inferential statistics. As the name suggests, the aim of such statistics is **to make inferences from known characteristics of a small group to unmeasured characteristics of a larger group.** There are many different kinds of inferential statistics, varying from relatively simple procedures to complex and sophisticated procedures. This chapter focuses on stastistical tools used specifically for inferential purposes.

Basic Concepts

Statistical techniques exist which permit comparison of groups in terms of characteristics other than the group means. However, the simpler inferential statistics use different ways of comparing groups in terms of their means. In this chapter, all of the inferential procedures examined have this feature in common. They all make comparisons bsed on the mean. In so doing they ask whether the differences between the group means are great enough to assume that the corresponding population means are different.

This concept will make better sense if the logic behind it is exposed. Commonly researchers find it impossible to measure a group they wish to study simply because the group is too large. They are left with no choice but to draw a smaller group from this large group and study what they can. We have already seen that this is the work of creating a **sample.** If they draw the small group wisely, they will be confident that it is **representative** of the large group. That means that the characteristics they observe in the smaller group should hold true for the larger group from which they were drawn.

Researchers use precise names for the large group and the small group taken from it. The large group, which the researcher wants to study, is called the **population.** By definition a population contains all of the possible members of a group the researcher wants to examine. But usually the scholar must content her/himself with the small group; it is a subgroup of the population. Since it is vitally important to obtain a sample representative of the population, a great deal of time and attention typically is given to the process of sampling.

Remember, the most favored way of ensuring that the sample is representative is to randomly select it from the population. A **random sample** makes for a representative sample because every member of the population has an equal chance of being selected for the sample. Tables of random numbers are easy to come by to facilitate this procedure. Occasionally, random sampling is modified by the needs of the study or some unusual features of the population. Thus a **stratified random sample** might be used where the characteristics of the population properly fall into strata (e.g., height, weight, age). A random sample is drawn from each strata.

It is not always possible to draw random samples. If a study wants to incorporate certain features in the sample, then a **nonrandom stratified sample** might be used. Where a researcher wishes to incorporate the extremes of a population, random sampling may be inappropriate because it tends to eliminate the extremes. But when random samples are not used it generally is because the population is not accessible to such a procedure. Many studies are limited in their approach to sampling by the availability of data. In such cases, the researcher must do the best he or she can in creating a sample. Of course, in such instances it is not possible to have the same confidence in generalizing to the population.

As the above consideration implies, **size** is a critical factor in any sample. How large must a sample be to be representative? As we have seen, sometimes the sample is determined as to both size and representativeness simply by what is available to the scholar from the population. Where this is not the situation two factors must enter into the researcher's thinking. First, the sample must be **manageable** in size. It might be nice to be able to state a range of numbers that could be guaranteed to satisfy this consideration, but that is not possible. The features of the study, including the time the researcher has to give to the study, his or her ability, and the methods being employed, all contribute to determining what is manageable or not. Second, the sample size must be **meaningful**. Once again, no number or range of numbers can be established arbitrarily. Meaningfulness is the idea which relates size to the ability to generalize. In essence, it is representativeness. A sample is meaningful only if it is representative, that is, if it is large enough to permit reasonable inferences to the population.

Thus far, this review of sampling should recall what was said in the chapter on content analysis. Now, when representative samples have been obtained, it is possible to estimate the mean of the population from the mean determined for the sample. However, a scholar may want to compare two or more groups to determine if the corresponding populations are similar. To accomplish this the researcher follows a definite pattern. He or she draws samples and then formulates an **hypothesis**, or proposed explanation, for what will be obtained. The hypothesis is stated as a **null hypothesis**, which, as the name suggests, asserts that no difference exists between the populations the researcher is studying. Or, he or she might state an **alternative hypothesis**, which asserts that a difference does exist between the populations. With the hypothesis the scholar establishes a level of significance which, it will be remembered, reflects the degree of probability that the researcher's results are the product of chance. If the .05 level is accepted, then he or she is stating that statistical results at or below this level reflect more than chance at work. If an outcome is a rare event when just chance is at work (which the level of significance assumes), then it makes sense to say that more than chance is operating when the specified level exists. Thus the null hypothesis is rejected and the alternative hypothesis accepted, for the difference which has been found between the groups does not seem to be attributable to chance alone.

In testing the hypothesis to determine whether to accept or reject it, the researcher's statistical test will yield what is called a **calculated value**. This value is a numerical index which can be used in conjunction with a **critical value** to make his or her decision about the hypothesis. The critical value is a criterion which constitutes a dividing line for all the possible values of the sample mean. This value is truly "critical" because whether the calculated value falls on one side of it or the other determines whether the scholar accepts or rejects the hypothesis he or she has set. If the calculated value is smaller than the critical value, the researcher accepts the null hypothesis. She or he concludes that no significant difference exists between the populations. If the calculated value is greater than the critical value, the null hypothesis is rejected. Thus, the critical value serves to divide the realm of all possible values of the sample means into an acceptance region (where the null hypothesis is accepted) and a rejection region.

The critical value is related to the level of significance set by the researcher. For the different inferential procedures there are available tables of critical values. These vary somewhat from each other but the principle is the same. Knowing the level of significance the scholar must compare the calculated value with the critical value given by the table. Having determined which side of the critical value the calculated value falls upon, the researcher makes the appropriate decision, either to accept or reject the hypothesis that has been made. (Examples of this procedure are included in the discussion of statistical tests below.)

The t Test

The t test, while amenable to more than one use, generally is employed to compare the means of two groups. The t value obtained is a calculated value to be compared against a critical value, with a level of significance in mind. On the basis of this comparison the researcher makes a decision to reject or accept his or her hypothesis. In other words, if the two sample means prove to be far enough apart to yield a significant statistical difference using the t test, then the scholar will conclude that the two populations from which the samples were removed (assuming, of course, that they are representative samples), most likely do not have the same mean. So the researcher, using the t test, makes an inference about a population he or she may never actually see in its totality. He or she must not only believe that the samples are representative, but that the scores in one group have about the same variance as the scores in the other group.

The t test is limited to comparing the means of two groups. However, there are two distinct forms of the test. The **independent samples t test** is the proper choice whenever one group's scores have no logical relationship with the other group's scores. The **correlated samples t test** (or **matched t test**, or **paired t test**), is used when the data of one group is logically connected to that of the other. It is easy to envision such situations: the group measured twice, or two different groups where each subject in one group is matched to a subject in the other group. The formula for the statistical test is different for the two forms, but each yields a calculated t value. The manner in which this is compared to the critical value does not vary between the forms.

There are any number of possible studies using the t test which might be of interest to a theological researcher. Suppose, for example, a scholar became interested in the debates between Bible translators over the relative merits of exact translation (the classical method) as compared to dynamic equivalency (a modern method). She or he might devise several ways to approach the debate, including a couple of studies using t tests. In one study, the researcher simply limits her/himself to asking the basic question whether one of the methods actually increases success in selecting proper translation alternatives among different linguistic choices. She or he does not ask if the method makes for selecting the best choices, only if its increases a translator's ability to make acceptable choices.

The translator finds 14 students who had participated in a classical translation training program. All had graduated previously from an introductory course in translation. Prior to their receiving the classical training the students were tested on making linguistic choices (this test is called a **pre-test**). After the training they received another test (called a **post-test**). The researcher realizes that the appropriate procedure to use is a correlated t test, since the same group is being measured twice.

The scholar either could use a computer or calculate the value by hand. He or she finds the correct formula for t:

$$t = \frac{\text{the mean difference}}{\text{the standard error}}$$

which means that the calculated value is determined by finding the mean (average) difference between the group's pre-test and post-test scores, and dividing that by the standard deviation of the sampling distribution (called the **standard error** and symbolized as s_D).

This involves straightforward mathematics. The scores, remember, are paired. The researcher notes the differences between each pair of scores, adds all of the differences, and divides by the total number of pairs (14 in this case), in order to obtain the mean difference. The standard error is a little harder to arrive at. The formula to calculate it is:

$$s_D = \frac{\text{the standard deviation of the difference}}{\text{the square root of the number of subjects}}$$

but, recall, the standard deviation can be calculated only from the variance (see chapter 15).

When the appropriate data has been placed in the right spots, the scholar obtains a calculated t value of, say, 2.40. This must be compared to the critical value from an appropriate table. Such a table might appear, in part, as follows:

CRITICAL VALUES OF THE t DISTRIBUTION

df	Level of significance for one-tailed test			
	.10	.05	.025	.01
	Level of significance for two-tailed test			
	.20	.10	.05	.02
1	3.078	6.314	12.706	31.821
2	1.886	2.920	4.303	6.965
3	1.638	2.353	3.182	4.541
4	1.533	2.132	2.776	3.747
5	1.476	2.015	2.571	3.365
6	1.440	1.943	2.447	3.143
7	1.415	1.895	2.365	2.998
8	1.397	1.860	2.306	2.896
9	1.383	1.833	2.262	2.821
10	1.372	1.812	2.228	2.764
11	1.363	1.796	2.201	2.718
12	1.356	1.782	2.179	2.681
13	1.350	1.771	2.160	2.650
14	1.345	1.761	2.145	2.624

(Table from Hinkle, Wiersma, and Jurs, **Applied Statistics for the Behavioral Sciences**, p. 466.)

Obviously, there are some things that must be known in order to use this table. First, the scholar must know how many degrees of freedom (df) there are. For correlated samples t tests this is determined merely by subtracting one from the total number of pairs of scores, or data observations, upon which the study is based. In this example, df=13. Second, the researcher must have a level of significance. For this example, it is set at the .05 level. Finally, the researcher must have decided whether the t test is one-tailed or two-tailed. A **two-tailed test** is one that is sensitive to significant differences of a sample mean where it is either much greater or much less than the hypothesized value. With respect to the example, the two-tailed test can answer whether students score significantly higher on the pre-test or the post-test. On the other hand, a **one-tailed test** is needed by the researcher who predicts the direction of the results. In this case, the scholar is interested in the question, Do students score significantly higher on the post-test? By examining the table it can be seen readily that the same difference with a two-tailed test is significant at the level of significance twice as large as that associated with a one-tailed test. Thus, what is significant at the .05 level for a one-tailed test is significant for a two-tailed test only at the .10 level. The use of the one-tailed test is most appropriate when the researcher is concerned only about a difference in one direction (or if he or she is certain of the direction of the difference between the populations). To use a one-tailed test and report results in the opposite direction of the one predicted would be to misuse and misunderstand the test. Where there is doubt, the two-tailed test is a safe alternative.

In the example, the scholar has used a one-tailed test because he or she is concerned only with the difference of direction from pre-test to post-test. He or she predicts that a significantly higher score will obtain for the post-test. Now, having made his or her decisions and calculations, the scholar looks for the critical value from the table. It is 1.771 (if a two-tailed test had been used, at .05 the critical value would have been 2.16). Since the calculated value of 2.40 is greater than the critical value, the scholar has found a significant difference at the .05 level. He or she rejects the null hypothesis that the mean of the pre-test group will be the same as that of the post-test group. This means an acceptance of the alternative hypothesis (or **research** hypothesis), namely, that a significant difference exists between the means. In short, classical training in translation has made a difference; students acheive a higher level of success in making choices among linguistic alternatives after receiving this training.

Now the researcher embarks upon a second study. This time he or she has in mind an independent samples t test. The scholar wishes to compare two groups, each trained under a different system. One group has the task of selecting the proper translation alternative among linguistic choices after receiving traditional (classical) training. The other group has the same task, but after receiving modern (dynamic equivalency) training. The 29 students participating in the study are assigned randomly to the two groups, with the result that 13 end up in the classical group, and 16 in the modern group.

Again the researcher has to decide whether to use the computer or do the mathematics by hand. He or she looks at the formula:

$$t = \frac{\text{difference between the group means}}{\text{standard error of the difference between the means}}$$

and recognizes how much work is involved. The calculation of the difference of the means is not too difficult. Each group's mean is found and then they are compared. But to find the standard error of the difference between the means is a more imposing task. It involves calculating the pooled estimate of the population variance, a tedious procedure to do by hand. The researcher decides to let a computer do the figuring. It will provide figures for the mean, standard deviation, and the standard error for each group. Other data likely is to be given, too, including the most important, the calculated **t** value. But, lo!, the computer is 'down,' and the work must be done by hand.

Since the first imposing task is the pooled estimate of the population variance (symbolized by s^2), the scholar turns to its formula, which in symbols appears as:

$$s^2 = \frac{(N_A - 1)s^2 + (N_B - 1)s^2}{N_A + N_B - 2}$$

In words this formula can be expressed as follows:

$$s^2 = \frac{\text{the sum of the squared deviations of both groups}}{\text{the degrees of freedom}}$$

The degrees of freedom for an independent samples **t** test is determined by subtracting two from the total number of subjects, or data observations. In the example study, df=27.

With the pooled variance estimate in hand, the standard error of the difference between the means now can be derived. The variance estimate (s^2) is multiplied by the sum of the numbers for both groups ($N_A + N_B$) divided by the total derived from multiplying the number of scores in each group together ($N_A N_B$). This product's square root is divided into the difference between the sample means ($\overline{X}_A - \overline{X}_B$) to yield **t**. The symbolic formula for **t**, then, is:

$$t = \frac{\overline{X}_A - \overline{X}_B}{\sqrt{s^2 \frac{N_A + N_B}{N_A N_B}}}$$

With everything in place, the researcher finds the value to be 3.98. Is this significant? The scholar has done a two-tailed test since he or she is intersted in any significant difference, irrespective of direction. The level of significance has been set at .05. The degrees of freedom equal 27. A quick consultation of the appropriate table produces a critical value of 2.771. The researcher therefore concludes that a significant difference does exist between the two groups trained by different translation methods. The difference of this direction can be seen from examining the means for each group. To make this obvious, the scholar set out the results in a table:

SUCCESS IN SELECTING THE PROPER ALTERNATIVE AMONG LINGUISTIC CHOICES FOLLOWING TWO TRAINING METHODS

Training Method (Group)	Mean	SD	t
Classical	1.7692	2.242	3.98*
Modern	5.8750	3.117	

*$p < .05$

From this table can be garnered the calculated t value, and whether it is significant (and at what level). Each group is identified, and both its mean and standard deviation reported. The mean is critical here as the point at which the two groups are compared. The standard deviation is useful in the evaluation of any particular score, or evaluating the variance around the mean. Here it can be seen that the modern group's mean is higher than the classical group's mean. Since it is significantly higher, it can be inferred that training under this method is relatively more successful than training under the classical method. When the result of this study is set alongside the result of the first study it appears that while training in the classical method increases translation skills it does not do so as successfully as training under the modern method. (But remember that these are only imagined studies.)

One-Way ANOVA

The abbreviation ANOVA represents "analysis of variance," another inferential procedure. The one-way ANOVA, so named because the researcher is interested in the possible effects of a single factor, shares with t tests the aim of comparing groups in terms of their means. However, one-way ANOVA is more versatile than a t test because it can compare more than two groups. Like t tests, a one-way ANOVA tests a null hypothesis that states that there is no difference between the population means the researcher is interested in. Also like t tests, one-way ANOVA tests this hypothesis by determining a calculated value (F instead of t), then comparing it to a critical value. It would not be inaccurate to think of the one-way ANOVA as an extension of the logic of the t test so that more than two groups may be treated in a study.

To further explain one-way ANOVA, and illustrate its applicability to theological research, let us consider a specific problem. Suppose a scholar is interested in religious phenomenology. He or she desires to see if religious persons' responses in worship settings are significantly different in various situations. Since he or she is interested particularly in a definite religious tradition, the test subjects are drawn from that tradition alone. Then they are randomly assigned to one of five groups, with each group being placed in a different worship setting. One setting is very normal, that is, identical to what the people in that religious tradition are accustomed to. This group is a **control group**, one that provides a baseline against which to evaluate the effects of the experimental treatments rendered to the other groups. Since the other four groups are receiving what could be termed an experimental treatment, they can be called **experimental groups**. One such group finds itself in a setting keyed by baptism (i.e., a baptismal service), another by the eucharist, a third by very demonstrative charismatic expressions, and the last by meditative prayer. In each instance the worship setting and accompanying service is quite dominated by the individual motif. All 40 volunteers are given a "phenomenological response" test measuring their reactions.

After the researcher has collected the raw data (the test scores), he or she is ready to analyze them according to a one-way ANOVA. The calculated F value is determined according to the formula:

$$F = \frac{\text{the mean square between groups}}{\text{the mean square within groups}}$$

Still not having access to a computer, the scholar must do the work by hand. He or she follows three steps to acquire the numbers needed for the above formula. First, he or she finds the total **sum of squares** following the formula:

$$\text{Total sum of squares} = \Sigma X^2 - \frac{(\Sigma X)^2}{N}$$
$$\text{(Symbolized } \Sigma x_t^2)$$

which, in words, means taking the scores for each group, adding them to produce a sum total score for each group (ΣX), then squaring each separate score and adding the squares together. That produces the sum of group scores squared (symbolized in the above formula as ΣX^2). The process might look like this:

	Group 1	Group 2	Group 3	Group 4	Group 5	
scores	21	35	45	32	45	
	35	12	60	53	29	
	32	27	33	29	31	
	28	41	36	42	22	
	14	19	31	40	36	
	47	23	40	23	29	
	25	31	43	35	42	
	38	20	48	42	30	
ΣX	240	208	336	296	264	= 1,344
ΣX^2	7,948	6,030	14,724	11,556	9,112	= 49,370

The number subtracted from 49,370 is obtained easily now. This number is the sum of all the group totals squared, then divided by the total number of scores. The sum of all the group totals already is known: 1,344. This number squared is 1,806,336. The total number of scores is, of course, 40. So, 1,806,336 ÷ 40 = 45,158.4, which is $\frac{(\Sigma X)^2}{N}$. Now the two numbers needed to calculate the total sum of squares are available, and the result is: 49,370 - 45,158.4 = 4,211.6 = Σx_t^2.

The second step is to find the between groups sum of squares. Another imposing formula appears:

$$\Sigma x_b^2 = (\frac{(\Sigma X_A)^2}{N_A} + \frac{(\Sigma X_B)^2}{N_B} + \frac{(\Sigma X_C)^2}{N_C} + \frac{(\Sigma X_D)^2}{N_D} + \frac{(\Sigma X_E)^2}{N_E}) - \frac{(\Sigma X)^2}{N}$$

which, in words, means that the between groups sum of squares is found by subtracting the sum of the group totals squared and divided (45,158.4), from the sum of each group's sum of scores squared, then divided by the number of scores in each group, then added to the corresponding numbers for every other group. The equation in symbols, and a straight-forward verbal translation, probably make the work appear more imposing than it really is. The actual operation looks like this:

$$\frac{(240)^2}{8} + \frac{(208)^2}{8} + \frac{(336)^2}{8} + \frac{(296)^2}{8} + \frac{(264)^2}{8} =$$

$$7,200 + 5,408 + 14,112 + 10,952 + 8,712 = 46,384$$

As can be seen, the formula is not yet complete. What has been done so far is that the sum of squares for each of the five groups has been squared, then each of those five results divided by the number of scores in each group (8), then those five results added together (46,384). Now this sum has subtracted from it the sum of the five groups' scores squared and divided by the total number of scores (45,158.4). So the between groups sum of squares is now found by a simple subtraction: 46,384 - 45,158.4 = 1,225.5 = Σx_b^2.

The last step is to find the within group sum of squares.

This is an exceedingly easy operation, for which the formula is:

$$\Sigma x_t^2 - \Sigma x_b^2 = \Sigma x_w^2$$

In words, the within groups sum of squares is found by subtracting the between groups sum of squares from the total sum of squares. Since both the between groups sum of squares and the total sum of squares already have been calculated, finding the within groups sum of squares is a matter of just one subtraction: $4,211.6 - 1,225.6 = 2,986 = \Sigma x_w^2$.

The basic numbers to calculate the F value are now in hand, but the researcher must be able to convert them into mean squares for both between groups and within groups. To accomplish this he or she must know the degrees of freedom for the between groups sum of squares and for the within group sum of squares. The formula for determining the degrees of freedom for the between groups sum of squares is 5-1 (or, the number of groups minus one). Since there are five groups, the degrees of freedom is equal to 4 for between groups. The formula for within groups is N-r, or the number of scores minus the number of groups. There are 40 subjects (hence 40 scores), and five groups: $40 - 5 = 35$. The degrees of freedom for within groups is thus 35.

By dividing the between groups sum of squares by the degrees of freedom for between groups $(1,225.6 \div 4)$, and the within groups sum of squares by the degrees of freedom for within groups $(2,986 \div 35)$, the mean squares for the formula for the calculated F value are obtained. Thus F is equal to: $306.4 \div 85.3 = 3.5920$.

The F value must be compared to the appropriate critical value drawn from a table. Unlike the table of critical values for a t test, this table requires knowledge of two degrees of freedom and the accepted level of significance. The two different degrees of freedom, of course, correspond to those found for between groups and within groups. On the table, these are called the degrees of freedom (df) for the numerator (the df for between groups), and the denominator (df for the within groups). So the df for the numerator is 4, and the df for the denominator is 35. Consulting a table yields a critical value of 2.64 at the .05 level of significance (3.91 at the .01 level).

The calculated value of 3.5920 is greater than the critical value of 2.64 so the researcher concludes that there is a significant difference between the means of the samples (groups). He or she reports this finding, along with some other relevant information, in a convenient summary table:

ANALYSIS OF VARIANCE OF PHENOMENOLOGICAL
RESPONSE SCORES FOR BAPTISM-KEYED, EUCHARIST-
KEYED, MEDITATIVE PRAYER-KEYED, CHARISMATIC-
KEYED, AND CONTROL GROUPS

Source	Sum of Squares	df	Mean Square	F
Between	1,225.6	4	306.4	3.592*
Within	2,986.0	35	85.3	
Total	4,211.6	39		

*$p < .05$

Of course, one problem still remains. Which group means differs from which other(s)? A significant **F** ratio does not supply the answer. However, there are follow-up **tests** (called **multiple comparison** tests, or **post hoc** tests) to help the scholar discover precisely where the significant differences are located. Some of these tests are rather liberal, that is, they are able to find a significant difference between two relatively close means. A very conservative post hoc comparison, like **Scheffé's test**, shows only significant differences where the means are far apart.

The researcher in our imagined example selects this conservative test. Still lacking the use of a computer, he or she must resort once more to doing the mathematics by hand. The scholar follows an established order of steps, which begins by determining the mean score for each group. Since he or she already has the sum of the scores for each group, he or she merely divides each by the number of scores in the group (8 in each case):

$$240 \div 8 = 30 \quad 208 \div 8 = 26 \quad 336 \div 8 = 42 \quad 296 \div 8 = 37 \quad 264 \div 8 = 33$$

Next, the standard error of the difference among the means, which is the square root of two times the mean square within groups divided by the number of scores per group is derived. The symbolic formula looks like this:

$$\text{Std. error} = \sqrt{\frac{2ms_w}{n}}$$

The actual operation appears as follows:

$$\sqrt{\frac{2\ (85.3)}{8}} = \sqrt{\frac{170.6}{8}} = \sqrt{21.3} = 4.62$$

Third, he or she either determines the critical value, or reasserts it. Since the table already has been consulted, all the scholar does now is set it down in an easy-to-read summary:

Critical value for $p < .05$ (df 4, 35) is 2.64.

Fourth, the scholar multiplies the critical value by the number of groups minus one (i.e., 2.64 x (5-1)): 2.64 x 4 = 10.56.

264

Fifth, the researcher takes the square root of the number obtained in step four and multiplies it by the standard error found in step two. This yields the critical difference needed to compare the different means. Thus:

$$10.56 = 3.25 \text{ and, } 3.25 \times 4.62 = 15.02$$

The critical difference, then, is 15.02.

Finally, the differences between the various means can be tested. Whenever the difference between any two of the means is larger than the critical difference, then the means should be assumed to be significantly different. A glance back at the means for each group (determined in step one) shows that in only one instance is the difference between the means for two groups larger than the critical difference. That exception is between group two (say, the control group; mean = 26), and group three (say, the charismatic-keyed group; mean = 42). The difference between means is 16, exceeding the critical difference, so the researcher states that the difference between these two groups' responses is significant.

The researcher now can infer that only the experience of the very demonstrative charismatic service produced a significantly different phenomenological response from the baseline (control) group. Such a finding is bound to prove interesting not only to the researcher, but to members of the religious tradition from which the subjects were drawn and, probably, to the wider reaches of various religious groups.

The post hoc test also can be presented pictorially in a table:

SCHEFFÉ MULTIPLE COMPARISON TEST

Keyed Group:	Charismatic	Eucharist	Prayer	Baptism	Control
	N=8	N=8	N=8	N=8	N=8
Mean:	42	37	33	30	26

The lines running beneathe the mean scores show the range of nonsignificant differences. There are no significant differences between the experimental groups, or between the control group and three of the experimental groups. The only two groups not so connected in the table (Charismatic and Control) have a significant difference between them.

The one-way ANOVA and the two forms of the t test are simple inferential statistics. Their use is appropriate where the scholar is interested in seeing if differences exist between the means of groups. This concept can be applied to many situations of interest in theological research. Where computers and statistical programs are available to guide the scholar the analysis of the data is relatively easy. Even where such aids are not present, a patient approach will yield the statistics desired.

265

Suggested Exercises

Exercise 1. The aim of this exercise is to test your understanding of calculated and critical values.

Suppose a scholar does an independent samples t test and obtains a calculated value of 3.65. With the level of significance set at .05 for 8 degrees of freedom (df), what is the critical value for a one-tailed test? For a two-tailed test? (Remember, the critical value can be found using the Table provided in the chapter.) Is the calculated value larger or smaller than the critical value in each instance? What does this mean?

Exercise 2. The aim of this exercise is to work through a one-way ANOVA.

Suppose a researcher desires to compare five of the Pauline epistles on five specific concepts. Because of the varying lengths of these books, each concept is rendered as a score representing its relative frequency of occurrence. The documents and concepts are charted as follows:

	Book 1	Book 2	Book 3	Book 4	Book 5
scores for	13	11	2	10	9
concepts	18	10	1	12	10
	15	12	1	9	8
	14	12	3	11	11
	15	10	2	9	10

Calculate the one-way ANOVA using the steps provided in the chapter. Then, present the results in a table (such as that shown in the chapter).

If statistical significane is found,* conduct Scheffé's test and present it in a table as shown in the chapter.

*Set your level of significance at .05. The degrees of freedom are 4, 20. Consulting a statistical table yields a critical value of 2.87.

Answers: Ex. 1. Critical value for one-tailed test: 1.860. Critical value for two-tailed test: 2.306. Calculated value is larger in each instance. There is statistical significance in both cases. Ex. 2 The one-way ANOVA will yield F = 4.70. Since significance has been found, the Scheffé test should be conducted. The critical difference is 27.92.

18

Christian Faith and Criticism

Faith and Reason

Very early in this text I wrote, "Faith cannot fear reason because faith engenders a renewed reason. Reason, if the thought be portrayed poetically, is the child of faith." Quite obviously, reason and the processes it creates stand at the forefront when various scholarly methods are discussed. What happens to faith? Do researchers give lip service to faith and then in practice abandon belief for the shallow skepticism of modern criticism?

If I have been understood, then the answer already should be known. Faith initiates reason, prompting it and supplying to it the questions that reason then pursues methodically. But faith's operation does not cease at this point. Faith is present continually, accompanying reason as a partner. The dominant role faith assumes is necessary because the knowledge of God requires faith (cf. 2 Co. 5:7). Faith is the point of contact with the revealed God which makes theological knowledge possible.

But faith's dominance does not mean a **fideism**. On the contrary, the preeminence of faith means the complete freedom of reason within those natural boundaries prescribed by the object under study, namely God himself. Thus reason and faith are complementary, and the dominance of faith cannot mean the bondage of reason or an artificial limiting of its proper reach. Reason is free to conceive and carry forth even the most radical programs of inquiry, provided these preserve faith's aim of securing real knowledge.

God is far less threatened by criticism than the average Christian. He who gave to humanity both the gifts of faith and reason has no need to worry over either. On our side, however, our consciousness of the fallen condition of mankind, together with our deep awareness of our rebellion against God makes us worried and afraid about critical methods. We face the concern that our imperfect faith and faulty reason will lead us away from a dependable knowledge of God rather than toward it. In our efforts to preserve faith's certainty and a perceivable Christian spirituality we often succomb to the temptation to rein reason in and permit it only the most meager effort on our behalf.

Our instinct to protect faith is so strong that rather than risk faith we are willing to sacrifice reason. But this must be resisted as an unacceptable tactic, since it establishes a false dichotomy between faith and reason. Yet, if this means of security is denied us, then what protection can faith have against the onslaught of criticism? Certainly, much of what comes down from the scholastic mountains of research seems more like an unhappy law than a joyous grace. Our desire to know God first is threatened, then blunted by pronouncements about God, the Bible, and Christian life that make us feel like throwing our arms up in despair and retreating to the inner sanctum of meditation and prayer. Is there any way out?

There is a way that honors both faith and reason. That way is what this book is about: responsible scholarship in theological research. Our certainty of faith need not be threatened by criticism. Indeed, if we take the initiative and learn the processes of critical scholarship, then we will be able both to understand what is claimed in its name and to assess accurately the credibility of those claims. More importantly, we will ourselves be able to undertake research and discover to our own satisfaction the actual situation of a given matter. Reason can be answered on the grounds of reason, without faith being opposed to reason (which quickly results in a perception of faith as irrational in nature).

The Bible

Now does this course of action, taken in the interest of keeping faith and reason in partnership, actually result in the ascendancy of reason to first place? It may seem so when we consider the actual state of affairs in biblical criticism. There the conviction that the Bible is God's Word, is in fact more than a merely human collection of documents, often seems to have been denied. In place of this conviction is a cynical analysis of the text that breaks down all of our childhood's acquisitions. No longer is the Bible God's word-for-word pronouncement. Its history seems suspect, the authenticity of Jesus' words in doubt, and all of our comfortable assumptions about its message seem like spoiled milk. If such is scholarship, who needs it?

Unfortunately, the case is made worst by those whose knowledge of criticism comes by hearsay. A careful attention to the biblical critics usually reveals quite a bit more than what was first heard. Radical and surprising assertions often become more palatable when all of the reasoning behind them comes into view. Even when they still appear too far distanced from reality to be acceptable, they at least can be understood on their own terms when they have been carefully examined. Those who have acquired an understanding of scholarship can dialog meaningfully with the critics. They can separate for themselves the gold from the lead, and answer the critics on their own ground. The simple reality of today's situation in biblical criticism is this: it is a menagerie. The diversity in scholars is astonishing, and the participation in scholarly research by liberals and conservatives alike is greater than ever before. The only reasonable chance anyone has of sorting through the confusion is to become a practiced and competent researcher also. This does not necessitate becoming an expert, but merely an intelligent consumer of theology and an able lay theologian. We cannot afford to let anyone do our thinking for us.

It is the responsibility of each of us to judge soberly the measure of faith God has given to us (Rom. 12:3). Each of us is accountable to God for the way we use the gifts of faith and reason. We must do the best we can with what we have, which is exactly what any good scholar aims at. I cannot deny that reason is permitted by some to take a place above faith, but I do deny that this is ever necessary. Scholarship in theology demands otherwise, since the object of research (God) has established faith as the **sine qua non** of knowledge; no dependable knowledge of God can be gained apart from faith.

But still we are left with some very real problems about the Bible. Is it not the case that biblical criticism generally seems to proceed without any consideration of the Bible's unique character and divine origin? Does not this situation suggest we should refrain from biblical criticism, or at least the more radical methods within it? These are serious questions and deserve careful attention.

First, we ought to recognize again that the diversity in critical studies makes it impossible to generalize fairly that all biblical criticism ignores the Bible's uniqueness or treats it, "like any other book." Many scholars are quite concerned to acknowledge the Bible as a holy book, and reverently study it. Virtually all who call themselves Christian scholars confess the necessity of understanding the Bible not only according to the processes applied to any book, but also in accordance with some standard of faith, one generally given shape by that researcher's own religious tradition and community.

The difficulty, however, is in applying scholarly methods to things which by their very nature are not readily susceptible to the means at hand. For instance, form criticism can take ancient documents and analyze them in a reasonable attempt to uncover the history of their different forms and the communities behind these. This is a part of its proper reach. But form criticism cannot assess these forms as conceptions in the mind of God delivered by one or another means of divine inspiration. It cannot do this because such things are beyond its reach. There are at present no scholarly means of testing an assertion like: "An apothegm is a divine form created by God and given to certain communities and editors (e.g., Mark) through such-and-such kind of inspiration." This kind of assertion can be confessed, but it is not open to form criticism. Thus, one who takes form criticism to task for neglecting such a matter is not being fair.

It is because scholarship is limited, and scholarly researchers accordingly reluctant to make dogmatic assertions of untestable items, that modern biblical criticism often seems to leave too much aside. This is a significant problem only if it is thought that biblical criticism should do more than it does, or if criticism is made the entirety of our approach to seeking knowledge. Criticism cannot do everything, and it should not try.

What biblical criticism is left with as its proper sphere is the Bible as a collection of documents. If it cannot fully assess matters like inspiration or the divine nature of the text, if it can at best approach such things indirectly, is it thereby made valueless? Of course not, for within its proper sphere there is much that can be learned that definitely contributes to our theological understanding. Biblical criticism, then, must be taken on its own terms, measured and judged in that way.

Method, Not Madness

But what of the question of leaving aside the more radical methods of research? Hardly anyone these days questions the use of textual criticism, but both source and form criticism (among others) have been very controversial. Many conservative Christians either do not engage in such methods or practice them only with the severest restrictions in force. What should be said about this situation?

I think it is imperative to distinguish between method and madness. What I mean is that we must remember that methods are tools and that tools do only as much as we allow them to do. It is madness to blame methods for irresponsible scholarship. It is madness to confuse the philosophical conceptions of the researcher with the essential elements of the method **per se.** Madness throws the baby out with the bathwater by rejecting a method because it dislikes some or even most of its practitioners.

Someone may rejoin that what I have said is all fine and well, except that it misses the essential point. Are not the method's premises and processes themselves suspect? Does not form criticism, for example, presume some things that are in themselves unacceptable, and so make it imperative that the method be rejected? A question like this can be made into an issue, and sometimes is, much to the misfortune of someone who may come to a different conclusion on the subject than the majority of his or her peers within the community. The issue is quite alive in some circles and cannot be lightly dismissed.

One way of defusing the situation might be to rethink the method with the express goal in mind of rescuing it for use. Thus, the points at which source or form criticism appear to be faulty or inadequate may be amenable to some adjustments so that, in some measure at least, the methods can be used profitably. There are some conservative scholars who have attempted to do precisely this. The strategy is not without risk, though, because some people will remain firmly convinced that the method under question is beyond rescue, or is wrong-headed in the first place.

This last objection should, I think, be overthrown if at all possible. Who denies that either sources or forms are in evidence in the Bible? If they exist, then they can and should be studied. This means, by definition, doing something that passes by the names "source" and "form" criticism. What is needful is defining these methods as well as possible, and that means doing so in such a manner that dialog can take place with others interested in the same kind of study. I am not claiming this task is always easy, especially for the most conservative, but it does seem necessary. We all must do the best we can with what we have at hand.

Every scholar needs to be mindful of his or her assumptions, personal philosophy, and how these bear on the work at hand. In assessing scholarly work it may sometimes be necessary to distinguish between a scholar's method and his or her "madness." So, for example, a conservative can read, with some degree of appreciation, Bultmann's **History of the Synoptic Tradition** or **Theology of the New Testament.** He or she can examine Bultmann's method, assess the faithfulness with which this is tied to his conclusions, and interact with his existential philosophy when this intrudes. Of course, a person can do this fairly only if he or she has bothered first to understand form criticism as a method and learned to understand Bultmann's philosophy. Otherwise, the criticism is mere carping.

If it is true that some manner or another of source and form criticism must be practiced, and if it is also true that contemporary means of doing so are inadequate, then it follows that those who most sharply disagree with the present state bear a heavy responsibility for pointing out a better way. No method is sacred, and none is without flaw. Only the efforts of serious practitioners and equally serious dissenters can hope to provide a measure of progress. But, even as the practitioners ought to listen to the concerns raised by those who find fault with their methods, so the dissenters ought to learn those methods well in order to point out most helpfully their shortcomings.

In this text, I have tried to focus on methods and stay away from madness. Doubtless, this text will have its critics. Some may come from those who practice the methods as well as those who take issue with the methods themselves. I am petitioning all of these well-intentioned critics to make their judgments based on what I have said. Please, understand the methods first, then correct them (and/or me).

Scholarship Without Fear

Scholarship seeks after truth, and truth cannot be opposed to faith and its certainty. So research and faith should not be opposed. But if the logic seems unassailable, the reality is far different. The fact is that many Christians remain afraid of research, and if they do not understand what they fear, it is because they are afraid to understand it. To risk understanding is to risk faith, or so it seems. What can we do to rectify this situation?

First, we must work to establish a proper understanding of Christian faith. This requires acknowledging its priority over reason, its creation of questions for reason to pursue, and its continuing partnership with reason as a valid gift from God. If we can comprehend that faith and reason rightly may be correlated, we will become free to let reason have its place.

Second, this means we must establish the proper place of reason. This necessitates an acknowledgement of reason's limitations, but also an appreciation of its genuine possibilities. Specifically, this requires a comprehension of what research is, and what it attempts. If research is understood as a human process, but also one which in theology is tied to the Word of God, then perhaps many of the misunderstandings which lead people to view it with suspicion, mistrust, or fear can be overcome.

Third, by establishing the place of theological research, we shall be able to see what lies beyond or outside its concerns. We can distinguish between those matters research can address directly and the many things it can address only indirectly. In understanding research we can become wise users of its processes and products. Through our own practice we can contribute to the knowledge of the Church. We can find satisfaction in realizing that we really are doing the best we can with what we have. More, we can have this satisfaction without also thinking that our efforts replace God's grace. Research never can supplant faith; it is not in its nature even to try.

Faith's certainty is disturbed by scholarship only when either faith or scholarship have been seriously misunderstood. If and when we are successful in freeing the Church from misunderstanding on these things, then we will have scholarship without fear. Until such a happy time arrives, we must work toward that end by beginning with ourselves. We must seek individually a proper understanding of faith, reason, scholarship, and research. Having attained a comprehension that permits us to study and serve freely, we also must be diligent not to abuse that freedom. Conscious of the concerns of those around us, we should not retreat to private places, but advance to meet those concerns in a spirit of tolerance, humility, and love. For without these things, scholarship, like faith itself, is empty and void.

PART THREE

A Sample Study

INTRODUCTION

Purpose

Part Three is a sample research study. All of the material is from an actual research project. The chapters cover the entire project, though in an abbreviated fashion. Thus, while the report given here addresses what prompted the study, how it was designed, conducted, and evaluated, it does not reproduce all of the documentation and other material used to flesh out the study. The deletion of footnotes, references, quotes, and reviews of pertinent other studies was done in order to keep a sharp focus on the essential outline of this research.

While this part may seem unduly lengthy, despite its actual size reduction from the original study, it has its present shape for good reasons. Each chapter focuses on a particular aspect of the whole. Enough information is given that the study can be replicated. More importantly, enough information is given in each chapter to permit the reader to see what the essentials are for each stage of the study and to engage in practice evaluation of this research. Through such an exercise the reader should become more aware of how research studies might be constructed. By evaluating this research some facility can be gained in reading, understanding, and critiquing the research of others. If needed, the reader should review earlier chapters covering the methods used in this study and, especially, the chapter on understanding the research of others.

When all of the chapters in this part have been read and evaluated, the reader should take the time to write a formal review. If this material is used in a classroom setting it would be useful to prepare this report and then exchange it with someone else's report to compare and contrast. In preparing the formal review some of the advice set out in the chapter on reporting research might prove helpful. The point of such an exercise, of course, is to begin immediately to be engaged meaningfully with research work. An important part of any researcher's labors is interacting with other scholars. While this interaction is barely hinted at in the report of this study (a fact which can be assessed in a review), the reading of this research gives the reader a chance to engage firsthand in a dialog about the study.

In this dialog the reader should examine what has been

learned from the study. What does the research say about how it originated, was set into a design, and conducted? Does this process seem to be an appropriate one? Is critical information lacking? Is the study reported clearly? Is it understandable? (The proper question is not, Is it easy to understand?, but, Is it understandable? Much research takes patience to understand even when it is presented clearly. Clarity does not equate with ease, though without clarity even simple things become difficult to understand.) Put the study to the test and assess it as honestly as possible.

By a careful appropriation of these chapters the information given in the first two parts of this book can be supplemented greatly. In all likelihood, the challenge of this study will force the reader to review concepts and processes advanced in earlier chapters. This is beneficial to the reader and should not be viewed negatively. When this part is placed in relationship to the rest of the book it should be clear that this text provides all of the basic materials needed to start someone on the road of using research profitably.

Multiple Regression

The research that is presented in the following chapters has used a technique of analysis known as multiple regression. This is a statistical test not discussed earlier in this book. In order to understand the discussion of the research results it is necessary to know some things about multiple regression. Therefore, this brief section introduces this technique in summary fashion. Only enough information is given here to permit a following of the study.

Multiple regression is a general statistical technique used to study relationships between variables. It is a kind of measure of association. A multiple correlation involves the analysis of the relationships of more than two variables; a multiple regression combines several variables in order to use some to predict others. The variable being predicted is known as the **criterion** (dependent) **variable**. The variable used to make the prediction is called the **predictor** (independent) **variable**. The main focus of a multiple regression is on determining the overall dependence of a given variable on other variables.

A formula for multiple regression is given in the study. The regression equation looks like this:

$$X_1 = a + b_2 X_2 + b_3 X_3 = \ldots b_m X_m$$

Here X_1 is the dependent variable, that is, the one being predicted. The independent variables, those being used to make the prediction, are designated by X_2, X_3, . . . X_m (the "m" means the number of such variables is an undetermined one in the equation; there might be three predictor variables, or forty). The letter "a" represents a constant, which is a predetermined number that does not vary (as given in the study, this number is .1894). The letters "b_2, b_3, . . . b_m"

are the coefficients of regression.

The formula, then, can be rendered in words as: "the predicted variable is equal to the sum of the constant, plus the sum of the first coefficient times the second predictor variable, . . . and so forth until all the predictor variables have been accounted for." The words are more confusing than the equation. The essential idea to remember is this: multiple regression studies the dependence of a given variable on a set of other variables.

A multiple regression analysis also will yield an index of the accuracy of the prediction equation. This index is known as the **coefficient of multiple correlation** (R). One way to regard R is as a simple product-moment correlation between the actual dependent variable scores and the predicted scores for those variables. Besides this coefficient, a multiple regression will produce **regression coefficients** and **beta weights**. The former are numbers that cannot be compared without translation into comparable units; the latter is the name for these comparable units. The beta weights are numbers; each predictor variable has a beta weight. The predictor variable with the largest beta weight is judged to be the one that is the best single predictor of the dependent variable (i.e., the variable being predicted). Although beta weights appear with positive or negative signs these do not affect the determination of the largest beta weight. Thus, a beta weight of -.5567 designates a better predictor variable than one of +.3324. In this study, where the researcher shows an interest in determining the best predictor variable, the beta weights are quite important.

Other aspects of multiple regression, such as the use of multiple R to account for variance, should be comprehensible from the context. If not, a review of the pertinent discussion of such matters from Part Two of this book is advised.

19

On Dating the Book of James

Background to the Problem

The New Testament is composed of literary texts. All of these texts originated in a span of time with relatively definable borders. Each of the documents can be expected to reflect, to some degree, those circumstances instrumental in calling forth the production of the text. In simple terms, every book gives some idea of its place in the history of the early Church.

Obviously, the placement of the biblical documents in their proper setting is of great value in accurately interpreting their message. Thus, while matters such as authorship, audience, and date typically are considered as introductory to the study of the textual material itself, they must not be undervalued in regard to the interpretive process. These matters are considered first precisely because they occupy a fundamental and irremovable place in the task of understanding the message of the Bible. Identification of the author, his audience, the date, and other particulars of historical circumstance enable the modern interpreter to place texts in relationship to one another and so not only grasp the intent of any specific writer but also to sense the development and sophistication of the entire New Testament gospel.

But a variety of obstacles can complicate this work. Some documents may not specify authorship (e.g., Hebrews), or may pose difficulties that make acceptance of the ascribed author a problem in interpreting the text (e.g., the Pauline authorship of the Pastorals). The declared audience of the document may not have been always the actual audience, or the entire audience (e.g., Ephesians). The date is never stated in so many words and must be inferred. Because the evidence upon which the dating is based is often fragmentary or uncertain, most dating carries only the weight of greater or lesser probability.

The value of the work outweighs its costs. But the difficulties mean that cautious and even provisional conclusions are often necessary. This has been long true in the study of James. This present research into the dating of James belongs, then, to New Testament introduction, and intends a contribution to a better understanding of the issue and the field. As such it may yield indirect light on the literary development of the

New Testament, the conceptual progress of early Christian thought, and the probable dating of other texts.

The principal significance of this study probably lies in extending the borders of the methodological tools employed within the field of New Testament research. The actual dating of James, however, should not be minimized. The point of the research is to objectively measure those factors necessary to determining this date. The use of quantitative tools and strategies **and** the conclusions on date are inseparable.

Purpose of the Study

James has an uncertain date. Most scholars place its date at one or the other end of the period in which the New Testament documents were composed, that is, roughly A.D. 50 to A.D. 150. Yet there is no general consensus as to which end of the spectrum James belongs. The formal purpose of this study is simply to attempt an indication about which extreme end of this century of composition is more likely for James.

The material purpose, and the uniqueness of the study, however, lies in another direction. The study advances the thesis that quantitative research techniques can be used profitably in questions of biblical introduction.

The first purpose is a very limited one, although not without a degree of significance. Many studies have attempted to date James. This study's aim is more modest. It seeks only to indicate a direction toward one or another extreme. In this effort, the only creativity is in the limitation to a consideration of extremes and, of course, in the methodology.

But it is the methodology which justifies the study's claim to a certain uniqueness and a definite importance. Little effort has been given in the past to applying strictly quantitative tools to biblical research. Even less attempt has been made to subject such research to a formal statistical analysis. Rare, if not nonexistent, are studies which feature both complexity of quantitative analysis and consistent statistical analysis. This study incorporates both.

Moreover, the formal and material purposes are intrinsically linked. The material purpose is to introduce clearly a new perspective on an ancient problem. That perspective is one admittedly unfamiliar to most biblical researchers. Thus a substantial emphasis has been placed on clarity and simplicity of style and explanation. The success of the material purpose depends on the achievement of the formal purpose.

The idea that this study is only a model cannot be overstressed. If the study is successful in demonstrating the usefulness of this kind of work it may also succeed in enticing other scholars into extending, refining, and propagating quantitative studies in the field. In this respect the study is truly educational in nature. Most biblical scholars have not been trained to consider quantitative methodologies or statistical analyses as appropriate tools for their research.

In summary, the content of the study aims at indicating the more probable pole of James' date, either at an early extreme (c. A.D. 50) or a late extreme (c. A.D. 95 or later). The form of the study intends an argument by example for the usefulness and possibility of new perspectives for biblical research. Together these purposes find unity in my own conviction that only the conscientious application of all the tools at our disposal will allow us to proceed and progress as scholars, whatever our field of endeavor. By undertaking to address a wide audience, one comprised of educational leaders and biblical scholars, it is my hope that the study will not only contribute something to the specific research question under consideration, but also to the stretching and growing of minds committed to learning.

The book of James is perhaps the single classic example of the problems associated with introductory study of New Testament documents. Its authorship, date, style, and audience have all been disputed. From the Apostolic period down to today these subjects have been debated. An impressive array of figures have contributed to the discussion, including Origen (185-254/5), Eusebius (c. 270-340), Jerome (c. 340-420), Luther (1483-1546), Calvin (1509-1564), Michaelis (1717-1791), Baur (1792-1860), Mayor (1828-1916), and Dibelius (1883-1947). Recent debate has been continued by such figures as Ropes, Reicke, Oesterley, Adamson, Davids, and Laws. All of these scholars have recognized that a resolution of the problem of James' date is elusive.

These scholars do not share a common view about the date of James, or, for that matter, most other problems of introduction. However, the positions they do represent with regard to date can, for the most part, be grouped into two general and opposing extremes. On the one hand are those who assign to the book a very early date (with a range of approximately A.D. 47-66). These individuals include, among others, J. B. Mayor (40-50), J. A. T. Robinson (47/8), D. Guthrie (50), T. Zahn (50), and A. Plummer (53-62). On the other hand, there are those who date James quite late (A.D. 90-110, or later). This group includes such diverse figures as G. W. Kümmel (80 – 100), A. Harnack (120-150), J. Ropes (75-125), and M. Dibelius (80-130).

Current publications on James continue to reflect such a division. Thus Adamson in his recent commentary (1976) argues for an early date; Laws in her commentary (1980) urges a late date. Participants in the discussion find themselves at an impasse with no readily apparent way forward. Clearly there is need for a new approach to collecting and evaluating the data. But what has brought the dialog to this impasse?

The answer, very likely, rests in what these scholars do share in common. They agree in the manner in which research is conducted, that is, along qualitative lines. Inevitably their differences in approaching the problem fade against the brighter light of the mutuality they share in adhering to research methods generally confined to qualitative practices. In short, a premium is placed on the value of expert opinion. Certainly, this, too, has its place. Nor is qualitative research to be dismissed as prescientific. But it does have its limitations, principally in its less objective character when contrasted to quantitative methods.

Of course, some utilization of quantitative tools does occur. Many biblical scholars routinely take into account the frequency of recurring lexical items or concepts; some even proceed so far as to contrast these frequencies with others, or to calculate relative frequencies. A little use is made of the idea of correlations, but rare indeed is the biblical scholar who knows how to apply such an idea to some particular task with a definite statistical analysis. The more sophisticated, and difficult, quantitative strategies simply do not appear anywhere in the mainstream of discussion on biblical research.

This study proposes to move beyond the impasse created by an adherence to qualitative research by adapting selected quantitative strategies to the problem. To this point the history of debate over James' date can accurately be characterized by two observations: first, scholars have utilized the same family of research techniques; second, their conclusions have polarized into opposing extremes. Therefore, simply stated, the problem confronting this study is twofold. On one side, it is apparent that James has no fixed date within the circles of New Testament scholarship. On the other side, traditional approaches to the problem have proven insufficient. An impasse exists. Perhaps the introduction of new perspectives, rooted in quantitative rather than qualitative research thinking, may provide substantial aid in resolving the impasse.

Research Questions

Perhaps the most natural way to get at any problem is to find appropriate questions to ask about it. Naturally there exists a wide range of acceptable questions around which a research effort can center itself. In this study there is a focus upon three general research questions: 1) Given the contradictory and confusing conclusions about the dating of James, are there any reasons to hope that further study will resolve matters, or even contribute significantly? 2) What factors must be considered in dating James? Finally, 3) how shall these factors be examined and evaluated?

The first of these questions addresses the purpose of this study, and also its justification. There are reasons to hope that further study will be productive. The scholarly passion to know continually shows in the ability of individuals to seize upon different, innovative approaches to a problem and apply them in such a manner as to extend the horizons of knowledge. In this particular case, the study of an ancient problem is turned to quantitative methods for help; the selection of content analysis, product-moment correlations, and multiple regression analyses are not intended to be exclusive of other, as yet unapplied, research tools. Nor are they put forward with any guarantees about their efficacy for this particular problem. But they do provide a measure of hope and reasonable expectancy because these tools have been applied successfully to problems in many fields principally devoted to the practice of qualitative research.

The second research question narrows the prospective reach of the study. Only factors concretely relevant to the dating of James can be considered. Of course, some factors are more directly related than are others. A measure of selection along expert-opinion lines is necessary. The factors included by one researcher may not all appear in another scholar's study. In this study, questions of authorship, audience, and other factors frequently regarded in New Testament introduction are all considered, even if only briefly. The specific factors upon which the study more heavily relies are those most amenable to quantitative categorization. These factors include particulars of the text itself like lexical items, concepts, and historical allusions or citations. Even among these factors an inevitable degree of interpretation is included.

However, and it is this concern addressed by the third research question, the interpretive input to the study is carefully accounted for through calculated controls. In this manner the factors are examined and evaluated along as objective lines as possible. Thus, for example, concepts are regulated by their constituent lexical terms. This format is, admittedly, a narrow way of dealing with the problem of concept definition. But it does provide for a greater measure of objective selection and scores well in reliability. In fact, the replicability of the study is consciously kept in view, and the preference for quantitative methods in examining and evaluating James' text again commends itself in this respect.

Throughout these three research questions a unified concern is maintained. Simply stated, it is to move beyond the impasse of expert opinions locked in varying interpretations of James' date by keeping strictly to empirically verifiable data and interpreting it along the objective lines afforded through statistical evaluation. Therefore, less attention has been given to matters limited by their greater reliance on qualitative judgment. So a premium has been placed on data that can be measured and evaluated quantitatively.

Limitations and Delimitations

As expressed above, the study is a narrow one. It has both a tight focus and a restrained reach. The date of James is the focus, and the reach moves to grasp most firmly materials that can be quantitatively appropriated. This approach is not without its limitations. But these very limitations can be viewed as positive features of the study.

In the first place, no attempt has been made to replicate the extensive qualitative research already available on the problem. At the same time, some interaction is both desirable and unavoidable; no study is conceived or conducted in a vacuum. In this study, the literature review of materials on James aims at presenting a representative overview of the research on James' date. Inasmuch as other introductory questions have played a role in discussing the text's date, these have also been considered. This procedure allows the study to extend the valuable work of others, not replace it. But it also frees the study to ocncentrate on its own distinctive contribution.

Second, there are limitations inherent in the methods themselves when applied to the material of James. Content analysis is a scientific technique demanding a certain artistic flair. In other words, while invoking established and sensible guidelines for research, content analysis still places a strong measure of responsibility on the researcher to make basic decisions about how the material will be treated. Studies employing a content analysis of the same material may still vary widely depending on the specific decisions of the individual researchers. These decisions reflect the unique concerns of each researcher.

Correlation techniques also possess limitations. Of these, one in particular must be highlighted from the beginning. The results of a correlation do not necessarily or inherently indicate causality. Inferences of a cause and effect relationship must be either avoided or very exactly qualified. A correlation evaluation must not be made into something other than what it is: the measurement of the extent to which two variables are related.

Third, the availability of materials to which James could be fairly compared set boundaries to the study. There is not such an abundance of texts suitable to a study of this kind to make for an embarrassment of riches. James cannot be examined in isolation if the idea is to try to date it according to its degree of likeness to other bodies of literature which possess relatively fixed dates. To the degree that such other texts themselves are both few in number and perhaps debatable in date, the results of the study are limited by an inherent uncertainty.

Fourth, and as a natural consequence, the study makes no pretensions about its conclusions. There are no indisputable results argued here. The study is a model. The intended narrowness of focus, the tight boundaries, and the inherent limitations, all urge a cautious appraisal of the results. This is not a negative judgment, but an honest one.

Assumptions

In at least some respects, every study is also limited and delimited by its assumptions. Some presuppositions are obviously more important than others. For example, while it is assumed that the possibility exists of some history of literary composition for James and the other texts considered, the study itself is limited to the final literary documents only. But other assumptions are fundamental to the study and must be made explicit.

First, it is assumed that James most properly be assigned a date in one or the other extreme positions named above. On the one hand, an appeal can be made to the literature itself that only these two extremes are generally conceded as legitimate options. On the other hand, a testing of extremes makes it easier to see differences where they in fact exist and so indicate direction. For a study such as this, testing James against the extremes makes sense because it provides a greater susceptibility to seeing the text's date at one or the other end of a continuum. Later, more refined analyses may indeed narrow and further specify the date, but such is not the present goal.

Second, it is assumed that inferences about relationships between the content of a document and its origin can be made validly. This assumption itself must be qualified in the light of the use of correlations. But the qualification is one specifically for this study. If, in general, inferences cannot be made about date from content in a valid fashion, then the dating of all undated texts must exclude textual material itself, a patently absurd restriction.

Four corollary presuppositions undergird this primary assumption:

1) Literary documents bear specific stylistic characteristics that aid in their dating to the degree to which they reflect literary conventions of the period in which they were composed. Thus formulaic openings, parallels, and conventional format in the progress of a document from one part to the next may all betray an allegiance to the literary style (broadly conceived) of a period of time. If an undated document is established to belong to a body of literature sharing such features which has been dated, then a very probable date for the text in question can be given. Of course, this factor has a greater role whenever a longer span of time is open to consideration for a text. Where the span is short, as in the case of James, this means of dating is minimized because literary conventions within restricted periods of time change less perceptibly. Then, too, in the case of the writings of the early Church many documents have, like James, an uncertain date.

2) Literary documents often display literary dependencies. These dependencies may be seen in quotes, allusions, copying of style, or peculiar vocabulary usage. To some extent

dependencies may also be glimpsed in the extension or clarification of earlier literary concepts or forms. Of course, quite often the direction of a dependency cannot be definitely decided. Which document is dependent on the other? Only where direction is relatively clear is this factor weighty enough to use substantially. Even then it generally can only set a limit to how early a document can be, or if the undated text can be shown to be depended upon by another text, how late it can be.

3) Literary documents display particular expressions of popular concepts. While a concept itself may or may not be datable, specific expressions of it may be. Likewise, concepts rise and fall in popularity, sometimes even disappearing. The comparison of concepts between documents can often be misleading, but can also provide a substantiating body of evidence that a document belongs more probably to one group of texts than another.

4) Literary documents often name or allude to historical events and/or persons whose dates are known. An allusion is less certain evidence because of the interpretive element involved, but quite often allusions are present if actual names are not. An allusion reflects either a date contemporaneous to the event or person, or later.

Third, it is assumed that the study of the manifest content of literary texts is meaningful. Some would delete the qualifying term "manifest" in order to make room also for "latent" content. Since manifest content is more objective and reliable it is the object of this study. But the exclusion of any attempt to systematically account for the latent content does not mean an assumption that it is either worthless, or less meaningful than the manifest content. Rather, the content that is "between the lines" is on occasion the most valuable. Since much qualitative research concerns itself with this content, and because it demands a separate if parallel treatment in analysis, the latent content has not been included as a direct concern of the study.

Fourth, it is assumed that the quantitative description of content is meaningful. At heart, this means that the frequency of particular items reflects to some degree their importance to that document. Of course, some basic discrimination is necessary. Connecting words, stylized prepositional clauses, and frequent repetition of ideas all carry different weights in considering the meaningfulness of a given frequency. Obviously the frequent use of words like "a" or "the" (articles) are nearly always of less importance than frequent use of terms like

"God" or "faith" (nouns reflecting persons or concepts).

Finally, fifth, it is assumed that literary documents, when properly quantified, can appropriately be subjected to statistical testing. The key is in the proper quantification. Inappropriately handled data will yield statistical results of little, if any, value. Statistical tests are an acceptable, and often preferable way to assess such matters as relationships between documents when the more quantifiable elements of those documents have been identified, categorized, and otherwise satisfactorily handled. Each statistical tool has its aim, strengths, and limitations; all can be used rightly, or abused.

Hypotheses

The way is now prepared to discuss the hypotheses of this study. The general hypothesis is: the direction of James' date of final composition can be probabilisticly reflected in a comparison of the text with other literary texts whose dates of final composition are already relatively fixed at one or the other extreme time limits to which James must belong. Ancillary to this hypothesis might be one expecting the direction which will, in fact, be revealed, if any is at all. But such a hypothesis adds little to the intent of the study and shall not be set forward. Focus is reserved for the general hypothesis.

20

Description of the Samples

Sampling Procedure Considerations

Sampling procedures in research have come to be well regulated, yet still flexible to meet the different demands of various studies. The two parameters which characterize a well—chosen sample are manageability and meaningfulness. The first of these parameters addresses the size of the sample, the second concerns its representativeness.

For this study it has been decided to pursue the general wisdom that the sample be small. In one sense, at least, this decision was unavoidable: the universe itself, from which the sample was drawn, is not very large. The study actually utilizes two samples drawn from the same general universe but distinguished by a factor critical to the intent of the study. Thus the universe can be said to include all of the Christian documents produced between A. D. 40/50 and A. D. 140/150. But the two samples drawn from this universe are distinguished from each other by their location along this continuum of time. One sample represents documents belonging to the earliest years of the century span of the universe while the other sample represents documents belonging to the later years of the same span. Both samples number three documents.

Size of the samples is integrally related to the question of representativeness. For this study the four guidelines suggested by D. P. Cartwright have been adopted:

1) There must be a specification of the universe to which generalizations are to be made.
2) There must be guarantees that every unit of the universe has a known probability of inclusion in the sample.
3) The sampling procedure must be independent of correlation among the units.
4) The sample must be large enough.

The universe has already been specified. Because the sampling procedure known as stratified sampling has been utilized, the second guideline is qualified. Stratified sampling does not guarantee that there is an equal probability for every unit to be selected by random selection. Instead, it establishes specific criteria necessary for a unit to qualify for selection. But under this qualification every unit has a known probability of inclusion. The nature of the universe makes the sampled units relatively homogenous. However, the sampling criteria do not specify any correlation of content among the units. Finally, the size of the sample is as large as feasible for this study, particularly given the limited number of units available to choose from. Accordingly, all four guidelines are addressed by the sampling procedure utilized in this study, albeit the situation that the universe has applied its own unique restrictions and limitations on the sampling.

The sampling procedure used is stratified and purposive, too: stratified purposive sampling. Although sampling theory has established the desirability of random selection, there is a rationale against such use for this study. First, there is a lack of access to the theoretical population from which the samples are drawn. This fact renders attempts at random selection suspect immediately. Second, the purpose of the study clearly makes many of the texts of the universe unsuitable or undesirable for inclusion. A random selection that might include dated documents from the middle of the time span of the universe, or that could select undated texts would provide a sample representative of the entire universe (assuming the whole universe is sufficiently known), but of little value for this particular study. Third, random selection tends to eliminate the extremes, which in this study are precisely the focus of interest.

At the same time, there is a specific rationale for the use of purposive sampling. It permits a conscious and sustained shaping of the sample by the aims of the study, especially where other sampling procedures might allow units of little value to enter inappropriately. Obviously, this procedure has the cost of some sacrifice of generalizability, but it protects the meaningfulness of the study and, together with stratified sampling, does not lose the measure of objectivity essential to the research.

The stratified sampling procedure used in this study has adopted six criteria. First, the length of the texts selected must be comparable to the criterion text (James). Second, the units in each sample must have a relatively fixed date with sufficient scholarly support to provide a reasonable assignation of them to one or another of the two date extremes of the universe. Third, the genre of the documents selected must be non-Gospel. While the literary character of James is debated vigorously, it is clear that it is not a Gospel. Fourth, any specific hypothesized relationship between a document and James is not sufficient grounds to either include or exclude the document, but all other things being equal, it is better to have such documents than to not have them. This is a judgment based on the aims of the study, and subject to the methodological qualification that it clearly is preferable to find at least one such document from both samples to which James is to be compared. Fifth, the general content of the documents must be unspecified beyond the limited conditions suggested by criteria four. In other words, the sample must be selected prior to the content analysis of any documents. Sixth, the style also must be unqualified, except as provided for in criteria three.

The criterion text of the study is, of course, James. It is the criterion text in two fundamental ways. First, it is instrumental in establishing criteria for sample selection. Second, it is basic to the construction of categories for the sampling of relevant content (cf. chapter 21). Against James both samples drawn from the universe of which James is a part are compared. The aim is to establish what strength of measurable relationship exists between James and each sample, if any. Further, the aim is to discern what predictor variables are best applied to James relevant to these relationships.

Samples

The sample representative of the early extreme end of datable material in the universe is:

EARLY EXTREME (A.D. 40-66 approx.):
Galatians (A.D. 48-58)
1 Thessalonians (A.D. 40-52)
1 Peter (A.D. 60-66)

Other materials that possibly might have been included were 2 Thessalonians and Q. The latter, the hypothesized source underlying some of the Synoptic Gospel materials in Luke and Matthew, has no agreed upon form. As an independent document it does not exist. For these reasons, it was rejected, despite its hypothesized relationship to James and its probable early date and its relative shortness. Two reasons militated strongly against the inclusion of 2 Thessalonians. On the one hand, two Pauline documents already were available (Galatians and 1 Thessalonians), both of which have stronger claims to authenticity, but more importantly, relatively more certain dates. On the other hand, the very uncertainty of the date made it a less acceptable candidate, especially since the alternative possibility to an early date (if the book is by Paul) would place it outside the early extreme.

Each of the selected documents requires some justification. This is especially true of 1 Peter, but all three should be evaluated against the criteria of the sampling procedure. To simplify this process a few general remarks are in order. All three documents are comparable in length to James (1,736 words): Galatians (2,228 words), 1 Thessalonians (1,479 words), and 1 Peter (1,681 words). As the following comments should establish, all three enjoy considerable scholarly support with regard to their being dated in this early extreme period. All three are non-Gospels, each being either epistolary or pseudo-epistolary in nature. Two of the three enjoy a hypothesized relationship to James (Galatians and 1 Peter). None of them were content analyzed or style analyzed prior to selection beyond the concerns of criteria three and four.

Galatians is assigned a date between A.D. 48 and 58. It is, of course, true that the document can only be dated approximately; the decade range suggested generally represents the estimates the book has received. Opinions on the date have, on the whole, tended to cluster toward the early end of this range. The dating of Galatians generally is made in connection with a decision regarding its destination. In this matter, two major options have presented themselves, known as the North Galatian and South Galatian theories, respectively. Neither of these theories remove Galatians from the early extreme end of the New Testament period of composition, but do differ in that adherents of the South Galatian theory generally date the book earlier than do adherents of the North Galatian theory. The following list is quite representative of the diversity of scholarly opinion within the general fixed span of years 48-58:

H. D. Betz (50-55)	W. G. Kümmel (54-55)
E. G. Briggs (c. 48)	K. Lake (c. 48)
J. Calvin (before 48)	J. B. Lightfoot (57-58)
O. Cullmann (52-53)	J. Moffatt (53-55)
G. S. Duncan (c. 48)	N. Perrin (54)
C. W. Emmet (c. 48)	D. Round (c. 48)
D. Guthrie (49-50)	E. F. Scott (53-55)
H. J. Holtzmann (c. 54)	W. A. Shedd (c. 48)
A. M. Hunter (48-49)	T. Zahn (53)

1 Thessalonians is assigned a date between A.D. 50-52. It is no exaggeration to say that there is common agreement that the document should be dated about A.D. 50. Despite the span indicated above, almost all scholars date the book right around 50. Thus the following list is indicative of how scholars are ranged on its date:

E. Best (51-52)	D. Guthrie (50-51)
F. F. Bruce (c. 50)	A. M. Hunter (50)
O. Cullmann (50)	W. G. Kümmel (50)
J. G. Davies (50-52)	W. Michaelis (50)
C. H. Dodd (50)	N. Perrin (51)
E. J. Goodspeed (50)	M. Tenney (51)
K. Graystone (50)	T. Zahn (51)

1 Peter is assigned a date between A.D. 60-66/67. This document is, admittedly, the most suspect in the sample. Many possible suggestions have been made as to its proper period. The options tend to cluster around one or another of the reigns of the following emperors: Trajan (98-117, with composition c. 111), Domitian (81-96, with composition c. 90-95), or Nero (54-68, with composition c. 60-66). Despite the fact that it is impossible to fix the date with any exactness, there have been enough arguments advanced to support an early date that this view has continued to enjoy widespread support. Even those who prefer to leave the date relatively open (unspecified) tend

to weigh an early assignment of origin as more probable than a later one.

Among the many who have found in favor of the traditional early date for 1 Peter are:

H. Alford (63-67)	J. E. Huther (64-67)
J. F. Barth (64-67)	C. F. Kiel (63)
C. Bigg (58-64)	J. B. Lightfoot (64)
F. H. Chase (62-64)	J. B. Mayor (61-64)
J. G. Davies (c. 64)	A. H. McNeile (64-67)
W. H. L. DeWette (64-67)	W. Michaelis (64-66/67)
P. Feine (63-64)	B. Reicke (64-65)
L. Goppelt (c. 66)	G. Salmon (c. 66)
D. Guthrie (60-64)	L. Schultze (64-66/67)
B. W. Henderson (64)	E. G. Selwyn (62-64)
F. J. A. Hort (60-64)	A. F. Walls (63-64)
J. L. Hug (64-67)	B. Weiss (before 60)
A. M. Hunter (63-64)	T. Zahn (64)

Given the situation that the traditional view both has weathered the critical storms most successfully (as compared, for instance, to the position for a date during Trajan's reign, which has no base of support in recent literature), and garnered the most critical support, it is not unreasonable to fix the book's date at the early extreme. This situation, added to the document's suitability according to the criteria used for sampling, justifies its use. But the justification is made cautiously and with the qualification that it is indeed suspect.

To help offset the possible prejudicial influence of 1 Peter it has been deemed advisable to include 2 Peter in the sample for late extreme. Not only does 2 Peter fulfill the criteria for inclusion, but like 1 Peter it may be dated either early or late. Yet, also like 1 Peter, the weight of evidence and scholarly opinion tends strongly in one rather than the other direction. So it is that while 1 Peter is dated early, 2 Peter is dated late; this is due, too, in no small measure to the differences between the two texts, differences which regularly draw attention.

The sample representative of the late extreme end of datable material in the universe is:

LATE EXTREME (A.D. 90-115 approx.)
2 Peter (A.D. 90-150)
1 John (A.D. 90-140)
Ignatius to the Ephesians (A.D. 90-120)

Other materials that might have been included were the **Didache** and the other letters of Ignatius. But to preserve a balance between the samples, and include the best available documents, these were set aside in favor of the ones named above. Obviously, to make such a decision makes it needful to justify the units selected for the sample. All three documents are comparable to James in length: 2 Peter (1,098 words),

1 John (2,140 words), and Ignatius to the Ephesians (1,775 words). Balanced with the other sample, the two samples and James appear as follows:

> 2 Peter (1,098)
> 1 Thessalonians (1,479)
> 1 Peter (1,681)
> JAMES (1,736)
> Ignatius to the Ephesians (1,775)
> 1 John (2,140)
> Galatians (2,228)

> EARLY EXTREME: 5,013 words
> LATE EXTREME: 5,387 words

With regard to other criteria, all three enjoy considerable scholarly support for a late dating; all three are non-Gospels; one has a hypothesized relationship to James (2 Peter); none were content or style analyzed prior to selection (except, again, as regards criteria three and four).

Of the three, 2 Peter is the most controversial, but at the present time it is not greatly controversial. Even those who continue to accept its authenticity and early date do so cautiously. They cannot escape the conclusion that it is the most problematical of all the New Testament books. By far, the majority of scholars reject it as a genuine work of the apostle Peter and assign to it a late date. Indeed, many scholars who ordinarily are quite conservative in their dating of the books of the New Testament have found themselves compelled to give to 2 Peter a late date (so, for example, Mayor dates both 1 Peter and James very early, but places 2 Peter after 125). Late dating of 2 Peter has not been a recent development. Doubts about the book's authorship have been around a long time, and by the start of this century the prevailing opinion was for a late date. Certainly the distribution of scholars on the topic is not as pronounced as is the case with 1 Peter.

The following scholars are representative of the range of opinion among the majority of scholars:

R. Bultmann (100-150)   R. Knopf (c. 150)
F. H. Chase (c. 150)   W. G. Kümmel (c. 125)
O. Cullmann (c. 150)   J. B. Mayor (after 125)
J. G. Davies (c. 150)   J. Moffatt (c. 150)
M. Dibelius (130-150)   N. Perrin (c. 140)
E. J. Goodspeed (c. 150)   W. Ramsey (100-130)
L. Goppelt (100-110?)   B. Reicke (c. 90)
J. E. Huther (90-100)   H. F. D. Sparks (100-150)
A. R. C. Leaney (90-100)   H. von Soden (c. 150)

1 John generally is agreed to fall somewhere in the period 90-110, although sometimes it is dated later. There has been little suggestion of alternatives placing the book earlier than the range of the late extreme. Like most New Testament texts, it

is impossible to fix the date more closely than a limited span of years. Hence the following scholars represent the range of opinions on its date:

A. Baumgarten (130-140)	A. Harnack (90-110)
A. E. Brooke (90-110)	J. Henshaw (c. 100)
R. E. Brown (c. 100)	A. Higenfeld (130-140)
B. Bruckner (130-140)	W. G. Kümmel (90-110)
R. Bultmann (90-130)	A. F. Loisy (130-140)
J. G. Davies (90-100)	J. Marty (120)
C. H. Dodd (96-110)	N. Perrin (90)
L. Goppelt (90-100)	O. Pfleiderer (125-130)
D. Guthrie (95-100)	E. F. Scott (100-110)

The Letter of Ignatius to the Ephesians perhaps is the least disputed document of any in the two samples with regard to date. It is customarily assigned to the period of Trajan's reign, 98-117. The following scholars show this consensus:

H. Conzelmann (c. 110)	J. B. Lightfoot (c. 110)
J. G. Davies (98-117)	P. Schaff (107-108)
E. J. Goodspeed (c. 107/8)	J. Sparks (98-117)
L. Goppelt (110-120)	B. F. Westcott (107-117)

Despite the continuing relative uncertainty about the dates of the documents of the universe of which James is a part, these six texts can be assigned, with probability, to one or the other extreme end of the universe. Inarguably, the samples are subject to disagreement and criticism; the availability of texts make any other outcome unlikely. But the samples are not unreasonable. They are, in fact, as good as might be expected, and they are the product of an intentionally conceived stratified purposive sampling procedure. Here, as elsewhere, the aims of the study have achieved a preeminence in the decision process.

21

Design of the Study

Categorization Considerations

It has already been observed that category construction rests at the heart of a content analysis study. The parameters bounding such construction should therefore be sound. Four parameters have been established for the task of constructing categories for this study: 1) they must be clear, 2) they must be relevant, 3) they must be logical, and 4) they must be simple without sacrificing comprehensibility. Within these parameters, three criteria are at work: do the categories meet a standard of pertinence (to the aims of the study), function, and manageability? Also certain specifications are necessary concerning the system of organization, the particular variables named, and the exact rules governing assignment of content to categories. Finally, a recognition must be made that all of the possible alternative ways in which a content characteristic may be expressed may not be known and accounted for; in other words, the categories are always limited by the analyst's knowledge.

These various considerations have all been accounted for in the construction of the categories of this study. For the sake of clarity all of the categories are subject matter categories, and are defined by simple descriptors (e.g., actual lexical terms or groups of terms). To ensure relevancy, all of the categories were constructed using James as a criterion text. In this way also the material could be kept simple, yet comprehensive. This process also helped ensure a high degree of pertinence, function, and manageability to the categories. In the face of questions about the logic of constructing certain categories and not others, the use of James as a criterion text provided one-half of the answer while another decision provided the rest of the solution. Only subject matter prominence, as measured by, for example, repetition of lexical items in more than one basic unit, or stylistic attention (as in thematic selection of paragraph-bound concepts), could justify category construction. This decision likewise aided manageability since James has only twenty-three basic units. The whole system of categories was organized into five major divisions, of which the first two are relatively weightier than the others. These are: 1) lexical item categories, 2) concept categories, 3) allusions or special reference categories, 4) person categories, and finally,

5) historical allusion categories. The particular variables and the rules for assignment to the various categories is clear in the discussion on categories below.

Categories

The categories for the lexical items are defined by the actual Greek terms themselves. The variables within these categories are the various forms of these lexical items, although in coding a reference to location in the appropriate text was used rather than the specific form of the term. The essential rule governing selection of the lexical items for inclusion was that it must appear in more than one basic unit in James. This rule is both simple and logical. It yielded the following list of items for categories:

ἀγνίζω	cleanse, purify
ἄγω	lead, bring, take
ἀδελφός	brother
ἀκούω	hear
ἀλήθεια	truth
ἀμαρτία	sin
ἀνθίστημι	set onself against
ἄνθρωπος, ἀνήρ	man
ἄνωθεν	from above
ἀποκυέω	give birth to
γῆ	soil, earth, ground
γλῶσσα	tongue
γραφή	writing
δαιμόνιον	demon, evil spirit
δίδωμι	give
δικαιοσύνη	righteousness, uprightness
δίψυχος	double-minded
δοκίμιον	testing
δύναμαι	able (able to do)
ἔλεος	mercy
ἐπαγγέλλω	to announce, to promise
ἐπιθυμία	desire, longing
ἐργάζομαι	bring about
ἔργον	work
ζηλόω	(neg.) to be filled with jealousy
ζωή	life
θεός	God
ἰδού	behold!
κακός	bad, evil
καλῶς	well, do what is right
καρδία	heart
καρπός	fruit
καυχάομαι	boast, glory, pride oneself
κλαίω	weep, cry
κόσμος	world
κρίνω	judge
κύριος	lord
λείπω	be in need

λόγος	word
μακάριος	blessed
νεκρός	dead
νόμος	law
ὅλος	whole, entire, complete
οὐρανός	heaven
πᾶς	each, every, all
πατήρ	father
πειρασμός	test, trial, temptation
πικρός	bitter
πίστις	faith
πλούσιος	rich
πονηρός	wicked, evil, bad
προσωπολημτέω	show partiality
πταίω	stumble, trip, sin
πτωχός	poor
πῦρ	fire
σοφία	wisdom
στόμα	mouth
σῴζω	save
σῶμα	body
ταπεινός	humble
τέλος	end, goal, outcome
ὑπωμένω	endure
φίλος	friend
φονεύω	murder, kill
χαρά	joy
ψυχή	soul, life

Obviously, many lexical items that could have been included were not. They include frequent, but less important terms, such as articles ("the") and prepositions ("in," "for," etc.). However, the existing list of 67 terms is comprehensive and representative of what can be termed the significant lexical items of the text.

The categories for the concept categories are defined in a different fashion than the lexical item categories. Here, the controlling English term(s) for a concept were used as a base and the resulting set of Greek terms established by reference to C. Brown's (ed.) work, **Dictionary of New Testament Theology**. However, the concepts, like the lexical items, were derived from James. The controlling concept of each paragraph was considered for inclusion, as well as certain others identified by scholars as significant to the author's thought. While it is recognizable that particular Greek terms, even though synonymous, may contain different meanings in different contexts, these categories stress the commonality of the sets under each controlling concept. The following list of 25 concepts was derived from James as representative of both the scope of its content and its major emphases:

1)	Controlling speech	γλῶσσα, λόγος, ῥῆμα
2)	Double-mindedness	δίψυχος
3)	Faith	πίστις
4)	Faith and works	πίστις, ἐργάζομαι, ποιέω, πράσσω
5)	God	θεός, Ἐμμανουήλ
6)	God as giver	ἀρραβών, δῶρον, κορβᾶν
7)	Humility	πραΰς, ταπεινός
8)	Judgment	κρίμα, παραδίδωμι, βῆμα, καταδικάζω
9)	Law	ἔθος, νόμος, στοιχεῖα
10)	Man	ἀνήρ, ἄνθρωπος, ἄρσην
11)	Mercy	ἔλεος, οἰκτιρημός, σπλάγχνα
12)	Partiality	πρόσωπον
13)	Rich vs. Poor	πλοῦτος
14)	Righteousness	δικαιοσύνη
15)	Servanthood	αἰχμάλωτος, δέσμιος, δοῦλος, λιβερτῖνος
16)	Sin	ἀδικία, ἁμαρτία, παράβασις, παράπτωμα
17)	Soul/life	ψυχή
18)	Steadfastness, endurance	ἀνέχομαι, καρτερέω, ὑπομένω, μακροθμία
19)	Temptation	πειρασμός, δόκιμος
20)	True religion	λατρεύω
21)	Truth	ἀλήθεια
22)	Wisdom	μωρία, σοφία, φιλοσοφία
23)	Word	λόγος, ῥῆμα
24)	Work(s)	ἐργάζομαι, ποιέω, πράσσω
25)	World	γῆ, οἰκουμένη, ἀγρός, χοῦς, κόσμος

The limitations of the text of James rendered the other three category divisions rather too small, and therefore relatively insignificant. However, for the sake of completeness they are listed below:

ALLUSIONS/SPECIAL REFERENCES

Dispersion	διασπορᾷ
Twelve tribes	δώδεκα φυλαῖς
Presbyters (elders)	πρεσβυτέρος
Synagogue	συναγωγήν

PERSONS

Abraham	Ἀβραάμ
Elijah	Ἠλίας
Isaac	Ἰσαάκ
Job	Ἰώβ
Rahab	Ῥαάβ

HISTORICAL ALLUSIONS

Discriminations in the synagogue
Rich persecuting (prosecuting) the poor
Rich keeping back wages from the fieldworkers
Anointing the sick with oil
Visiting orphans and widows

The rule governing inclusion of material was simple: all such variables in James were entered as categories. But with the discussion of any literature review in mind, it is obvious how many problems plague the determination of such categories as allusions and historical references (events). They suffer from both validity and reliability, although more from the former than the latter. Because of these problems, the study relies most heavily on the use of the first two subject matter divisions of categories (lexical items and concepts).

Unitization Considerations

Units and categories are intimately related. Much of the discussion about categories is relevant to unitization and will not be repeated here. However, it is necessary to note both the parameters and the guidelines adopted by this study and the visibility of the units. This latter parameter simply states that the units must be obvious, easily discernible. The guidelines are four, and have been discussed elsewhere: 1) the units must be large enough to yield meaning, 2) small enough not to contain too many meanings, 3) easily manageable, and 4) comparable in their total number for each sample.

The units are related only to the purpose of the study in their naturalness, that is, in their being natural divisions of the textual material. This aids their identification as well. Because they are (initially) paragraphs, the units are basic holders of related meaning; they are both large enough to focus on the main meaning, and small enough not to hold too many messages. Paragraphs also are easily manageable. To a lesser extent, all of these same ideas apply to the words and word sets that, as variables, also are units of analysis in the study. Finally, the documents of the samples are all comparable in the number of basic units, as the following shows:

2 Peter	11 units
1 Thessalonians	19 units
1 John	21 units
Ignatius to Ephesians	22 units
JAMES	23 units
1 Peter	23 units
Galatians	28 units

Units

Several distinctions need to be made with regard to the actual units. First, the basic coding units, or the recording units, are paragraphs. However, there are two instances in James where such units could be combined into one context unit (2:1-4 with 2:5-13; 2:14-17 with 2:18-26). In the interest of simplicity this was not done; such a neglect does not affect materially the study's results because of the manner in which the material was sampled for categorization (in fact, it could be argued that not using context units in this instance actually has strengthened the study's ability to see the content).

301

Other distinctions are more germane. Within this study are three different kinds of units; different, that is, in character, although similar in function. These are not basic recording units (paragraphs) for the establishment of categories for analysis, but are the (later) sampling units of the analysis itself. These units are syntactical (words), thematic (concepts), and referential (author allusion, historical allusions, place/event allusions). They share the common function of being an identifiable parcel of information susceptible of coding as a part of the analysis of content.

Variables

The term "variable" has more than one usage in this study. In one sense, each of the samples and the criterion text are treated as variables (or better, sets of variables) in the data analysis. Thus James, the criterion text, can be labelled the dependent variable; the samples are independent variables. In the multiple regression analysis this means James is the criterion variable which is being predicted; the samples are predictor (independent) variables.

In another sense, each of the sampling units coded by assignment to a particular category also are variables. It is in this sense that each sample, and James, are really sets of variables. These variables are coded at times by a very simple presence-absence scheme (e.g., in order to determine initial categories for lexical items from the criterion text). More important to the data analysis, though, is their coding on the basis of their relative frequency. This is the simple description of their occurrence, a number derived for each item by dividing the actual number of occurrences by the total number of words of the text or sample.

Procedure

Samples, units, variables, and coding all come together in a certain systematic procedure. This procedure encompasses two major divisions: the content analysis and the data analysis. The latter, which introduces the product-moment correlations and multiple regression analyses into the study, is considered separately. The former has, in this study, seven steps.

Step one is the selection of specific Greek texts to provide the raw content for analysis and specific divisions for unitization. While many suitable versions of texts are available, the **Greek New Testament**, published by the United Bible Societies (2nd and 3rd editions) was chosen for study. It represents sound scholarly judgment of the best readings of the New Testament documents, provides a reasonably full critical apparatus, and sets out the text in clearly discernible (paragraph) divisions. It does not, however, include the text of Ignatius to the Ephesians. For this document the work of J. B. Lightfoot was selected, since it still represents the most thorough and scholarly treatment of the Greek text. It, too, provides a critical apparatus and easily identifiable text divisions.

Step two includes the selection of referencing tools for different parts of the study in order both to increase validity and, more importantly, reliability. Thus, as already discussed above, the three volume dictionary edited by Colin Brown was used in establishing the rules for the inclusion of material in the concept categories. For the task of coding, two Greek reference tools were used, one for the New Testament documents, the other for Ignatius to the Ephesians. For the former, the analytical concordance of J. Stegenga was utilized bceause of its completeness. It uses the Greek text of Stephanus 1550 (also Elzevir 1624), commonly referred to as the Received Text (Textus Receptus), because of its greater word count. The author's intention was that users of other and later texts might find all the words listed in his comprehensive work. The system of organization was helpful, too, for it places all words under their root stems. For Ignatius to the Ephesians, the standard concordance of Patristic literature by E. J. Goodspeed was used, again because of its completeness. But these texts were not used exclusively; other Greek reference aids were consulted continually. Throughout the study a wide range of Greek grammars, lexicons, dictionaries, commentaries, and studies were constantly at hand.

Step three was the formulation of a descriptive outline of the criterion text according to its basic units. This outline, consisting of descriptive titles for each paragraph, served as a convenient summarizing tool for the content of James. It is reproduced below:

James	Title
1:1	Salutation
1:2-8	Testing and Steadfastness
1:9-11	The Poor vs. the Rich
1:12-15	Trial and Temptation
1:16-18	The Giving God
1:19-21	Receive the Saving Word
1:22-25	Be Doers of the Word
1:26-27	The Doers' Religion
2:1-4	Show No Partiality
2:5-13	Partiality and the Whole Law
2:14-17	Faith Without Works is Dead
2:18-26	Works Show Faith
3:1-5a	Controlling Our Words
3:5b-12	No One Can Tame the Tongue
3:13-18	Wisdom
4:1-10	Renounce Passion for Humility
4:11-12	Do Not Judge
4:13-17	Why Humility and Obedience are Necessary
5:1-6	The Coming Miseries of the Rich
5:7-11	Be Patient

5:12	Do Not Swear
5:13-18	Prayer, Praise, and Confession
5:19-20	Returning Wanderers to the Truth

Step four is the criterion text's basic units analyzed to produce: 1) lexical items recurring in more than one paragraph; 2) significant concepts (by concentration of attention in the unit); 3) historical allusions to events and persons; and, 4) special references, quotes, etc. Most of these have been discussed previously. It then was indicated that 3 and 4 above suffered from too many problems to render them very helpful. In the same vein, it was early on decided not to include any cross-references, text-critical matters, or style considerations in the main analysis. Determining literary dependencies or parallels is a risky business at best, and suffers greatly in reliability. Even a casual examination of the listed cross-references and discussions of dependencies/parallels reveals such a wide disparity among scholars as to render such an effort almost hopelessly subjective. The text-critical matters were not included simply because the three "D" readings (3:3, 4:14, 5:20) and six "C" readings (1:17, 2:3, 2:19, 4:5, 4:14, 14) did not materially affect anything in the content analysis. Finally, style proved impossible to quantify beyond the most rudimentary considerations of lexical items and concepts.

Steps five, six, and seven are all analysis steps taken after category construction. Thus step five analyzed lexical items for frequency of occurrence across samples and in James. Step six did the same for concepts, and step seven covered the remaining categories. All of these have been discussed above.

22

Data Analysis Procedure and Results

Level of Measurement

After the content from James and the samples was coded, the items in each category were converted to a frequency score. Thus, for example, the lexical item θεός ("God") occurs 94 times in the early extreme sample, 16 times in James, and 113 times in the late extreme sample. This actual count was divided in each instance by the total number of words in the samples or James. Thus, the actual proportion of text accounted for in the early extreme sample by this term is 1.745%; it is .922% for James, and 2.254% for the late extreme sample. This is a measure of relative frequency. Taken as a whole, all of the lexical items and concepts accounted for the following proportions of each sample and James:

Lexical items

Early extreme: 10.582%
James: 19.494%
Late extreme: 9.100%

Concepts

Early extreme: 7.535%
James: 11.767%
Late extreme: 6.585%

The use of relative frequencies permitted the establishment of an interval level of measurement. An interval scale is one where the values share a common quantitative foundation characterized by equal intervals between the successive scale values. This level of measurement is necessary for any product-moment correlations and multiple regression.

Analysis Techniques

Product-moment correlations and multiple regressions were conducted for four separate data analyses. Three of these concerned lexical item analyses, the fourth concepts. These data analyses stand central to the report discussed in the next section and only will be identified here. First, James was correlated with the early and late extreme samples for all lexical items (67 cases). A multiple regression was also conducted on these data. Second, James was correlated with the two samples after all lexical items unique to James had been factored out (58 cases). This, too, received a multiple regression analysis. Third, James was correlated with the two samples after all items common to all seven literary documents were deleted (56 cases). This analysis hypothesized that such items were indicative of the homogenous character of the universe, what might be called the "Christian vocabulary." Again, a multiple regression analysis accompanied. Finally, James was correlated with the two samples on the basis of concepts (25 cases), with the multiple regression once more added.

The purpose of the data analysis was first and foremost the establishment of the strength of relationship between James and the two samples based on measurements of the content from the literature. The multiple regressions focused on prediction. Inference, not causality, is a subsidiary aim. The actual results of the analysis are reported in the following sections.

Minor Analyses

Four items from James were selected as plausible references of a special character. They were set as categories and the two samples examined with the following results:

Item (Greek and English)		Incidence in:		
		James	Early	Late
διασπορᾷ	*diaspora*	(1:1)	1 Pe. 1:1	--
δώδεκα φυλαῖς	*twelve tribes*	(1:1)	--	--
πρεσβυτέρους	*elders*	(5:14)	1 Pe. 1:1, 5	--
συναγωγήν	*synagogue*	(2:2)	--	--

By sight alone there is an evident correlation with the sample of early literature. But the cases are too few to trust the results.

Five persons are named in James (excluding "God" and "Jesus"), and these names were established as categories for analysis of the two samples, with the following results:

Name (Greek and English)		Incidence in:		
		James	Early	Late
Ἀβραάμ	*Abraham*	2:21, 23	Gal. 3:6, 7, 8, 9, 14, 16, 18 29; 4:22; 1 Pe. 3:6	--
Ἡλίας	*Elijah*	5:17	--	--
Ἰσαάκ	*Isaac*	2:21	Gal. 4:28	--
Ἰώβ	*Job*	5:11	--	--
Ῥαάβ	*Rahab*	2:25	--	--

Again there evidently is no correlation between James and the late extreme sample, but a positive one between James and the early extreme sample. However, the cases still are too few. It also is noteworthy that of the 11 occurrences in the early sample, all but one are to the name of Abraham, and 8 of those occur in one limited space in Galatians.

Five plausible historical allusions were identified, set as

306

categories, and used in the analysis of the two samples, with the following results:

Item	James	Early	Late
		Incidence in:	
Discriminations in the synagogue	2:2-4	--	--
Rich persecuting the poor	2:6-7	--	--
Rich keeping back the fieldhands' wages	5:4	--	--
Anointing the sick with oil	5:14	--	--
Visitation of orphans and widows	1:27	--	--

No correlations between James and the samples were evident.

In each of the above three analyses insufficient data suggest great caution in interpreting results. For this study the minor analyses have been merely looked at. No inference from them has been attempted. At best, they might be used only as small corroborating information for the larger analyses to follow.

Product-moment Correlations

Four Pearson product-moment correlations were conducted. The results of the first, James with both samples, all lexical items included (66 cases), are summarized below:

PRODUCT-MOMENT CORRELATION MATRIX FOR JAMES, EARLY LITERATURE, AND LATE LITERATURE LEXICAL ITEMS

Variables	1	2	3
1 Early Extreme	--	.7078[†]	--[*]
2 James		--	.5511[†]
3 Late Extreme			--

N = 67   [†]$p < .01$ *Correlation for Early by Late deleted

The strongest association found on lexical items between James and either sample was .7078. This correlation between James and the early extreme is relatively strong, and positive. The weaker correlation between James and the late extreme also is positive. Variable 1 (Early Extreme) was discovered to account for 50.09% of variable 2 (James); variable 3 (Late Extreme), by contrast, accounted for only 30.37% of variable 2, a difference of almost 13%.

The second Pearson product-moment correlation attempted a refinement in the analysis of the data. Lexical items unique to James were factored out, leaving 58 cases. The results are summarized in the following table:

PRODUCT-MOMENT CORRELATION MATRIX FOR JAMES,
EARLY LITERATURE, AND LATE LITERATURE LEXICAL
ITEMS WITH ITEMS UNIQUE TO JAMES FACTORED OUT

Variables	1	2	3
1 Early Extreme	--	.6966[†]	--*
2 James		--	.5356[†]
3 Late Extreme			--

N = 58   [†]p<.01   *Correlation for Early by Late deleted

With nine lexical items factored out (ἀποκυέω, διαμόνιον, δίψυχος, κλαίω, λείπω, πλούσιος, προσωπολημτέω, φίλος), the strongest correlation between James and either sample was .6966. This correlation, between James and the early extreme sample, does not vary significantly from the prior correlation reported (.7078). The correlation between James and the other sample also remained much the same. Variable 1 accounted for 48.53% of variable 2, while variable 3 accounted for only 28.69% of variable 2, a difference of nearly 20%.

The third correlation attempted yet another refinement. All items common to all seven documents were deleted. The resulting correlations are summarized below:

PRODUCT-MOMENT CORRELATION MATRIX FOR JAMES,
EARLY LITERATURE, AND LATE LITERATURE LEXICAL
ITEMS WITH ALL COMMON ITEMS FACTORED OUT

Variables	1	2	3
1 Early Extreme	--	.6098[†]	--*
2 James		--	.4250[†]
3 Late Extreme			--

N = 56   [†]p<.01   *Correlation for Early by Late deleted

With 11 lexical items factored out (ἀδελφός, ἄνθρωπος, ἐπιθυμία, ἔργον, ζωή, θεός, λόγος, οὐρανός, πᾶς, πατήρ, πίστις), the strongest correlation proved to be between James and the early extreme sample (.6098). Variable 1 accounted for 37.19% of variable 2, while variable 3 accounted for merely 18.06% of variable 2, a difference of just under 20%.

The last correlation utilized concepts rather than lexical items as its content base. The results of this correlation are summarized as follows:

PRODUCT-MOMENT CORRELATIONS BETWEEN JAMES AND
EARLY LITERATURE, AND JAMES AND LATE LITERATURE,
AS MEASURED BY CONCEPT FREQUENCIES

Dependent Variables correlated to	Independent Variable	r^2
1 Early Extreme	.5989[†]	.3587
2 Late Extreme	.4119[†]	.1697

N = 25   [†]p<.01

308

The stronger correlation for concepts was found to exist between James and the early extreme sample (.5989). Variable 1
accounted for 35.87% of James, in contrast to variable 2 which
accounted for just 16.9% of James, a difference of approximately
19%.

All four correlation analyses were consistent in reporting
positive correlations between James and both samples. In each
instance the correlation between James and the early literature
was stronger than between James and the late literature. The
magnitude of the correlations for James with early literature are
relatively strong. All four correlations establish, therefore, a
strong, positive relationship between the content of James and
that of the sample of early dated material.

Multiple Regressions

A multiple regression analysis accompanied each of the
above correlations. For all lexical items (67 cases) the multiple
regression analysis can be summarized as below:

REPORT OF REGRESSION EQUATION AND VARIANCE
ACCOUNTED FOR BY THE COEFFICIENT OF MULTIPLE
CORRELATION

The regression equation is as follows:

$$x_1 = a + b_2 x_2 = b_3 x_3 + \ldots b_m x_m$$

The equation for the prediction of James' lexical
items is as follows:

James = .1894 + .9454 Var. 1 - .3197 Var. 3

The multiple R for this equation is .733, which
accounts for 53.7% of the variance in the criterion
variable.

More to the point of prediction is the following:

SET OF BETA WEIGHTS AND MULTIPLE CORRELATION
COEFFICIENTS FOR THE CRITERION VARIABLE

Criterion Variable	Multiple Correlation	Beta Weights for Predictors	
		Early Extreme Literature	Late Extreme Literature
James	.733	1.094	-.431

The relative predictive value of the Early Literature
is greater for James, with regard to lexical items,
than is that of Late Literature.

The predictor variable of Early Extreme is significant at the α
level p<.01 (69.27); the other is not (5.007, p>.01).
The second multiple regression analysis utilized 58 cases,
with items unique to James factored out. It can be summarized
as the next table shows:

SET OF BETA WEIGHTS AND MULTIPLE CORRELATION
COEFFICIENTS FOR THE CRITERION VARIABLE: 58 CASES

| Criterion Variable | Multiple Correlation | Beta Weights for Predictors | |
		Early Extreme Literature	Late Extreme Literature
James	.723	.9269	-.3150

The relative predictive value of the Early Literature
is greater for James, with regard to this situation,
than is that of Late Literature.

The prediction equation for this situation is: James = .1986 +
.9269 Var. 1 - .3150 Var. 3. The multiple R of this equation
(.723) accounts for approximately 52.3% of the variance in the
criterion variable. The predictor variable of Early Extreme
(variable 1) is significant at the α level $p < .01$ (55.77); the
other is not (4.32, $p > .01$).

The third multiple regression analysis utilized 56 cases,
with all common items factored out. For this analysis the prediction equation is: James= .1721+ .7244 Var. 1+ .1561 Var. 3.
The multiple R for this equation (.617) accounts for some 38.19%
of the variance of the criterion variable. The predictor
variables can be summarized as follows:

SET OF BETA WEIGHTS AND MULTIPLE CORRELATION
COEFFICIENTS FOR THE CRITERION VARIABLE: 56 CASES

| Criterion Variable | Multiple Correlation | Beta Weights for Predictors | |
		Early Extreme Literature	Late Extreme Literature
James	.617	.5444	.1149

The relative predictive value of the Early Literature
is greater for James, with regard to this situation,
than is that of Late Literature.

Variable 1 is significant at .01 (31.78); the other is not.
Like all four correlations, the four multiple regression
analyses highlight the relatively greater value of the early extreme literature sample for James than the other sample. In
each instance, the predictor variable that was significant was
the early extreme. It consistently accounted for more variance
in the criterion variable (James), and provided greater predictive ability.

Excursus

Before proceeding to the summary of these results, it is
necessary to consider one interesting feature that emerged in
some of the correlations. It may have been observed that in
the report of the first three correlation analyses the correlation
for early extreme by late extreme was deleted. In part this

decision was made to facilitate the reading of the correlation in relation to James, which is, after all, the interest of the study. But, it also was decided that the inclusion of these figures might prove confounding apart from some additional and directed comment.

For all cases (67), the correlation between the two samples was .8973, stronger than between James and either sample! The most plausible explanation for this fact is that James is a relatively heterogeneous document in a relatively homogenous universe. In other words, the texts of both samples are more like the universe from which they were drawn than James is like the universe. This correlation figure, then, substantiates the homogeneity of the universe and highlights, indirectly, the observable difference from that universe so characteristic of James.

When items unique to James were factored out (58 cases), the strongest correlation remained between the two samples (.8938). This, of course, was not unexpected because of the nature of the change in the analysis.

However, when items common to all the documents were deleted (56 cases), the situation changed. Now the strongest correlation was between James and the early extreme sample (.6098). The correlation between samples was .5967. This change corroborated the hypothesis formulated above.

Summary

Every analysis conducted pointed in the same direction: James' content is related more closely to literature dated at the extreme early end of the period of New Testament composition (A.D. 40-66) than to literature from the extreme late end of the same period (A.D. 90-115, or later). The correlation analyses established a relatively strong and positive relationship between James and the early literature sample. The multiple regression analyses confirmed that early literature, as a predictor variable, not only was a better predictor than late literature, but also was a consistently significant predictor.

The inferences to be drawn from these results must be cautious. The problems of sampling, and the difficulties of the minor analyses already have been noted. Still, it does not seem unreasonable to suppose that some general inference from the results to the universe can be made. The overall tests for goodness-of-fit of the regression equation in each instance yielded significance (37.14, 30.12, 16.29, 7.31 respectively; alpha level $p < .01$). In other words, the tests indicated the likelihood that the samples are indeed representative of the universe from which they were drawn.

Thus, despite the several inherent limitations of the study, it is not unreasonable to suggest that, on the basis of literary content, James belongs rather better in the time period 40-66 than 90-115, or later. This suggestion is undergirded by every test. James is, probably, an early Christian document.

23

Discussion and Conclusions

Discussion of Results

In the presentation and summary of results some discussion of them was inevitable. That discussion must now be supplemented. The results must be considered in the light of several matters, beginning with the research questions that prompted the study, and its general hypothesis.

The first research question asked, Given the contradictory and confusing conclusions about James' date, are there any reasons to hope that further study will resolve matters, or even contribute significantly? At the time this question was posed an answer was put forward on presuppositional grounds. The results of the study substantiate this hope. It is apparent that such an approach as the one advocated herein can indeed contribute helpfully to the discussion about James' date. In fact, the analyses reveal many possible extensions of the approach to such related introductory issues as authorship, theology, and literary form. The uniform direction of the results, their statistical strength, and their generalizability, all contribute to a resounding "yes" to this first question.

The second research question queried, What factors must be considered in dating James? This issue has proven to be a major concern threaded throughout the study's several parts. The literature review, discussion of methodology, presentation of results, and addendum all address this question. If the proper factors cannot be identified, or are not utilized, the study is in vain. The literature review, in part, helped identify these factors. The methodology carefully clarified them and their use in the study. The results indicated that the factors had been properly selected (e.g., in their showing the homogeneity of the universe, and James' observable departure from it), were representative (e.g., in accounting for adequate proportions of the texts, and in being adequately generalizable), and were susceptible to refinement and some discrimination in order to render more trustworthy analyses.

The third research question posed, How shall these factors be examined and evaluated? Content analysis provided a partial solution to this question. It permitted an analysis which quantified the content in order to evaluate that content by statistical means. Product-moment correlations evaluated relationships;

multiple regression studied the predictive powers of various variables. Together, the three component parts resulted in a rather compelling picture: the book of James should probably be dated quite early. This picture is not without its flaws. But it is quite striking in its overall unidirectional emphasis. The factors when examined and evaluated say the text is early.

The general hypothesis of the study stated: the direction of James' date of final composition can probabilisticly be reflected in a comparison of the text with other literary texts whose dates of final composition are already relatively fixed at one, or the other, extreme time limits to which James must belong. Obviously, the results point to this event actually having occurred. A probable date for James in the period c. A.D. 50 is indicated. This conclusion did result from the establishment of procedures designed to test the hypothesis. It would seem, then, that the hypothesis is confirmed.

Significance of Study

If it accomplishes little else, it should be noted that the study does indicate the plausibility of applying quantitative strategies to perplexing problems of biblical research. This fact alone more than justifies the study. There is a way past certain impasses like that on James' date, and that way is by the careful application of quantitative methods, tools, and analyses.

But what if the study has, in fact, contributed even more? Perhaps it has, in two regards. First, it can serve as a model. A high premium has been placed on the value of replicability. Consistently, decisions were made to include more rather than less material and explanation. Naturally, the study is neither a primer in statistics nor an introduction to the New Testament; some background in each of these areas had to be presupposed. Yet the material should be clear enough and comprehensive enough to provide a guide useful for consultation to others attempting the same or a similar work.

Second, it must be weighed seriously whether the study sufficiently overcomes its limitations to contribute an answer to the problem of dating James that cannot be safely ignored. Certainly, further work should add to the validity of the study's results, or call them into question. Yet as it stands, the study is methodologically sound enough to warrant some weight given to its results. This seems particularly true given the uniformity and strength of the results. While it is obvious that the study cannot have answered every question applicable to dating James, it has directly addressed the literary content of the book and, by comparison with other literary texts, concluded that James may be assigned a probable date.

Validity and Reliability

Without a certain assurance that the results are both valid and reliable, the study cannot be trusted. Thus it is important to review the steps taken by the study to help ensure that both of these concerns were satisfactorily taken into account. Proper methodological construction to preserve validity and reliability also substantially aids valididity and reliability of results.

Validity, it will be recalled, asks if a measurement technique measures what it is supposed to measure. On one hand, this is related to certain assumptions. This study, for example, assumes that relative frequencies are good indicators of what is important to a writer (within certain parameters, of course), and that similarities of content between documents reflect, within certain boundaries, a common background (date). On the other hand, validity is also related to the purpose of the study. Here the purpose has been to measure items of the manifest content of specified documents, as categorically determined by James as a criterion text. It is against this dual backdrop that validity must be understood.

Validity in this study depends upon the efficacy of the categories determined by James, and the usefulness of relative frequencies. If the categories do not represent in an adequate manner the content of James, the study is not valid. Validity also depends on the suitability of correlations and multiple regression analysis to measure relationships and predictive variables. But these have been quite substantiated and greatly aid the overall validity of the study.

Reliability asks whether similar results would occur if the analyses were conducted again in the same fashion, or if another researcher were to follow the same procedures. Often content analysis studies use inter-rater reliability to help answer this concern. That approach was considered for this study but rejected finally because it did not add enough to the reliability to warrant the time and effort it required. In this study, inter-rater reliability was replaced by the intentional use of certain reference tools at critical points. However, this alone was not all that was done to help ensure reliability.

Reliability and objectivity are closely related. To control the subjective element in coding, it was decided to create categories and coding requirements so objective as to render coder disagreement nearly impossible. This was accomplished by first using James as a criterion text to provide categories in accordance with simple frequency of occurrence. This one criteria eliminated selection on the basis of personal preference. The definition of lexical items and concepts according to specific Greek terms also made coding a matter, not of judgment, but of simple presence or absence, and actual number of occurrences. Coding thus became a matter of simple observation, not sophisticated and arguable judgment.

The use of comprehensive and reputable reference tools further simplified and clarified the process. The careful specification of these tools makes replicability much more likely. Moreover, the checks placed upon these tools by the use of other comparable reference aids constituted an internal check on the reliability of the instruments themselves. In the final outcome, the study appears about as reliable as is reasonable to expect.

Rival Hypotheses

Alternative explanations for observed situations can arise virtually at any time in any place. It may be a truism without being trite, that there are always alternative explanations for things seen or discovered. So it is that at every stage, and in every part of this study, it was not uncommon to find that some other reason might exist for what was found.

Some alternatives, however, are stronger, or relatively more plausible than others. In particular, eight such rival hypotheses continue to linger at the conclusion of this research. While these may have implications in more than one area, each seems to relate most particularly to one or another of three concerns: assumptions, methodology and data, and results. Thus, although any assumption is open to challenge, all methodologies have their structural weaknesses, and any result might be due to chance, some ideas remain so persistently troubling that they deserve articulation.

What if literary analysis, especially that proffered by content analysis, is still too imperfect a science to trust? Of course, it is a practical assumption to suppose that such analysis is, essentially, trustworthy. But maybe the new methodologies in literary analysis circles reveal a deep and distressing discontent with present limitations. If content analysis has not yet "arrived" as a science, at least for endeavors like the one undertaken by this study, then some reserve should attach to the results. Maybe, after all, the results can be explained as predetermined by the assumption.

Or, perhaps, the methodology is too flawed. Five rival hypotheses can be mentioned in this regard. It may be that the variables are insufficient or inadequate. It might be that they were improperly selected, finally revealing themselves as extremely artificial, with too little resemblance to the world of the texts themselves. Or, second, it is a possibility that the data from James is simply too ambiguous to warrant subjecting it to even "probable" conclusions, let alone "firm" conclusions. Third, it could very well be that more weight should have been given to anomalies in the data, since an exception (or an extreme) may prove much more than a battery of conformities. Fourth, the observer/rater effect may have, despite all safeguards, introduced an unwarranted degree of subjectivism into the study. Finally, fifth, it is arguable that a wrong choice of texts for the samples to which James has been compared inordinately biased the study. At this point, both assumption and method meld; what if the book of James in fact originated c. A.D. 75?

The remaining pair of rival hypotheses can be formulated in relation to the data analysis procedures and results of the study. First, the preference for including texts with a supposed relationship to James may have biased the correlations so much that some other sample, without such texts, would reveal a considerably weaker set of associations. Then, second, the correlations may reflect just the homogeneity of the universe, and the differences between them (recall they are all positive correlations) are really less consequential than supposed. Is a century too small to yield enough discrimination? Is the obvious homogeneity too profound to overcome in the analysis?

Obviously, these rival hypotheses have all been limited to just that status: rival, or competing, alternatives. The study, consciously and unconsciously, has attempted to create an instrument which can intelligently reject these alternative ideas on the basis that they are, after all, not as plausible as the ones adopted, or sufficiently answered by the design of the study. The fact that some rival hypotheses will persist to claim attention is inevitable and beneficial. Such ideas help keep research honest and humble.

Recommendations

This study is disturbingly incomplete. It is a model that is itself in the process of coming into a more perfect form. The limitations and weaknesses that became apparent during the course of research await further address. In particular, there is need to expand and refine the samples, if possible, and to add other data analysis procedures. So, for example, some nonparametric statistics like Chi Square and Spearman-rho correlations are worth examining closely. Also, additional categories, beyond subject matter categories, would add balance and weight to the overall analysis. Still, the incompleteness is principally a matter of refinement and addition. Essentially, as it stands, the study is adequate to its purposes. Ultimately, that is all that reasonably may be asked.

ADDENDUM:
Actual Occurrences and Frequencies

The following system has been used in collating this raw data: it is gathered into three groups (the two samples and James), and for each term (or concept) there are two divisions. These divisions are: actual number of occurrences and relative frequencies. Text references to each Greek term may be found in Stegenga's **Concordance**. The chart displays the scheme:

Term	Early Lit.	James	Late Lit.
Greek word	# of occurrences	----------	
	Relative frequencies	--------	

Term	Early Literature	James	Late Literature
ἁγνίζω	2	2	3
	0.037	0.115	0.060
ἄγω	2	2	0
	0.037	0.115	0.000
ἀδελφός	31	17	21
	0.575	0.979	0.419
ἀκούω	3	3	20
	0.056	0.173	0.399
ἀλήθεια	5	3	12
	0.093	0.173	0.239
ἁμαρτία	12	8	19
	0.223	0.461	0.379
ἀνήρ	4	6	2
	0.074	0.346	0.040
ἀνθίστημι	2	2	0
	0.037	0.115	0.000
ἄνθρωπος	26	7	8
	0.483	0.403	0.160
ἄνωθεν	1	3	0
	0.019	0.173	0.000
ἀποκυέω	0	2	0
	0.000	0.115	0.000
γῆ	0	5	5
	0.000	0.288	0.100
γλῶσσα	1	5	1
	0.019	0.288	0.020
γραφή	4	3	2
	0.074	0.173	0.040

319

δαιμόνιον	0	2	0
	0.000	0.115	0.000
δίδωμι	9	6	7
	0.167	0.346	0.140
δικαιοσύνη	6	3	7
	0.111	0.173	0.140
δίψυχυς	0	2	0
	0.000	0.115	0.000
δοκίμιον	1	2	0
	0.019	0.115	0.000
δύναμαι	3	6	4
	0.056	0.346	0.080
ἔλεος	2	3	0
	0.037	0.173	0.000
ἐπαγγέλλω	11	2	9
	0.204	0.115	0.180
ἐπιθυμία	10	3	8
	0.186	0.173	0.160
ἐργάζομαι	3	3	0
	0.056	0.173	0.000
ἔργον	12	15	8
	0.223	0.864	0.160
ζηλόω	4	3	0
	0.074	0.173	0.000
ζωή	24	3	21
	0.445	0.173	0.419
θεός	94	16	113
	1.745	0.922	2.254
ἰδοῦ	2	7	0
	0.037	0.403	0.000
κακός	5	3	1
	0.093	0.173	0.020
καλῶς	2	3	1
	0.037	0.173	0.020
καρδία	7	5	6
	0.130	0.288	0.120
καρπός	0	4	1
	0.000	0.230	0.020
καυχάομαι	2	4	0
	0.037	0.230	0.000

κλαίω	0	2	0
	0.000	0.115	0.000
κόσμος	6	5	23
	0.111	0.288	0.459
κρίνω	7	18	7
	0.130	1.037	0.140
κύριος	40	14	30
	0.742	0.806	0.598
λείπω	0	3	0
	0.000	0.173	0.000
λόγος	17	5	12
	0.316	0.288	0.239
μακάριος	3	3	1
	0.056	0.173	0.020
νεκρός	7	4	0
	0.130	0.230	0.000
νόμος	32	10	0
	0.594	0.576	0.000
ὅλος	4	4	4
	0.074	0.230	0.080
οὐρανός	5	2	8
	0.093	0.115	0.160
πᾶς	52	12	63
	0.965	0.691	1.257
πατήρ	14	4	24
	0.260	0.230	0.479
πειρασμός	6	6	1
	0.111	0.346	0.479
πικρός	0	2	0
	0.000	0.115	0.000
πίστις	48	21	26
	0.891	1.210	0.519
πλούσιος	0	6	0
	0.000	0.346	0.000
πονηρός	2	2	7
	0.037	0.115	0.140
προσωπολημτέω	0	2	0
	0.000	0.115	0.000
πταίω	0	3	1
	0.000	0.173	0.020

321

πτωχός	2	4	0
	0.037	0.230	0.000
πῦρ	1	2	3
	0.019	0.115	0.060
σοφία	0	5	2
	0.000	0.288	0.040
στόμα	1	2	0
	0.019	0.115	0.000
σῴζω	1	5	0
	0.019	0.288	0.000
σῶμα	3	5	1
	0.056	0.288	0.020
ταπεινός	3	4	0
	0.056	0.230	0.000
τέλος	7	7	7
	0.130	0.403	0.140
ὑπομένω	3	3	1
	0.056	0.173	0.020
φίλος	0	2	0
	0.000	0.115	0.000
φονεύω	2	4	0
	0.037	0.230	0.000
χαρά	6	2	2
	0.111	0.115	0.040
ψυχή	8	2	4
	0.148	0.115	0.080

Concept	Early Literature	James	Late Literature
Controlling speech	19	10	14
	0.353	0.576	0.279
Double- mindedness	0	2	0
	0.000	0.115	0.000
Faith	48	21	26
	0.891	1.210	0.519
Faith and works	43	36	27
	0.798	2.074	0.539
God	94	16	113
	1.745	0.922	2.254
God as giver	0	2	4
	0.000	0.115	0.080

Humility	7	6	1
	0.130	0.346	0.020
Judgment	9	19	10
	0.167	1.094	0.199
Law	34	10	2
	0.631	0.576	0.040
Man	31	13	12
	0.575	0.749	0.239
Mercy	2	4	1
	0.037	0.230	0.020
Partiality	1	2	0
	0.019	0.115	0.000
Rich vs. Poor	0	4	0
	0.000	0.230	0.000
Righteousness	6	3	7
	0.111	0.173	0.140
Servanthood	13	1	4
	0.241	0.058	0.080
Sin	17	12	23
	0.316	0.691	0.459
Soul/Life	8	2	4
	0.148	0.115	0.080
Steadfastness	6	7	5
	0.111	0.403	0.100
Temptation	7	8	1
	0.130	0.461	0.020
True Religion	0	3	0
	0.000	0.173	0.000
Truth	5	3	12
	0.093	0.173	0.239
Wisdom	0	5	2
	0.000	0.288	0.040
Word	19	5	13
	0.353	0.288	0.260
Work(s)	31	35	21
	0.575	2.016	0.419
World	6	10	28
	0.111	0.576	0.559

APPENDICES

APPENDIX A

Library Classification Systems

Dewey Decimal

What follows is a general summary of the classification system, plus a complete listing for religion.

100   Philosophy
      110   Metaphysics
      160   Logic
      170   Ethics
      180   Ancient & Medieval Philosophy
      190   Modern Philosophy
200   Religion
      201   Philosophy & Theories of Religion
      202   Handbooks & Outlines
      203   Dictionaries & Encyclopedias
      204   Essays & Lectures
      205   Periodicals
      206   Organizations & Societies
      207   Study & Teaching
      208   Collections
      209   History
      210   Natural Theology
      211   Knowledge of God
      212   Pantheism
      213   Creation
      214   Theodicy
      215   Religion & Science
      216   Good & Evil
      217   Worship
      218   Immortality
      219   Analogy
      220   Bible
      221   Old Testament
      222   Historical Books
      223   Poetic Books
      224   Prophetic Books
      225   New Testament
      226   Gospels & Acts
      227   Epistles
      228   Revelation
      229   Apocrypha
      230   Doctrinal Theology
      231   God
      232   Christology
      233   Man
      234   Salvation

Library of Congress

The major classifications of most likely interest to a theological scholar are:

B   Philosophy. Psychology. Religion.
D   History: general and Old World

The following provides a more complete breakdown of B:

B   Philosophy (General)
      B69-5739 includes individual philosophers and various schools of philosophy
BC   Logic
BD   Speculative Philosophy
      BD10-41   General Philosophical Works
      BD95-131   Metaphysics

	BD143-236	Epistemology
	BD240-241	Methodology
	BD300-450	Ontology
	BD493-708	Cosmology
BF	Psychology	
BH	Aesthetics	
BJ	Ethics	
BL	Religion. Mythology. Rationalism	
	BL175-290	Natural Theology
	BL300-450	Mythology
	BL425-490	Doctrines (General)
	BL500-547	Eschatology
	BL550-619	Worship
	BL660-2670	History and Principles of Particular Religions
BM	Judaism	
BP	Islam. Bahaism. Theosophy, etc.	
BR	Christianity (General)	
	BR45-85	Collections (including early Christian documents)
	BR140-1500	Church History
	BR1690-1725	Biography
BS	Bible and Exegesis	
BT	Doctrinal Theology. Apologetics	
BV	Practical Theology	
	BV5-525	Worship
	BV590-1650	Ecclesiastical Theology
	BV2000-3705	Missions
	BV3750-3799	Evangelism . Revivals
	BV4000-4470	Pastoral Theology
	BV4485-5099	Practical Religion. The Christian Life
BX	Denominations and Sects	
	BX1-9	Church Unity. Ecumenical Movement
	BX100-750	Eastern Churches. Oriental Churches
	BX800-4795	Roman Catholic Church
	BX4800-9999	Protestantism

A Simple Guide to Textual Changes

The changes that may be discerned in textual variants stem from a variety of causes. These were discussed briefly in the chapter on Textual Criticism (ch. 9). The following outline is provided as a supplement to that discussion.

I. Intentional Changes:
    1) Errors arising from faulty eyesight:
        (1) Confusion of letters:
            a) In uncial script, many capital letters are sometimes confused for one another:
                -capitals sigma (Σ) and epsilon (E);
                -capitals theta (θ) and omicron (O);
                -capitals gamma (Γ), pi (Π), and tau (T)
            b) Uncial lambda (Λ) errors: two written too closely together (e.g., $\Lambda\Lambda$) might resemble mu (M). Lambda followed too closely by an iota (I) might appear as nu (N). Sometimes lambda and delta (Δ) were confused.
            c) Uncial kappa (K) was sometimes mistaken for the abbreviation of the conjunction KAI ("and").
            d) In cursive script, the letters beta (β), mu (μ), and nu (ν) were sometimes confused.
        (2) Wandering eye (accidental omissions) called **haplography**:
            a) Due to a similar ending of lines (**homeoteleuton**).
            b) Due to a similar beginning of lines (**homoioarchton**).
            c) Due to a looking to the side so that a line or more is skipped (usually caused by homoioarchton and called **parablepsis**).
            d) Due to the same word, or group of words, occurring later (**dittography**).
    2) Errors arising from faulty hearing (from soundalikes):
        (1) Confusion of vowels, e.g., omicron (o) and omega (ω).
        (2) Confusion of consonants, e.g., kappa (κ) and xi (χ).
        (3) Confusion of diphthongs, e.g., $\epsilon\iota$, $o\iota$, and $\upsilon\iota$.
        (4) Confusion of vowels and diphthongs, e.g., upsilon (υ) with $o\upsilon$; epsilon (ϵ) with $\alpha\iota$;

eta (η) with ει; or, iota (ι) with υι . This process is known as **itacism**.
  (5) Confusion of rough (') and smooth (') breathing, with rough breathing eventually losing its distinctive force.
  (6) Confusion of verb forms where the consonants are doubled.
  (7) Confusion of different words with similar sounds.
  (8) Interchanged consonants.
 3) Errors of the mind (memory):
  (1) Substitution of synonyms.
  (2) Variations in the sequence of words.
  (3) Transposition of letters.
  (4) Influence of a parallel passage.
 4) Errors of judgment:
  (1) Copy a more familiar word for a less familiar one.
  (2) Misunderstood or overlooked abbreviation.
  (3) Failure to include something omitted from the text but preserved in the margin.
  (4) Failure to exclude something included in the margin but not belonging to the text.
II. Intentional Changes:
 1) Spelling, grammatical, linguistic changes:
  (1) "Correction" of first aorist endings on second aorist verbs.
  (2) Alterations of forms (from less desired to more desired forms, including assimilation of non-assimilated forms).
  (3) Alleviation of rough, incomplete, or incorrect syntax.
 2) Liturgical changes: conforming the text to actual cuurent Church usage.
 3) Elimination of apparent discrepancies:
  (1) Those due to faulty references (i.e., attributing a quote to an incorrect author or source).
  (2) Those due to historical difficulties.
  (3) Those due to harmonization of parallel passages.
  (4) Those due to errors of fact.
 4) Harmonization.
 5) Conflation.
 6) Addition of natural complements and similar adjuncts to round off phrases.
 7) Attempts to correct a manuscript error.
 8) Doctrinal changes.
 9) Addition of miscellaneous details.

Texts for Sources

There have been many hypotheses advanced concerning the specific extent and character of the various sources of the Old and New Testaments. The following constructions offer a contemporary persepctive on the JEDP sources (Old Testament), and Q (New Testament). Their inclusion here is not meant to suggest that these designations are universally accepted, but to provide a definite example of the biblical texts sometimes assigned to one or another source. Both J. A. Soggin and A. M. Hunter have earned respected reputations in their fields of study.

JEDP (Texts as assigned by J. Alberto Soggin in **Introduction to the Old Testament** (Phila., Westminster Press, 1976). Old Testament Library series. Cf. pp. 103, 107, 114, 144.)

J: Gen. 2:4b-4:26; 6:1-8; 9:18-27; 10:8-19, 28-30; 11:1-9, 28-30; 12:1ff.; 13:1ff. (each with what is probably a small insertion from P); 18:1ff.; 19:1ff.; 28:13-16; 29:2-14, 31-35; 43:1ff.; 44:1ff.; 49:1-27; 50:1-11. Ex.: The situation is so complex that it is impossible to assign material to sources with any degree of certainty.

E: Gen. 20:1ff.; 21:1-14; 22:1-19; 24:1ff.; 27:1ff. (combined with J); 28:10-12, 17-22; chs. 29-34 (with J elements); 35-37 (with J and P). While Gen. 15 often is cited too, it is difficult to make precise distinction of sources in the chapter. Ex. 3:1ff. (with J); 11:1-3; 17:1ff.; 18:1ff.; 19:1ff. (with J, but generally doubtful); 20:1-23:33; 32:1ff. Num. 12:1ff. Deut. 32:1ff.; 33:1ff.; 34:1ff. (with J).

D: Coincides for the most part with the book of Deuteronomy (except for the poems of chs. 32 and 33, and ch. 34).

P: Gen. 1:1-2:4a; 5:1-27, 30-32; 9:1-7, 28f.; 11:10-27, 31f.; 17:1ff.; 23:1ff.; 25:7-20; 27:46-28:9; 35:9-13, 15, 22-29; 46:6-27. Ex. 1:1-7, 13f.; 6:2-30; 7:1-13, 19f., 23; 8:1-3, 12-15; 11:9-12, 20, 28; 12:40-51; chs. 25-31; 34:29f.. Lev.: all. Num. chs. 1-10; 13-14; 16:1-19, 20 (in part); 22:1ff.; chs. 28-30 (?); chs. 33-36.

Q: (Texts as assigned by A. M. Hunter in **The Work and Words of Jesus** (Phila.: Westminster Press, 1973), p. 165).

Q: Luke 3:7-9, 16-17, 21-22; 4:1-13; 6:20-49; 7:1-10, 18f., 22-35; 9:57-62; 10:2-16, 21-24; 11:9-13, 14-52; 12:2-12, 22-34, 35-39; 13:18-30, 34-35; 14:11, 15-27, 34-35; 16:13, 16-18; 17:1-6, 22-37. Matt.: parallels with Luke (Matthew further from the original Q).

Select Bibliography

This bibliography does not aim at exhaustiveness. In fact, it is intended as merely a suggestive list. The selections represent a variety of perspectives, and cover the range from liberal to conservative. Each entry provides at least partial entrance to some key aspect of the theological enterprise. Start with these, but use them as springboards to a much wider reading.

Books and Articles

Aune, David E. *Jesus and the Synoptic Gospels.* TSF-IBR Bibliographic Study Guide. Printed by Inter-Varsity Press, 1980.

Barth, Karl. "On Systematic Theology," *Scottish Journal of Theology,* XIV: 225-228 (September, 1961).

Barth, Karl. *Church Dogmatics,* I/1: 1-50. Edinburgh: T. & T. Clark, 1936.

Bollier, John A. *The Literature of Theology: A Guide for Students and Pastors.* Phila.: Westminster Press, 1979.

Brown, Colin. Ed. *History, Criticism & Faith.* 2nd ed. Downers Grove: Inter-Varsity Press, 1977.

Cantor, Norman F. and R. J. Schneider. *How to Study History.* N. Y.: Thomas Y. Crowell Co., 1967.

Cox, Harvey. "Theology: What Is It? Who Does It? How Is It Done?" *The Christian Century,* 97:874-879.

Danker, F. W. *Multipurpose Tools for Bible Study.* 3rd ed. St. Louis: Concordia, 1970.

Ebeling, Gerhard. *The Study of Theology.* Phila.: Fortress Press, 1978.

Everett, William W. and T. J. Bachmeyer. *Disciplines in Transformation: A Guide to Theology and the Behavioral Sciences.* Lanham, MD: University Press of America, 1979.

Griffiths, Robert B. "Is Theology a Science?" *Journal of the American Scientific Affiliation,* 32: 169-173.

Hahn, Herbert. *The Old Testament in Modern Research.* Rev. ed. Phila.: Fortress Press, 1966.

Hall, T. William. Ed. *Introduction to the Study of Religion.* N.Y.: Harper & Row, 1978.

Healey, F. G. Ed. *What Theologians Do.* Grand Rapids: Wm. B. Eerdmans, 1970.

Huck, S. W., W. H. Cormier, and W. G. Bounds, *Reading Statistics and Research.* N. Y.: Harper & Row, 1974.

Kennedy, James. *Library Research Guide to Religion and Theology: Illustrated Search Strategy and Sources.* Library Research Guides Series, No. 1. Ann Arbor: Pierian Press, 1973.

Kepple, Robert J. *Reference Works for Theological Research: An Annotated Selective Bibliographic Guide.* 2nd ed. Lanham, MD: University Press of America, 1981.

Ladd, G. E. *The New Testament and Criticism.* Grand Rapids: Wm. B. Eerdmans, 1967.

Marrow, Stanley B. *Basic Tools for Biblical Exegesis.* Rome: Biblical Institute Press, 1976.

Pannenburg, Wolfhart. *Theology and the Philosophy of Science.* Phila.: Westminster Press, 1976.

Schleiermacher, Friedrich. *Brief Outline on the Study of Theology.* Atlanta: John Knox Press, 1977.

Sheehy, Eugene P. *Guide to Reference Books.* 9th ed. Chicago: American Library Association, 1976. See pages 252-283.

Soulen, R. N. *Handbook of Biblical Criticism.* Atlanta: John Knox Press, 1976.

Swidler, Leonhard. "History, Sociology and Dialogue: Elements in Contemporary Theological Method," *Journal of Ecumenical Studies,* 17: 57-62.

Thielicke, Helmut. *A Little Exercise for Young Theologians.* Grand Rapids: Wm. B. Eerdmans, 1962.

Tucker, Gene M. Ed. *Guides to Biblical Scholarship.* A series of volumes. Phila.: Fortress Press, 1971ff.

Waardenburg, Jacques. *Classical Approaches to the Study of Religion: Aim, Methods and Theories of Research.* Religion and Reason Series, No. 4. Hawthorne, CT: Mouton, 1974.

Walterstorff, Nicholas. "Theory and Praxis," *Christian Scholar's Review,* 9: 317-334.

Wiersbe, Warren. *A Basic Library for Bible Students.* Grand Rapids: Baker Book House, 1981.

Wiles, M. F. *What is Theology?* N. Y.: Oxford University Press, 1977.

Representative Periodicals to Note

Biblical Research. Chicago: Chicago Society of Biblical Research.

Christian Scholar's Review. Wenham, Maryland.

Interpretation: A Journal of Bible and Theology. Richmond, VA: Union Theological Seminary in Virginia.

Journal for the Scientific Study of Religion. Storrs, CT: Society for the Scientific Study of Religion.

Journal for the American Academy of Religion. Chico, CA: Scholars Press and the American Academy of Religion.

The Journal of Theological Studies. London: Oxford University Press.

New Testament Studies: An International Journal. Cambridge, Eng.: Cambridge University Press.

Religious Studies. N. Y.: Cambridge University Press.

Religious Studies Review. Waterloo, Ont.: Council on the Study of Religion.

Review of Religious Research. N. Y.: Religious Research Association.

About the Author

Gregory G. Bolich is an administrator and theologian-in-residence at the Christian Studies Institute, Spokane-Cheney, Washington. He holds three Masters degrees, including the M.Div. He earned his doctorate from Gonzaga University after completing a dissertation in the field of New Testament introduction. In addition to shorter works, he is the author of *Karl Barth & Evangelicalism* and *Authority and the Church*.

Dr. Bolich earnestly solicits questions, comments, and criticisms about this text. Please send these to him at the address given below.

Christian Studies Institute

Incorporated in 1979 as a non-profit institution, CSI exists to serve the Christian churches of the Inland Empire region (an area encompassing Eastern Washington, Northern Idaho, and Western Montana). The Institute's purpose is expressed by its motto, "Developing a Christian perspective through theological excellence in service of the Church." Its operations are designed to further the comprehensive educational ministries of churches throughout the region, and to facilitate Christian scholarship.

Please address all queries or comments about this text, or about the Institute, to Dr. Bolich.

Gregory G. Bolich
c/o
Christian Studies Institute
Rt. 2 Box 74
Cheney, WA 99004